English-Only Instruction and Immigrant Students in Secondary Schools

A Critical Examination

English-Only Instruction and Immigrant Students in Secondary Schools

A Critical Examination

Lee Gunderson
University of British Columbia

LAWRENCE ERLBAUM ASSOCIATES, PUBLISHERS
2007   Mahwah, New Jersey   London

Lawrence Erlbaum Associates, Inc., Publishers
10 Industrial Avenue
Mahwah, NJ 07430

Cover design by Tomai Maridou

Library of Congress Cataloging-in-Publication Data

English-only instruction and immigrant students in secondary
schools: a critical examination / Lee Gunderson

     p. cm.

Includes bibliographical references and index.
ISBN 0-8058-2513-4 (cloth : alk. paper)
ISBN 0-8058-2514-2 (pbk. : alk. paper)
ISBN 1-4106-1495-6 (E book)
1. Immigrants—Education (Secondary)—United States. 2. Multicultural
education—United States.   I. Title.
LC3726.G86   2006
373.18396'912—dc21   2006004927
                                                          CIP

Books published by Lawrence Erlbaum Associates are printed on
acid-free paper, and their bindings are chosen for strength and
durability.

Printed in the United States of America
10 9 8 7 6 5 4 3 2 1

This book is dedicated to
Catherine Eddy
Friend, Mentor, Researcher, and Caring ESL Advocate

Contents

Preface: Hopes and Aspirations

This is a book for teachers, teacher educators, school and district administrators, policymakers, and researchers who want to know about literacy, cultural diversity, and students who speak little or no English. A central hope is to present a picture of the incredible diversity of students who are entering as immigrants—to describe their abilities, their needs, and their aspirations. It is my hope that the contents of the chapters that follow will lead those who care to understand the incredible difficulties immigrant students face in schools where they struggle to learn English and academic content at the same time. It is also my hope that those who care will assess the issues raised in the following pages and will help to design programs that will improve the lives of students.

The results of a number of studies are presented in this book. Each study forms a part of a large longitudinal study of the success of about 25,000 immigrant students in a school district in which the policy is English-only instruction. The separate studies result in multiple views of the lives of immigrant students and their success in schools where the language of instruction is different from the languages they speak with their friends and families.

The studies were also designed to explore students' views of teaching and learning, to describe the potential differences between their views and their teachers' views. They were designed to explore issues related to students' views of their identities as they worked, studied, and socialized in a new environment.

Another hope is to explore different reading models designed to represent the learning of English as a second language (ESL). Educators and researchers will find the descriptions of students' learning of English and of academic content such as physics or social studies at the same time as important to their view of whether instruction should be English-only or bilingual. For teachers who view multicultural education as an important endeavor, the contents of this book will on occasion shock them and at other times confirm their views.

The methodology used in this book varies according to the purpose of the particular studies. Different methodologies are used to describe and measure the English and academic achievement of large groups of students, small groups of students, and an individual student. They are designed to produce different views of immigrant students and their lives in schools in an English-only teaching and learning environment.

The studies described in this book do not attempt to develop a particular political viewpoint about which approach works best with immigrant students. Instead, the studies describe immigrant students and their success in schools in which the unwritten policy is English-only instruction. The objective of the studies in this book was neither to support nor to refute the outcomes of English-only programs. Rather, the purpose was to develop a full, rich description of the lives of immigrant students enrolled in classes where the medium of instruction is English. The reader is left to evaluate the results.

ORGANIZATION OF CHAPTERS

Part I: Background and Design

Chapter 1: Increasing Diversity and English and Academic Achievement.
In this chapter a description of the rapidly changing demographics in schools in the United States and Canada is presented. Classrooms are becoming more diverse as more school-age students immigrate. This diversity is reportedly responsible for a lowering of students' achievement and for their tendency not to graduate from secondary school. The chapter ends with a rationale and focus of the research.

Chapter 2: Reading, Language, and Immigrant Achievement. This chapter contains a review of first-language (English) and second-language (ESL) reading models. The controversy concerning English-only and bilingual education is presented: a controversy that concerns which approach works best with second language students. The debate is so intense that it takes on political overtones, as some states have passed laws to make English-only instruction the official policy. Second-language reading models are described and a model is proposed. The chapter ends with the conclusion that first cultural language and developmental features will predict English and academic achievement in the English-only context in which the studies are conducted.

Chapter 3: The Setting, the Population, and the Measures. The study procedures and instruments are described in this chapter. The Oakridge

Reception and Orientation Center (OROC) where immigrant families are interviewed and the 25,000 students in the study were assessed is described and procedures are reviewed. The chapter describes issues related to the various locally developed assessment instruments used in the studies. It reviews coding and observations approaches and procedures, including a review of data coding and recording. The chapter concludes with a series of hypotheses that predict the findings of the various studies.

Part II: Findings of the Studies

Chapter 4: Demographic and Descriptive Findings.   Background findings for the 24,890 immigrant students interviewed and assessed at OROC are presented. These findings include such information as home countries, first languages, personal developmental information, schooling history, and English language and literacy scores. Results are described and discussed for 1,309 primary students assessed. Results for the recognition and naming of lower case letters, upper case letters, colors, school items, body parts, and prepositions are presented. Cross-linguistic and geolinguistic comparisons are presented. The fuzzy nature of some of the comparisons is discussed. It is found that on the basis of standardized reading assessment the overwhelming majority of immigrant students entered their new schools with what could be most accurately described as significant learning disabilities.

Chapter 5: Reading Models and Traditional Analyses.   In this chapter the efficacy of the common underlying proficiency (CUP) model, the interdependence principle, the Bernhardt model, and the proposed differential base model is explored through the use of multiple factor analyses and regression analyses. A proposed categorization of first orthographies is developed to allow languages to be grouped for analysis. Findings of the study are surprising in that they suggest a new model related specifically to the learning of English as a second language.

Chapter 6: Multiple Case Studies, Students' Views, and Secondary Achievement.   In this chapter, data from interviews of 412 randomly chosen immigrant students enrolled in high school are presented. In addition, the academic achievement of 5,000 randomly selected immigrant students and 5,000 randomly selected Canadian-born students is presented and discussed. The voices of the students are broken down by first cultures and represent their lives in secondary schools as immigrants. Disaggregated achievement data reveal the underlying first-cultural differences that are associated with success and failure. Data are used to measure their predictive power with grades in academic subjects from Grade 8 to Grade 12. Interesting relationships among first languages are discussed and a number of possible universals are described. Economic background is found to be a predictor of academic and language achievement.

Chapter 7: One Immigrant—One Story.   A case study of an individual immigrant student is presented to reveal the complexities that exist between first and second languages. The student is diagnosed by a school psychologist as someone with a reading disability. Interestingly, in after-school courses his Chinese language reading ability seems to be intact and progressing well. The chapter ends with a discussion of the role of first culture in learning in English-only schools.

Part III: Conclusions and Implications

Chapter 8: Summary, Conclusions, Speculations, Observations, and Conundrums.   In this chapter, results of the various studies are presented and discussed. The scientific approach to reading research is presented. The fuzzy nature of conducting research in school settings is described, and it is suggested that school settings are not good environments to assure scientific rigor. It is concluded that effect size, in the present study, is probably better measured by study mortality rather than the traditional effect size of a significant statistical finding. The chapter concludes with a number of conundrums or issues that are extremely difficult to address, but without doing so schools will continue to be places of struggle and failure for immigrant students.

ACKNOWLEDGMENTS

This book and the studies described in it would not have been possible without the help and support of Catherine Eddy, Supervisor of the Oakridge Orientation and Reception Center (recently renamed the District Reception and Placement Center). She was the one who conceived of the center as a place to welcome immigrant students and their families. She is the one who has inspired a number of research endeavors. Thank you also to Dr. Valerie Overgaard of the Vancouver School Board for her consistent support of the research reported here. Thank you to Mike Garcha and all of the other individuals who work so diligently for the good of the thousands of immigrant students who have passed through the center over the years.

Two individuals worked tirelessly to enter data into computer files. I thank them in spirit, but not in name, because they were part of a data-entry company and I never actually met them, just their work. The study would not have been possible without the diligence of Debra Clarke, Julie Fine, Dan Lui, Jérémie Séror, Louis Chen, David Ward, Eiji Hashimoto, Lynn McGivern, Renee Cohen, Jumin Hu, and Fatima Pirbhai-Illich, who served as research assistants.

Thank you, Martin Guardado, for your Spanish translation and thank you Reg D'Silva for your Hindi translation.

Thank you, Dr. Bruno Zumbo of the University of British Columbia, who provided expert guidance on the use of multiple factor analyses used to explore interdependence or common underlying proficiency and for being willing to answer my inane statistical questions. Thank you, Kim Koh, for being the consummate number cruncher that you are.

Acknowledgment must be made of the financial support provided by the Social Science and Humanities Research Council of Canada, the British Columbia Ministry of Education, the UBC Faculty of Education Office of Graduate Programs and Research, and the UBC Hampton Fund. Without their support the studies reported here could not have been undertaken.

Thank you, Erica Kica and Tanya Policht of Lawrence Erlbaum Associates for all your help with this manuscript. Thank you, Naomi Silverman, Lawrence Erlbaum Associates editor, for your extreme patience and strong belief in this book and its topic. And finally, thank you to the thousands of students whose lives are chronicled in the pages that follow.

Part I

Background and Design

1

Increasing Diversity and English and Academic Achievement

Give me your tired, your poor,
Your huddled masses yearning to breathe free,
The wretched refuse of your teeming shore
Send these, the homeless, tempest-tossed to me.
I lift my lamp beside the golden door.[1]

The headline reads, "Anger simmers among youth in Paris Projects" (Keaten, 2005, p. A12). Fourteen hundred vehicles were burned in one night as immigrants and children of immigrants rioted in France in 2005. The President of France concluded there was an, "incapacity of French society to fully accept them" (Arab and African immigrants; Gecker, 2005). He also deplored their "ghettoization" (Gecker, 2005, p. A12). The number of immigrants has increased significantly across Europe over the last ten years. As their numbers have increased the problems they faced in their new countries also increased. Their new countries, it appears, were not prepared to provide the needed support for their increasingly diverse populations. Immigrants and children of immigrants complained bitterly about being "marginalized by French society" (p. A12). Populations in the United States and Canada are becoming more diverse. It is not clear that either country is providing appropriate programs to account for the increasing diversity of its school populations.

---

[1] Liberty Enlightening the World, inscription, Statue of Liberty, New York Harbor.

3

LINGUISTIC DIVERSITY AND SUCCESS IN SCHOOLS

Many students speak languages other than English at home in Canada and the United States. The problem is that students who speak a language other than English at home are less likely to succeed in schools (Statistics Canada, 2001; NCES, 2004). There is also an unfortunate differential in that certain groups are less likely to graduate or to go on to college or university than others. In British Columbia, Canada, for instance, about 14% of the English-speaking students who successfully graduate from high school go on to enroll in universities in the province (PAIR, 2001). Many, of course, find this statistic to be an indictment of the system in and of itself. In comparison, however, 47% of those who are successful graduates who have "Chinese" as their primary language spoken at home attend university. On the other hand, only 8% of Spanish-speaking successful graduates go on to university. This is a significant disparity in that a university credential is seen by most as a key to higher paying jobs and success in society.

In the United States, Spanish-speaking students are less likely to complete high school than English speakers and are also less likely to go on to a university (NCES, 2004). The number of non-English speakers is increasing in both Canada and the United States. As immigration increases their numbers, the problems they encounter in schools increase. Rumberger (1995) noted that immigrants in the United States have a higher dropout rate than native-born students. Hispanic students have alarmingly high dropout rates, varying from 14% to 30% (Zehr, 2003). In Canada, Radwanski's (1987) Ontario study revealed that 53% of the ESL high school population left early, while Watt and Roessingh's (2001) study showed a 73% dropout rate in Alberta. Pirbhai-Illich (2005) concluded that both American and Canadian studies have indicated that students likely to drop out "come from families from low socioeconomic backgrounds, are from various ethnic and linguistic groups, perform poorly academically, perform poorly on standardized tests, demonstrate signs of disengagement, have been retained at grade level, take on adult roles prematurely, work more than 15 hours per week out of school, have family structures that are not stereotypically middle-class, and have at least one parent who has not graduated from high school" (pp. 38–40).

It is vital to explore the success immigrant students from various cultural and linguistic backgrounds have after they leave their home countries and have enrolled in schools where the language of instruction is English. The French riots were, in many respects, a result of the failure of the system to account for the needs and abilities of the immigrants the country gladly accepted as laborers. Educators must be concerned about immigrant students. The consequences for not doing so are obvious and ominous.

IMMIGRANT STUDENTS

Every year millions of human beings—the rich, the destitute, entrepreneurs, refugees, the young, the old, laborers, scientists, law-abiders, criminals—freely or under duress, driven by political, familial, economic or social motives, uproot themselves and by first-class, coach, steerage, on foot or by stealth, cross the political boundaries that mark the margins of the greener pastures they earnestly seek, only to face the revelation that the cultural, linguistic, economic, and social borders of the pastures themselves are often more difficult to cross than the invisible geographic and political boundaries protected by the armed guards and police dogs they met on their first day as immigrants. The transition from citizen to immigrant is difficult, especially for the teens who cope with acne and awkwardness, social insecurity and self-doubt, linguistic and social alienation, and deep-seated feelings of personal and cultural loss and disenfranchisement. They enter their new countries filled with hope but mostly with trepidation. Often, they are disappointed, unhappy, and confused about their new homes, their new schools, their new lives.

Very young students, those in primary grades, kindergarten to Grade 3, are often enrolled in classrooms and schools where they are immersed in an unknown language with a teacher and students they cannot understand. The are left to "sink or swim" because of the belief that they will learn English quickly and become assimilated into the culture of the classroom because, after all, the primary curriculum is based, in part, on helping students to learn how to get along with each other, with groups, and to be socialized into the community of schools. Most suffer from a sense of isolation and loneliness. In many schoolyards the very young immigrant students can be seen on the peripheries, looking abandoned. In many cases, they are the lost ones (Gunderson, 1983).

Seeking refuge, older students, on the other hand, search out other teenage immigrants who speak the same languages and share the secrets known within the teenage cultures of their home countries.

> The youngest members of the newest and most visible diasporas cling together in litter-strewn secondary school hallways amidst lockers filled with the delicious and dangerous tokens of the dominant culture and Discourses. (Gunderson, 2000, p. 694)

And their thoughts and feelings are as confused as they themselves look as they are pushed through crowded school hallways toward classrooms filled with other human beings they do not or cannot understand. "The schools are so bad in Canada, you get too much freedom and all the parents think it's bad" (male, Hong Kong, 14 years). "In El Salvador it's bad, in Canada it's healthier, it's different, it's good" (female, El Salvador, 14 years). "I don't know, I never go school, I spend time in refugee camp hiding from bullies" (male, Afghanistan, 18 years). "It's completely different in Canada, teachers are humans not dictators" (female, India, 16 years). "I like Hong Kong better because the teachers tell you everything you have to know" (female, Hong Kong, 13 years).

The United States, Canada, England, Australia, and New Zealand are the putative lands of opportunity for immigrants seeking the best for their families: opportunities for their children. Opportunity is the beguiling promise of the Western world, one often broken by the ineluctable reality of being a stranger in a new and unknown land. Many immigrants know they will fail in school and fail in their new society. Indeed, their failure is almost assured by the vast differences that exist between their needs and abilities and the teaching and learning going on in schools. Being teenagers, their lives are also filled with the physical and psychological difficulties human beings experience as they transition from child to adult. In many cases, it appears that "the deck is stacked against them."

Immigrants whose stories most often make the press are usually criminals or, on the other hand, incredible success stories. The morning newspapers regale us with stories about illegal immigrants, immigrants who are criminals, and, on the other hand, immigrants who become outstanding success stories, usually winning spelling bees or making vast fortunes. We hear of the refugee who immigrates and becomes a fabulously rich businessperson, such as Hassan Khosrowshahi, who in 20 years became a multimillionaire (Jamieson & Lazaruk, 2001). These individuals are, indeed, noteworthy. Their stories should be told. The difficulty is that the majority of immigrants will not become criminals, nor will they become as successful as Mr. Khosrowshahi. For most immigrants, life represents a struggle against a number of hurdles and obstacles.

Canadian immigration policy is designed to give "points" to individuals who wish to immigrate. Points are awarded to individuals who have skills that will be useful, it is thought, to Canada's society and economy. The points system changes regularly depending upon some bureaucrat's view of the changing value of certain professions or skills and higher points are allotted to individuals and families. There was a time when "trained chefs" were given added points because the industry appeared to need them. English proficiency becomes particularly important for immigrants who are professionals, such as engineers, doctors, or scientists, who must pass a professional examination to practice legally. However, after they enter the country, many immigrants learn there is no way for them to upgrade their English skills because programs are not available.

> Learning English is a matter of survival for Xin Chen, 26, who came to Canada 3 months ago. And if there's one thing she has learned about her new home, it's the importance of communication. "My husband is a computer programmer. He's working in a restaurant," Chen says. Canada offers newcomers much opportunity, she adds, "If your English is good." (Tanner, 2001, p. A3)

English is the key to success in most of Canada (not Quebec), regardless of immigrants' special talents and skills. The engineer who cannot pass the qualifying examination in English is unable to use his or her skills to gain a good job and to participate in society. In the meantime, the government that grants people extra points for their special expertise cuts back the funding for the programs designed to teach them the English skills they need to succeed. Immigrants face similar challenges in the United States. School-age immigrant students do not fare much better.

Immigrants and School Failure

Immigrant students, on the average, do not do well in schools in North America. Cummins (1981a), for instance, suggested that ESL students are 2 or more years behind their native English-speaking classmates by the time they reach sixth grade. Gunderson and Carrigan (1993) reported that 80% of the 4,416 immigrant students who enrolled in secondary schools in a suburban area in western Canada between 1989 and 1991 at the end of 3 years were 2.5 or more years behind in reading as measured by the Gates-MacGinitie reading test. At the end of 3 years ESL students scored significantly lower than their native-English-speaking classmates in reading achievement at all grade levels.

Reading scores in the 1990s in California fell dramatically. Various reasons for this decrease were proposed. Asimov (1997), reporting on a study conducted by *Education Week*, noted that it had been concluded that California's dismal results were because, in part, "Vast numbers of students speak little English, and one in four lives in poverty" (p. A2). Some authorities have thought that one answer to this pattern of failure is that immigrant students should be instructed either bilingually or in their first languages. The debate is described in some detail in chapter 2. The difficulty is that schools are becoming more complex in many ways. It is clear they are becoming more culturally and linguistically diverse.

THE INCREASING CULTURAL AND LINGUISTIC DIVERSITY IN SCHOOLS

Schools and school districts across Canada and the United States have become more diverse as a result of rapidly increasing immigration. Increasing immigration has also resulted in many schools and school districts in Canada and the United States having majority populations that come from homes in which students speak a language other than English. "The number and percentage of language minority youth and young adults—that is, individuals who speak a language other than English at home—increased steadily in the United States between 1979 and 1999" (NCES, 2004, p. iii).

The report also notes that, "Accordingly, of all 5- to 24-year-olds in the United States, the percentage who were language minorities increased from 9 percent in 1979 to 17 percent in 1999." The Ministry of Education in British Columbia, Canada reported that the percentage of students whose primary language spoken at home is not English increased from 15.40% in 1995 to 20.70% in 2005 (Ministry of Education, 2005). What is interesting about this finding is that the increasing percentage of language minority students took place against a general backdrop of decreasing school-age enrollments.

There is strong evidence that students who speak a language other than English are not successful in learning to read English or in completing their high school studies. There is also a great debate about what works for immigrants and those native-born students who speak a language other than English. Some advocate bilingual programs, whereas others argue strongly that English-only programs are the preferred way to teach the skills they need to succeed in a society in which the official language is English. The debate between English-only and bilingual advocates is often vitriolic. The English-only advocates seem to formulate their views on political principles rather than research evidence. On the other hand, bilingual advocates appear to base their view on the putative results of research. On close inspection, however, the research base seems sparse, especially as it relates to high school students.

Slavin and Cheung (2005) note that "The reading education of English language learners (ELLs) has become one of the most important issues in all of educational policy and practice" (p. 247). Immigration continues to grow in both Canada and the United States, which puts more pressure on teachers and educational policymakers to try to design and implement programs to account for the needs and abilities of all their students. The increasing diversity makes bilingual programs extremely difficult to design and implement because of a lack of trained teachers, appropriate instructional materials, and programs. Gunderson (2004), for instance, reports that there are 158 first language groups in the school district he researched. Bilingual programs could be designed for the largest language groups, but not for the many smaller groups. It seems that the only practical alternative is an English program. However, there is a lack of systematic research on the appropriateness of English programs for students who speak a language other than English, especially at the high school level.

Considering the significantly increasing enrollment of students who speak a language other than English in schools in North America, it is essential that English-only programs be investigated, especially with a focus on secondary schools. In many respects, secondary schools represent immigrant students' last best chance to learn the skills to allow them to participate in society, to learn, and to gain employment to contribute to their new communities. Secondary school English-only programs must be investigated to see how they are meeting the needs of immigrant students, those who speak a language at home other than English, but who must read and learn in English contexts. The studies in this book are designed to explore the language and academic achievement of immigrant students in secondary schools.

2

Reading, Language, and Immigrant Achievement

What helped me to learn English was speaking with teachers and friends. I think reading too. Reading, reading, lots of reading.[1]

This chapter is complex because it contains discussions of the literature related to immigrant students' achievement from a variety of viewpoints. Reading and reading-related research are central to the chapter; however, it also contains background information about such issues as identity, writing, achievement, and dropout rates. The purpose is to provide a context within which to assess the findings that result from the use of multiple research paradigms. Issues related to immigrant students and their success in North American schools are addressed first.

LITERACY LEARNING AND SECOND LANGUAGE

It has been argued that learning to read and write is basic to become a contributing, participating member of society. Many in North America view learning to read and write as the prerequisite that allows both native-born and immigrant students' participation in schools, socialization into society, ability to learn, and academic and professional success. Indeed, some individuals are convinced that the learning of English is a basic requirement of citizenship for immigrants; their democratic responsibility.

Olson (1992) notes that proponents have proposed the "somewhat overblown" notion that "learning to read and write is not only necessary to permit one to participate in literate society, but also necessary for the full

---

[1] Female, Cantonese, 16 years, Hong Kong.

development of one's intellectual resources" (pp. 18–19) and that "literacy has come to be seen as an interesting problem in its own right rather than being seen as the solution to every other problem" (p. 19). Olson (1989) concludes that "Literacy is a resource that is particularly appropriate to some forms of discourse, to solving a certain range of problems and to functioning in contemporary social institutions. But literacy does not exhaust the range of valued forms of discourse and valued forms of rationality" (p. 13).

Learning literacy skills most often, but not always, is accomplished at school. Teachers generally appear to hold the view that teaching literacy skills is central to their missions—that literacy is the basic foundation of learning. They are often convinced that their most important role is to develop independent critical readers. They appear to hold a view of learning, an extremely complex model of language learning, that is literacy-centered, that views reading and writing as integral activities of thinking human beings designed to produce independent critical learners. These are fairly well engrained North American views not necessarily shared by individuals from other cultures (Anderson & Gunderson, 1997; Early & Gunderson, 1993). Anderson (1994) concludes "that parents from different cultural groups held different perceptions of literacy learning" (p. 13).

CURRICULUM AS NORTH AMERICAN TEXT

Cummins (1985/1991) proposed that "students from 'dominated' societal groups are 'empowered' or 'disabled' as a direct result of their interactions with educators in the schools" (p. 375). Indeed, teachers consciously or unconsciously reproduce the political system of domination. Eurocentric views and beliefs form the core of the educational thought that guides curriculum development and instructional practice. Although the demographic data indicate that "five out of six people in the world are non-White" and that the "vast majority of the world's population is non-Christian" (Banks, 1991), North American educators appear to view education within a "mainstream" viewpoint, one that focuses on European values and beliefs, even though their school populations grow increasingly multicultural. Teachers generally hold a view of teaching, learning, and the role of text that is imbued with features of their culture. The Primary Program in British Columbia, Canada, for instance, begins its section on children's intellectual development with the following quotation:

> "If intelligence develops as a whole by the child's own construction then what makes this construction possible is the child's curiosity, interest, alertness, desire to communicate and exchange points of view, and a desire to make sense of it all." (YEAR 2000, 1988)

The underlying assumption is that the development of "questioning" children is something that is valuable to do. However, this viewpoint is by no means universally shared, neither by all Western teachers nor by students. As Oster (1989) explains:

> When we ask students who come from such diverse places as the Middle East, the Far East, Africa, or Latin America to argue an opinion, especially an opinion different from that of a teacher or a text, or more threatening yet, to take a stand when there has been no direction from the teacher, we are often reversing assumptions deeply ingrained in the value system of their culture, implicitly telling them, for example, that a younger person has something new to say to an older one (Anderson & Powell, 1988, p. 208), that words can have value in argument (Barnlund, 1987, p. 164; Becker, 1988, p. 251), that no one will be offended or feel personally attacked (Becker, 1988, p. 245; Osterloh, 1987, p. 81) if a pupil or fellow student openly disagrees with her or him. (p. 86)

These generalizations are based broadly on the interpretations of research conducted in classroom environments. They are, therefore, not necessarily indicative of students' behaviors in noneducational settings. However, in many countries books are the embodiment of knowledge, wisdom and truth. Many of the texts read by students from pre-industrial countries are exclusively sacred and not open to question. Recent Kurdish refugees to British Columbia, for instance, report that they and their children first learned to read using the Koran and that the only generally available reading material for them was sacred. Work by Maley (1985), Matalene, (1985), Parker et al. (1986), Valdes (1986), and Young and Lee (1985) has increased our awareness of intercultural differences in attitudes to learning in general and to the teaching of literacy in particular. They have shown how and why students from such education systems as that of the People's Republic of China rely on memory and quotation and find our insistence on originality and analysis difficult to embrace.

Teachers who encourage students to be curious, interested, critical, communicative, to hold a plurality of points of view, and to possess a desire to question and make sense of it all are teaching a value system. Moreover, it is a value system potentially in opposition to that held by the families of many of our students, both immigrant and native-born.

Heath's (1983) detailed report of literacy practices in three communities found literacy orientations different from the kind required in school, differences that divided along ethnic and class lines. This work, together with other research (Field & Aebersold, 1990, with Moroccan and Samoan students; Schieffelin, 1982, with Southeast Asian immigrants in Philadelphia; Scribner & Cole, 1981, with the Vai in Liberia), indicates that the social definition of literacy may vary as a result of the nature of the social and cultural context of literacy in the community and in the home (Early & Gunderson, 1993). Learning to read and write is a social activity and as such both students and teachers may vary in their views related to reading, writing, and learning.

Literacy is significantly related to a student's potential to learn and to succeed in school and society in North America. Learning English is important to the potential an immigrant student has in learning and in succeeding. However, it would appear that they are neither wholly successful in learning literacy skills nor successful in learning academic content.

IMMIGRANT STUDENTS' ACHIEVEMENT

Cummins (1981a) found that ESL students are 2 or more years behind their native-English-speaking classmates by the time they reach sixth grade. Gunderson and Carrigan (1993) reported that 80% of the 4,416 immigrant students who enrolled in schools in a suburban area in western Canada between 1989 and 1991 at the end of 3 years were 2.5 or more years behind in reading as measured by the Gates-MacGinitie reading test. At the end of 3 years ESL students scored significantly lower than their native-English-speaking classmates in reading achievement at all grade levels. Asimov (1997), reporting on a study conducted by *Education Week*, noted that it had been concluded that California's dismal achievement scores were due, in part, to the fact that "Vast numbers of students speak little English, and one in four lives in poverty" (p. A2).

Elley (1992) looked at the reading achievement scores of students in 32 countries who spoke a language at home that was different from the language of school. He found there were major discrepancies. Nine-year-old students in New Zealand, for instance, were on the average 70 points below their English-speaking classmates, a difference that increased to 81 points for 14-year-olds. Students in the United States were 61 points below their English-speaking classmates. Students in Botswana, Cyprus, Indonesia, Nigeria, Germany, Spain, and Thailand did not show the same pattern; nonnative speakers were reading about as well as their native-speaking classmates. In British Columbia, Canada, with an English-only school system with no bilingual or bilingual support programs, the study showed a difference of 14 points; only five countries showed lower differences. This study suggests that the students in British Columbia who were enrolled in programs taught in a language other than their L1 did not reveal the significant deficit in English that a number of other countries, including the United States, did. Second-language students in many countries are not learning to read L2 at their appropriate grade-levels, whereas some appear to have no difficulty achieving at or above grade-level norms, even though the programs they are enrolled in are second-language programs.

Many ESL students are not learning to read, especially in academic classes (Early, 1989) and the expectation that they can acquire the proficiency needed to succeed in just a few years is unrealistic (Cummins, 1984; Early, 1989; Gunderson & Carrigan, 1993; Leyba, 1978; Rossier & Holm,

1980; Swain & Lapkin, 1982; Wong-Fillmore, 1983). Unfortunately, there is little agreement on how to teach immigrant students. Additionally, there is an increasing problem related to the lack of ESL-trained teachers or qualified bilingual teachers. Dramatic changes in populations also make it difficult to find appropriately trained teachers. In one large school district in western Canada, for instance, there were 120 ESL students in 1988 and about 12,000 in 2000, whereas the number of ESL-trained teachers increased only about 5% (Carrigan, 2000). In California about 18,400 teachers without teaching credentials were hired (Asimov, 1997).

Lucas and Katz (1994) conclude, "Given the right circumstances (i.e., sufficient numbers of students who speak and are literate in the same native language and qualified bilingual staff), the development of native language skills and native language instruction in academic content areas give learners the best hope for building a solid foundation in content and cognitive development and support the growth of their self-esteem and the English abilities" (pp. 539–540). A number of strategies to help students learn have been suggested by various researchers and educators.

First-Language, Bilingual, and English-Only Instruction

A number of researchers some 25 years or more ago provided evidence that a student's initial reading instruction should be in his or her "mother tongue" (Gamez, 1979; Guttierrez, 1975; Hillerich, 1970; Kaufman, 1968; Lewis, 1965; Modiano, 1968; Mackey, 1972; Rosen, 1970; Yoes, 1967). Natalicio (1979) refers to the belief that students should learn to read their L1s first as the "native-language literacy axiom." She suggested that there is an underlying learning sequence: understanding, speaking, reading, writing. Some early researchers, particularly those who looked at French-immersion students who were native English speakers enrolled in French immersion classes, concluded that students don't necessarily learn to read best in their L1s (Barik & Swain, 1975; Tucker, Lambert, & d'Anglejan, 1973). Andrew, Lapkin, and Swain (1978) noted, "While it is not clear that the superior performance of the immersion centre students in these academic areas is due to the language environment of the immersion centres, it is clear that a French language environment in these schools has no detrimental effects in the achievement of the immersion students in any of the academic areas tested" (p. 27). This early research into French immersion was viewed as supporting the notion that students don't necessarily learn to read best in their L1. Generally the English-speaking immersion students in these early studies were from families in which both English and French were highly valued and the dominant language was English. Auerbach (1993) concludes that "Whereas research indicates that immersion programs can be effective in the development of language and literacy for learners from dominant language groups, whose L1 is valued and supported both at home and in the broader society, bilingual instruction seems to be more effective for language minority students, whose language has less social status" (pp. 15–16).

Bilingual Programs

The U.S. Supreme Court in 1974 concluded that all students had the right to access to educational programs in schools and that L1 was a key to such access (*Lau vs. Nichols*, 1974). Proponents of bilingual programs in the United States argue that the only effective way for students to have access to academic content is through use of their L1s, especially for students who have little or no proficiency in English (see, for instance, Moll, 1992; Ramirez, 1992; Ramirez, Yuen, & Ramey, 1991; Willig, 1985). Generally such researchers suggest that because it takes considerable time to acquire general and academic English language skills, then students immersed in English will not acquire the academic skills their English-speaking peers are learning. Further, it is likely they will lag further behind their peers in academic development as they concentrate on English (Lucas & Katz, 1994).

Issues relating to the use of languages other than English in the United States have become contentious and politically charged. Many American states have passed English-only laws, and a group called U.S. English has organized to lobby for an amendment to the U.S. constitution that would establish English as the official language (Crawford, 1989). In 1998, 63% of the voters in California supported an anti-bilingual proposition called Proposition 227 (Crawford, 1997). Arizona has also passed a similar law (Zehr, 2001). The passage of the law in California did not eliminate the debate concerning bilingual education, nor did it eliminate bilingual education. Moore (1998), a visiting fellow at Stanford University's Hoover Institute, noted:

> The bilingual lobby is now simply defying the law. A front-page story in the San Francisco Chronicle headline "Educators Working Around Prop. 227" reports that "in many Bay Area school districts, bilingual education lives." When kids got back to school "they found bilingual education waiting for them." The bilingual-education director in Contra Costa County defiantly said, "If a child is very limited in English proficiency, we will offer [native] language instruction. It's essentially the same as what we offered last year." (p. 23)

Students in jurisdictions outside of the United States are often enrolled in schools in which the language of instruction is different from their home languages. The language of instruction in the People's Republic of China, for instance, often differs from the languages spoken by students in different areas and provinces. The language of instruction has also been the focus of contention in places like Malaysia, where university programs were conducted in L1 until recently. In British Columbia the language of instruction at all levels is English, and bilingual programs, other than French and English, are not available. It is not clear from or well supported by research that English-only programs are necessarily detrimental to second-language students' language development in either L1 or L2. There is a great deal of contention and argument, however. The evidence related to bilingual programs is complex and often difficult to evaluate for various reasons. It appears that the proponents of differing viewpoints about English-only versus bilingual programs in many cases base their beliefs on strong conviction rather than research evidence.

Systematic bilingual programs in the United States first appeared in Dade County in Florida in the 1960s. Early bilingual programs were designed to be transitional, in that the use of first language was used to support students until their English skills developed and they could learn. The majority of students' early education in this model is conducted in first language, with a daily "period" reserved for English instruction. Students begin to transition to English after they have attained a degree of English proficiency. At this point they are taught to read and academic content is in English. These programs have come to be known as transitional bilingual education or TBE.

Rossell and Baker (1996) reviewed 300 studies of bilingual education and concluded that only 72 were "methodologically acceptable studies" and that they revealed "no consistent research support for transitional bilingual education as a superior practice for improving language achievement of limited English proficient children" (p. 21). They also concluded, "Seven percent of the studies show transitional bilingual education to be superior, 64% show it to be inferior, and 29% show it to be no different from submersion—doing nothing" (p. 22). They add, "Altogether, 93% of the studies show TBE to be no different from or worse than doing nothing at all" (p. 22). One of their most damning comments was, "One cannot trust an author's conclusion to be an accurate representation of the data on which it is supposedly based" and "Moreover, this is as true of studies done by supporters of bilingual education as it is of those done by its critics" (p. 25).

However, other researchers criticized Rossell and Baker, sometimes quite vociferously. Greene (1998) noted, "It is clear that Rossell and Baker's review of studies is useful as a pool for a meta-analysis, but the lack of rigor and consistency in how they classify studies and summarize results prevent their conclusions from being reliable" (p. 8). In addition, he argued that "unfortunately, only 11 of the 75 studies identified as acceptable by Rossell and Baker actually meet their own criteria for an acceptable study" (p. 4). Greene concluded, however, that "despite the relatively small number of studies, the strength and consistency of these results, especially from the highest quality randomized experiments, increases confidence in the conclusion that bilingual programs are effective at increasing standardized test scores measured in English" (p. 9). Greene (1998) asserted that scores on standardized tests were higher when children with limited English proficiency were taught using at least some of their native language than when only English was used to teach similar children. He also concluded that "the limited number of useful studies, however, makes it difficult to address other important issues, such as the ideal length of time students should be in bilingual programs, the ideal amount of native language that should be used in instruction, and the age groups in which these techniques are most appropriate" (p. 6). Finally, he noted that "the results from the 5 randomized experiments examined here clearly *suggest* [emphasis added] that native language instruction is useful" (p. 6). These five randomized experiments were among the 11 methodologically acceptable studies from the Rossell and Baker review. Thus, Greene's response to Rossell and Baker's review identified many problems, a critique that was echoed, if even less politely, by other authors (e.g., Crawford, 1999; Cummins, 1998; Krashen, 1999).

Bilingual immersion programs were designed "to rapidly introduce minority students to English in a meaningful fashion during the early years of school by sensitively integrating second language instruction into content area instruction" (Gersten, Woodward, & Schneider, 1992, p. 5). Gersten, Woodward, and Schneider compared the achievement of students enrolled in transitional bilingual classrooms to that of students in bilingual immersion programs and found that the immersion students showed an early significant advantage in achievement at Grade four that disappeared by Grade 7. There were a number of methodological problems with the Gersten et al. study, however, some of which the authors themselves acknowledged. They noted that they did not adequately describe the degree to which the two programs were implemented in the study. They also noted the difficulty of the use of standardized tests with second-language students. They concluded, however, that the results of the study were suspect because the design did not involve random selection of students; it included only those students who remained in the programs over 4 years. They noted that "Neither the bilingual immersion program nor transitional bilingual education brought its students up to the national norms, especially in the areas of reading (23rd-24th percentile for the bilingual immersion program and 21st percentile for the transitional bilingual education program) and vocabulary (16th and 15th percentiles respectively by the seventh grade" (p. 29). It is clear that many second-language students are not doing well in school.

Two-Way or Dual Immersion Programs

Howard and Sugarman (2001) define two-way immersion programs as the integration of language-majority and language-minority students in the same classrooms where: "1) language-minority and language-majority students are integrated for at least 50% of the day at all grade levels; 2) content and literacy instruction in both languages are provided to all students; and 3) language minority and language-majority students are balanced, with each group making up one third to two thirds of the total student populations" (p. 1).

One major difficulty in evaluating bilingual studies is that there are so many variations in programs across studies. A second major difficulty, as mentioned earlier, is that many studies are neither well designed nor well evaluated. A third difficulty is that authors often take for granted that what other authors claim is true of their findings is, in fact, true. Cazabon, Nicoladis, and Lambert (1998), for instance, state that "research on the most effective forms of bilingual education (usually in terms of English achievement) suggests two way programs may be the best" (p. 2). The research they cite to support this conclusion is that of Thomas and Collier (1997). It is not clear, however, that this conclusion is a valid interpretation of the results of their study.

Thomas and Collier (1997) reported on findings of their study of "700,000 language minority students, collected by five participating school districts between 1982 and 1996, including 42,317 students who have attended our participating schools for four years or more" (p. 30). Unfortunately, they did not identify or describe any of the demographics related to the school districts nor provide enough information to allow the reader to evaluate whether or not their results are valid, reliable, or accurate. The study does not appear to have been published in a refereed publication, so it has not received critical independent blind review. In addition, its dissemination by the National Clearinghouse for Bilingual Education adds the possibility that it is more a political document than an independent research effort. Thomas and Collier indicated that they only recorded data from "well-implemented programs in school systems with experienced, well-trained staff" (p. 28), but no data were presented to substantiate such claims. Although they themselves criticized other reports of studies of language minority education as frequently more "pseudo-scientific" than scientific, they did not provide enough information needed for the reader to judge whether or not they themselves had been rigorous in the application of what they called scientific methods. On the basis of their cryptic report, one that focused more on the methodology than on the details of their research results, it is difficult to conclude whether they have provided strong evidence to support their claims.

Rossell (1998) is less kind. In a review of Thomas and Collier (1997), she noted that "the methodology of the study is unscientific, as is the case with all of Virginia Collier's research" (p. 1). Crawford (1999), a proponent of bilingual education, remarked that "unfortunately, for reasons that remain unclear, Thomas and Collier have thus far declined to release sufficient data to support these findings" (p. 11). He added, "So, when asked about the Thomas-Collier study, bilingual education researchers usually respond that, whereas the early reports are intriguing, this remains *unpublished research* [emphasis in the original]" (p. 12). Thomas and Collier (2002) published a subsequent study through the Center for Research on Education, Diversity, and Excellence at the University of California in Santa Cruz. This more recent effort focused on data collected between 1985 and 2001 in five sites, but again, the data are not easy to interpret, and the report does not appear to have been subjected to the rigors of a blind review.

Greene (1998) concludes, on the basis of his analysis of eight studies, that "I find that children with limited English proficiency who are taught using at least some of their native language perform significantly better on standardized tests than similar children who are taught only in English" (p 1). He also concludes that "The limited number of useful studies, however, makes it difficult to address other important issues, such as the ideal length of time students should be in bilingual programs, the ideal amount of native language that should be used in instruction, and the age groups in which these techniques are most appropriate" (p. 6). He notes finally that "The results from the 5 randomized experiments examined here clearly *suggest* [emphasis added] that native language instruction is useful" (p. 6). Slavin and Cheung (2005) conducted a meta-analysis of studies comparing bilingual and English-only instruction. They note, "The most important conclusion from research comparing the relative effects of bilingual and immersion programs for English learners is that there are too few high-quality studies of this question" (273). Their study showed that of the 17 studies that fit their qualifications 12 revealed bilingual education resulted in higher scores, whereas English immersion resulted in no superior performances. The majority of their qualifying studies involved Spanish-speaking students in primary-level classes. One study involving secondary students found bilingual education superior to immersion in a ninth-grade program involving Spanish-speaking students. The research base related to secondary students is almost nonexistent.

A National Literacy Panel was established to review the literature of experimental studies comparing bilingual and English-only programs (National Literacy Panel, 2003). However, in August 2005 the U.S. Department of Education declined to publish the report of the National Literacy Panel, reportedly "because of concerns about its technical adequacy and the degree to which it could help inform policy and practice" (Staff Writer, 2005, p. 1).

The claims that one instructional approach is superior to any other appear to be founded on limited or questionable evidence. At best, inferences about best approaches appear to have limited empirical support. As

Ovando (2003) concluded, one reason it has been difficult to derive a clear view of the effectiveness of bilingual education programs is that often program evaluation research and basic research have been confused, and "much of the adverse publicity for bilingual education stems from a set of poor program evaluation results" (p. 15). Especially in terms of its effect on secondary-age immigrant students, the research on bilingual education is inconclusive about its effects.

What is clear, however, is that reading, and specifically learning to read English, is vitally important to a student's potential for success in schools and, perhaps, in society in North America.

READING

Olson (1992) concludes that "The ability to read critically is an important part of first and second language literacy" (p. 21). Attitudes about the teaching and learning of literacy have a profound effect on immigrant students' learning, especially on the learning of English. Researchers and teachers are faced with another significant dilemma, however. Although there is agreement that reading is an important part of literacy and that it is vital to students' success in school, there is little agreement concerning the basic nature of reading, what the components are that underlie reading, if there are any, and what pedagogical approaches are appropriate to teach them or even how to measure reading. Indeed, there is little agreement upon what language immigrants should first learn to read. Most often second-language educators have simply adopted models, approaches, and techniques developed for first-language learners. Those who advocate that students should learn to read in their first languages are often unable to accomplish the task because there are too many first languages or there are no trained teachers fluent in a particular language such as Papiamento or Kurdish (Lara, 1994).

Reading is viewed as significant and important to immigrant students' potential for success. Second-language researchers have opted to borrow and adapt first-language reading models for purposes of research and instruction. It is, therefore, crucial to review and understand first-language models. The review begins with a discussion of traditional views of reading, those usually supported by traditional empirical tests and measures.

First-Language Reading Models—A Traditional Viewpoint

The prevailing notion of reading in Western countries for about the last 2,000 years has been that it is decoding or reading aloud (Boyarin, 1993; Fabian, 1993, Howe, 1993; Mathews, 1966; Noakes, 1993), a view that has changed dramatically in the last 150 years. Huey (1908) helped to focus educators' attention on word meanings and silent reading, which greatly influenced the development of basal instruction that "met the expectations of a public and educational community enthralled with business, science, and psychology as they tried to find a remedy for the apparent crisis in reading instruction in schools at the turn of the century" (Shannon, 1989, p. 27).

Over the last 100 years or so the research community, primarily working within a behaviorist tradition, has learned a great deal about the processes involved in reading: about the recognition of letters, the recognition of words, the effects of type, context, development, ability, reader background, and so on. However, it has yet to develop a model that accounts for all of the theorized subprocesses in a coherent fashion. In fact, the major model types, bottom-up, top-down, and interactive, might be considered to be mutually contradictory. The "whole language" notion of learning, a popular view of literacy acquisition, cannot be said to be a model of reading; rather, it is a model of literacy instruction that proposes that "pedagogy should encourage the strategies observed in early readers—those who learn to read before ever going to school and should imitate conditions of early readers' learning environments" (Gunderson & Shapiro, 1988). Most whole language advocates posit a view of language learning that is psycholinguistic or top-down, whereas some have argued that it is a philosophy. Others have argued that whole language is not a philosophy (Gunderson, 1997).

Proponents of the different models support their theoretical positions with considerable evidence, often obtained from studies designed to test a particular model. There are problems, however, with this procedure. In addition, second-language researchers freely adopt first-language models, although there is little validity in doing so (Bernhardt, 1991, 2000), even though the supporting research involves first-language speakers.

Reading Models

A model, as a set of theoretical propositions, allows a researcher to analyze logically the possible relationships within a particular system. Further, it permits the design of procedures to isolate and to test empirically the association of variables in the theorized component relationships. In many respects, however, a researcher's model introduces a set of outcome probabilities. If one develops a model based on the theoretical position that processing is "top-down" one then often designs studies to explore "top-down" processing. Or, one looks about to find other research supporting the proposed propositions. As Leu (1981) notes, "Typically, investigators have constructed models of the reading process based on a set of specific empirical results, often from their particular paradigm, or investigative approach" (p. 96). The proponents of the three major model types often construct their models based on such results.

Bottom-Up Models

There are many models that can be classified as bottom-up (e.g. Gough, 1976; LaBerge and Samuels, 1974). One of the most widely discussed is the Gough model. Gough proposed, in an article titled "One Second of Reading," that reading is, in fact, a "letter by letter process" (Gough, 1976, p. 513).

Gough suggested that reading involves the processing of an icon, "a relatively direct representation of a visual stimulus that persists for a brief period after the stimulus vanishes," (p. 662) that explains the discovery he and his colleagues made that the time between showing a reader a word and the time at which the reader begins to pronounce the word aloud increases about 10 to 20 ms per letter (Gough, 1976). He proposed a stage model in which the icon is scanned and information is sent through various stages that decode and recode information until it passes through "the place where sentences go when they are understood." He concluded that poor readers have difficulty because their processing of print is too slow and items are lost from short-term memory.

Gough supports his model with evidence from studies involving letters and isolated words. He concludes that "letters of words are read out of the icon at a rate of 10–20 msec per letter" (Gough, 1976, p. 512). Gough cites two studies by Sperling (1960, 1963) to help support this contention. First, Sperling (1960) presented subjects with a vertical array containing three rows of letters. When asked to report as many letters as possible, subjects' recognition accuracy was about five letters. When Sperling increased the number of letters in the array, recognition accuracy did not increase. However, when he gave subjects an auditory tone to signal which row the target letters were in, subjects were nearly perfect in their responses. Sperling proposes that this finding reveals the existence of an icon: a VIS (visual information storage). Sperling's evidence suggests that an icon does exist in certain experimental situations. Do his findings suggest that letters are scanned one at a time in real reading? Subjects were asked to report as accurately as possible as many letters as possible. They were asked, therefore, to attend to as many letters as possible, and that's what they did, especially because they were unrelated letters. Gough (1972) notes that "Scarf, Zamansky and Brightbill (1966) found that the masked recognition threshold (using Sperling's own mask) for familiar five-letter words to be roughly 90 msec" (p. 334). Gough continues by suggesting that such a finding gives little support to the contention that meaningful words are read out of the icon any quicker than unrelated words. However, he fails to note that Scarf, Zamansky, and Brightbill themselves state that "At this rate, 50 to 90 msecs would be required to scan all letters in these five- and six-letters words. Of course, Ss would not always need to see all five or six letters to identify a word, a common word, but missed letters combined with misperceived letters would often lead to a false response, thus somewhat offsetting the contextual advantage" (Scarf, Zamansky, and Brightbill, 1966, p. 112). It would seem that some of the findings used to support this bottom-up model come from studies designed to observe particular outcomes. In addition, the bottom-up model fails to account for a considerable number of findings concerning letters and words (see Brewer, 1976). It also does not address issues related to context effects, graphic cues, individual differences of readers, differences in oral versus silent reading, or effects related to second-language learning. However, the bottom-up view has been pervasive in the way teachers view learning and the programs they design to teach literacy skills, both first- and second-language educators. The bottom-up model, although not specifically named as such, has been the view of reading that has guided instruction and research for many years.

The search for better methods during the first half of the 20th century focused on developing better materials and a better teaching approach. The work of such educators as Emmett and William S. Gray helped to develop systematic reading programs and approaches based on a bottom-up or skills-based model. Basal readers and the Directed Reading Approach have been predominant features of the teaching and learning of reading in North America during most of the 20th century (Gunderson, 1985a, 1985b, 1991a, 1997). Basal instruction is designed on the notion that reading is a series of subskills to be learned in a developmental order, a bottom-up model. Teaching students to read using basal readers has become associated with a basic lesson plan referred to as the Directed Reading Lesson (DRL) or the Directed Reading Approach (DRA), a basic lesson plan used widely around the world to teach students to read in many different countries and languages (Gunderson, 1991a). The basic plan includes five steps: (a) the introduction and discussion of the background of the story to be read; (b) the introduction and teaching of the new vocabulary items introduced in the story; (c) guided reading in which the teacher prompts students to read to discover certain items in the story; (d) a comprehension check in which the teacher asks questions or gives students a worksheet containing questions about the story; and (e) a skills-development exercises related in some way to the story. Basal readers are written to represent a hierarchy of skills imputed to be necessary to learn in sequence to become a mature reader. The underlying notion is that reading skills should be learned in order, an order prescribed by the skills hierarchy. Students learn such skills as letter names, phonics relationships, word recognition skills, and comprehension. The basic lesson plan has helped guide reading instruction for years, although teachers often do not strictly adhere to it (Durkin, 1978–1979). Many different pedagogical approaches use the basic DRA to teach reading. For instance, the Miami Linguistic Readers designed in the 1960s to teach ESL students to read, a program utilizing regular spelling patterns, was a basal series utilizing the DRA.

Top-Down Models

The last 30 years or so have seen the development of various models of reading during the same time that the behaviorist model has been increasingly viewed as unreliable, such as psycholinguistic models (e.g., Goodman, 1967, 1985; Smith, 1979, 1982), interactive models (Rumelhart, 1977), schema-theoretic models (Adams & Collins, 1979; Anderson & Pearson, 1984; Anderson, Spiro, & Anderson, 1977; Anderson, Stevens, Shifrin, & Osborn, 1978), and a series of models of integrated language learning and teaching referred to as whole language (Gunderson, 1997). Bernhardt (1991) notes that no other model has had the profound influence on second-language researchers that the psycholinguistic model has had: a top-down theory of reading.

Although there are several top-down models (e.g., Kolers, 1972; Levin & Kaplin, 1970; Neisser, 1967; Smith, 1973), the Goodman model has been and continues to be particularly influential. Bernhardt (1991) found that this model "has been the overwhelming conceptual framework within second-language reading for this period" (p. 22). Goodman (1981) insisted that his model is interactive; however, it is generally considered to be top-down. Goodman (1976) opposes the bottom-up view.

Psycholinguistic Models

Goodman published a study in 1967 that changed the way many viewed reading. He compared what students read aloud with what was actually in the text, their miscues. Miscues, instances in which responses deviated from what was written in the text, were used to make inferences about the reading process. Goodman (1967) suggested that reading was a "psycholinguistic guessing game" in which the reader samples text and makes predictions based on his or her knowledge of syntax and semantics. Mature reading, it is suggested, is an active and critical process in which the reader samples textual cues and produces hypotheses or predictions about the meaning or message in the text. This view of reading and other similar models are referred to as top-down models because the reader actively uses his or her complex background knowledge to make predictions about what is in text.

Goodman's early study involved asking students to read words written in a list and then in the context of a story. He found that students did not miss the words in context that they had missed in isolation. He concluded that this revealed the effects of context. Nicholson (1991) replicated Goodman's study; however, he randomized the presentation of the words in lists and in context and found no advantage for the recognition of words in context. He concluded that presenting students words in a list first had prepared them to read them in context.

A great deal of the data used to support top-down models is accumulated through analyses of miscue data. In order to ensure that sufficient data are generated, students are often asked to read aloud material that is too difficult for them. For instance, Goodman and Gollasch (1980) reported data obtained from a fourth-grade student reading a story. The student's mean number of miscues per 100 words was 9.35, and there were instances in which she paused for as long as 40 s. As early as 1946 Betts suggested that an error rate of more than 5 words per 100 was a sign of poor comprehension. The long periods of silence also suggest the student was not comprehending. Miscue data from such studies are used to support the view that readers operate in a top-down fashion. The paradigm, however, appears to assure that top-down processing will be observed. Goodman (1976) states that reading "involves partial use of available minimal language cues selected from perceptual input on the basis of the reader's expectations" (p. 498). However, because the texts are too difficult, the reader is not provided with a level of minimally meaningful language cues from the graphic input, and he or she must base his or her predictions predominantly on higher level processes. Leu (1982) concluded:

> Until errors are scored in a more reasoned and consistent manner, until differences in relative passage difficulty are controlled, and until we acknowledge the problems associated with multiple-source errors, the results of oral reading error studies are bound to reflect the particular effects of these unplanned variables as much as they reflect the effects of variables deliberately manipulated by the investigator. (pp. 430–431)

Goodman's model is complex, but it does appear to involve stages.

Top-down models have also been criticized because they do not adequately account for fluent reading or differences due to ability (see Stanovich, 1981). In addition, top-down models fail to specify the relationship between graphic cues and higher level cognitive processing. Bernhardt (1991) concludes, "It is remarkable that an area of disciplined inquiry such as reading in a second language could be so dominated by one conceptual framework" (p. 22).

The psycholinguistic model has been adopted by a number of second-language researchers to represent the processing occurring during the reading of second languages. Their views are presented later in this chapter. A third view of reading, one that has also been adopted by second-language researchers, is called the interactive model.

Interactive Models

The interactive view of reading suggests that both bottom-up processing and top-down processing contribute information to the reader (Rumelhart, 1977). Rumelhart's model, a parallel model in which the processing of input is simultaneous, includes a pattern synthesizer that assesses information from letter and word features, syntactic knowledge, semantic knowledge, orthographic knowledge, and lexical knowledge. As each of the sources of information provides input, hypotheses are generated. Rumelhart notes:

> The message center keeps a running list of hypotheses about the nature of the input string. Each knowledge source constantly scans the message center for the appearance of hypotheses relevant to its own sphere of knowledge. Whenever such a hypothesis enters the message center, the knowledge source in question evaluates the hypothesis in light of its own specialized knowledge. As a result of its analysis, the hypothesis may be confirmed, disconfirmed and removed from the message center. The procedure continues until some decision can be reached. At that point the most probable hypothesis is determined to be the right one. (1977, pp. 589–590)

Stanovich (1981) supports an interactive model, but adapts it to reflect his belief that reading is "interactive-compensatory." He proposes that "a process at *any* level can compensate for deficiencies at any other level" (p. 36). His comprehensive view of the literature reveals findings he suggests show that good readers rely less on context than poor readers in order to recognize words. Stanovich contends that poor readers are more sensitive to orthographic structure than good readers. The evidence he cites is quite comprehensive; a typical study is Stanovich and West (1979), involving 96 third-grade students who had been identified as good or poor readers by their teachers. These students were subsequently tested and found to be significantly different in "mean reading ability" (p. 260). Unfortunately, the test used by the researchers was the Wide Range Achievement Test (WRAT) Reading Subtest. In fact, subjects were significantly different in their ability to recognize words from a list—the reading behavior tested by the WRAT. The authors found that their poor readers took longer to search for word targets in lists of words, nonwords, and pseudowords than did good readers and they were less accurate. These results, of course, are not surprising considering their WRAT scores: The poor readers were different from the good readers in their ability to recognize words by sight from a list. The authors suggest that poor readers were more sensitive to orthographic structure because their performance differed significantly from word to nonword conditions so that they had twice as many errors in the word conditions than in the nonword condition. Stanovich (1981), referring to poor readers' "*greater* [emphasis in original] sensitivity to intraword structure," notes that their errors "almost always involved the children responding to a string that had several letters in common with a target or that had the same shape as one of the targets" (p. 40). In fact, it would appear that good readers were more sensitive to orthographic structure; they were not misled by gross likenesses, but were keenly aware of, as the author wrongly notes of the poor readers, "the internal structure of the strings" (p. 41). How could poor readers (for their grade) in the ability to recognize words in lists be expected to perform differently in the experimental situation? As Thompson (1981) suggests, such good/poor findings may disappear when good readers are given tasks that are as comparably difficult. Indeed, cueing on initial letter as a salient graphic cue appears to be a feature of beginning readers (Marchbanks & Levin, 1965; Williams, Blumberg, & Williams, 1970).

Stanovich (1981) also cites evidence from studies that show differences in context effects. One early study involved fourth and sixth graders with "mean reading ability" of 5.5 and 7.5 as measured by the WRAT. They concluded that "better readers (as indicated by a standardized test) make less use of context" (p. 721). Again, the criterion test of reading is a sight-word task, by definition the better readers were de facto better at word recognition tasks. Mabry (1995) comments on the WRAT by stating, "On no grounds can this be considered a test of reading" (p. 1108). In addition, she notes that the relationships between the WRAT reading subtest and other measures of comprehension are unclear.

The Stanovich model appears to be supported by evidence resulting from studies that in many cases are within a particular experimental paradigm. Goodman (1981) suggests that the Stanovich model is supported by evidence from studies of laboratory-like conditions ignoring the available miscue data from conditions that are more ecologically valid. The Stanovich model subsumes "lower-level" processing in the general area of orthographic structures. It does not describe the relationships between other factors such as word frequency or graphic input and higher level factors, nor does it represent variables related to second-language reading.

Schema-Theoretic Models

A related view of reading has been referred to as the schema-theoretic view, which suggests that reading involves making predictions based on schema or general outlines of spoken or written texts. Bartlett (1932), based on a concept developed by Kant, suggested that memory is organized into schemata: general or specific outlines of knowledge. According to schema theory a text provides directions to show how meaning is retrieved or constructed for a listener or a reader. A reader has background knowledge related to his or her experience and from that background knowledge constructs schemata (Bartlett, 1932; Adams & Collins, 1979; Rumelhart, 1985). The construction of meaning involves mapping input against some existing schema. Two basic modes of information processing are used, top-down and bottom-up. Schemata are hierarchically organized from the most general at the top to the most specific at the bottom. Bottom-up processing is called text-driven and top-down is called conceptually driven.

According to Rumelhart (1985), both kinds of processing should occur simultaneously. A schema consists of a description of a particular category of concepts. It consists of a hierarchy of schemata embedded within schemata. If the conceptual category is "going to the dentist," then its top-level representation would include such information as the general purpose of a visit to the dentist, which would contain such information as making appointments, and paying the dentist to care for one's teeth. At the level below this, schemata would contain items related to "dental checkups," the cleaning of teeth, drilling and filling, and extraction. Each schema at each level contains descriptions of its meanings and their interrelationships. The mention of a drill, therefore, is understood immediately as referring to the removal of caries, rather than practice as in "fire drill."

Research into schemata often involves presenting passages to adults wherein the "subject" or "focus" is not clearly stated. Anderson, Reynolds, Schallert, and Goetz (1977), for instance, had individuals from different backgrounds read passages that could be about wrestling or jail and playing music or playing cards. These authors found that physical education students read the jail/wrestling passage and understood it, because of their backgrounds, according to a "wrestling" schema, whereas most people viewed the passage as one about a jail break. A number of related studies looked at passage comprehension by individuals whose backgrounds differed. Other studies varied the schemata individuals applied as they read. Pichert and Anderson (1977) showed that individuals learned more about a passage when they were provided with a perspective or schema; for instance, individuals asked to read a passage about a house as though they were burglars remembered some items that those who were asked to read it as potential buyers did not, and vice versa. Burglar schemata made individuals more likely to remember that a side door was always unlocked than the home-buyers schemata.

Schank and Abelson (1977) produced a related model through an elaboration of Minsky's (1975) frame theory, a "script theory," which suggests that part of one's knowledge is organized in hundreds or thousands of stereotypic situations, which contain usual or routine activities. Scripts, it is suggested, organize individuals' activities and allow them to understand or comprehend conventional activities when they hear or read about them.

Most schema research involved short sentences or short, contrived passages that had more than one possible interpretation. Most written material is more complex, often less linear than the passages used in most schema research. Researchers posited that knowledge structures were complex, yet their research involved highly routinized or scripted events occurring in common situations such as trips to restaurants. However as Spiro and Myers (1984) note, "*One cannot have a prepackaged knowledge structure for everything!*" [emphasis in original]. Schema theory was developed primarily on the basis of the study of adults, so developmental differences in comprehension are not accounted for, nor is the acquisition of schemata. Indeed, little research on schema acquisition has been conducted. The relationships between lower level perceptual processes such as letter and word recognition and comprehension are not considered. Schema-theoretic models have been adopted and adapted for second-language learners. During the 1980s and 1990s a model of literacy, the whole language model, evolved.

Whole Language Models

A more recent development has been the application of emergent literacy research to investigations of the preschool development or emergence of literacy that occurs in some children, to the classroom. Harste and Burke (1977) first noted that whole language as a theoretical orientation "views reading as one of four ways in which the abstract concept of language is realized" (p. 37). Y. Goodman (1989), in a comprehensive review of the history of whole language titled "Roots of the Whole-Language Movement," details the multiple influences on whole language. She suggests the Harste and Burke reference is the first instance in which the term *whole language* appears in print. She also notes that Goodman and Goodman published an occasional paper in 1978 that discussed whole language comprehension-centered reading curricula. These early contributors to whole language had reading orientations, whereas the more recent view of whole language, sometimes referred to as whole literacy (Au, 1993), is that speaking, listening, reading, and writing are integrated language activities that develop in a mutually supportive parallel fashion. A major impetus for the development of the whole language model was the research by Read (1971), who looked at the spelling development of his preschool child and found that it was logical rather than random. Read showed that a child's early independent writing revealed a developing understanding of grapheme–phoneme correspondences. The results of Read's study have, in part, been used as evidence to support whole language. His orientation was to studies of the developing phonological awareness in the early spelling attempts of very young individuals. Whole language theorists believe, as a consequence, that children should be allowed to invent spellings and view the activities as meaningful language explorations. Many preschool children begin to write letters and letter-like forms spontaneously. Researcher after researcher has observed that there appears to be a sequence in the development of independent writing: scribbling (with meaning); perceiving print and drawing as synonymous; representing things with individual letters; writing initial consonants to represent words beginning with particular sounds; spacing between words; representing sounds with letters; inventing spellings; and producing mature conventions of spelling and writing (Dyson, 1981; Ferreiro, 1986; Gunderson, 1991a; Gunderson & Shapiro 1988; Hipple, 1985; Sulzby, 1986). In addition, preschool children learn that particular items of "environmental print" represent different things, certain logos represent products and certain letters represent items, like STOP. Most preschool readers and writers are fortunate to come from home environments where reading and writing are valued activities and parents actively encourage, indeed, reward the process of reading and writing. Many view whole language as a philosophy rather than a model, but Gunderson (1997) concludes that whole language is not a philosophy; rather, each teacher's view of whole language is "a composite propositional intertext," which contains beliefs concerning the teaching and learning of literacy. In essence, the whole language approach is to emulate in the classroom the environment of preschool independent learners (Gunderson & Shapiro, 1988). The basic whole language model is that literacy occurs through a child's meaningful interaction with language. Gunderson (1997) concluded that whole language as a model involves a minimum number of features, including: "that meaningful language is intact language; that active learning is meaningful learning; that speaking, listening, reading, writing, and watching are integrated, mutually reinforcing language activities; that the aesthetics of language are fundamental; that language is functional; that the learning of content and the learning of language are inseparable; and that literacy learning should involve the learning of process" (p. 226).

Whole language, as a literacy model, has changed the way many teachers view literacy and teach their students to read and write. Students are given a log book or diary on their first day of school and are asked to write. They are involved in learning to read using children's literature, books they are motivated to read. They learn basic skills such as spelling and phonics through meaningful interactions with reading and writing activities (Gunderson & Shapiro, 1988). Gunderson and Shapiro found that students learn basic phonics and spelling skills as they are involved in the activities of whole language classrooms. However, a number of researchers have suggested that whole language is based on a concept of literacy that is Eurocentric and biased toward middle-class White students.

Delpit (1988, 1991) argues that whole language involves a focus on process, one that benefits students from the middle-class, which denies minority students access to the "power code." Anderson (1994) found "that parents from different cultural groups held different perceptions of literacy learning" (p. 13). Indeed, he also found that "While parents from all three cultural groups supported some aspects of emergent literacy, parents from non-mainstream were less supportive of this perspective than were their mainstream counterparts" and "each of the non-mainstream groups unanimously rejected some aspects of emergent literacy" (p. 13). Whole language is a pedagogical approach uniquely imbued with mainstream North American cultural features (Anderson & Gunderson, 1997). Swiniarski (1992) proposed that whole language theorists in North America have credited the literacy program in New Zealand as being built on whole language principles; however, she notes of New Zealand teachers that "while many were familiar with whole language literature, they regarded the term as a purely American interpretation of their literacy programs" (p. 225). Anderson, Hiebert, Scott, and Wilkinson (1985) refer to the literacy instruction occurring in New Zealand as whole language. Ashton-Warner's (1963) language experience concepts have influenced whole language; indeed some researchers have considered the two to be synonymous (Stahl & Miller, 1989). Holdaway (1979) introduced the use of shared reading, a development that also influenced literature-based and whole language programs. Clay (1979, 1985, 1991) contributed significantly to the development of programs in New Zealand. In Australia, Cambourne developed a natural learning theory "from naturalistic research that sets out to describe and explain how language learning occurs in the everyday ebb and flow of human activity" (Cambourne & Turbill, 1990, p. 338). Cambourne (1988) sets out seven conditions for literacy acquisition: immersion, demonstration, expectation, responsibility, employment, approximation, and response. Cambourne and Turbill note, "Teachers who implement this theory create classrooms in which the conditions of learning that accompany natural language learning are simulated for pupils learning to control the written form of language" (p. 338). They suggest that such conditions can be used to teach both young students and those who are older. Cambourne and Turbill (1988, 1989, 1990) have also influenced whole language through their studies of "teacher-as-coresearcher."

Reading and writing are interactive processes; the mature reader relies on knowledge from multiple sources to read, understand, and interpret text and to think, create, and compose text. The student's initial reading activities involve his or her own initial writing activities and reading aloud with the teacher; the activities are co-interactive in that they are inseparable (Gunderson, 1994). In this view, learning to read and write involves exploration or, as Harste (1993) refers to it, "inquiry." Learning to read and to write involves the acquisition of a number of abilities, from the ability to decode orally individual letters to the ability to write syntactically complex and elegantly coherent and complex arguments. Whole language represents a model of language learning that posits that such skills are learned in environments that foster functional and meaningful language learning that varies from teacher to teacher as each constructs an individual propositional intertext (Gunderson, 1997).

McKenna, Robinson, and Miller (1993) opined that "Mainstream researchers are often frustrated by the lack of coherent, universally applicable definitions" (p. 141) and "If whole language varies from teacher to teacher, general definitions and generalizeable conclusions are difficult to make precise" (p. 142). Stahl and Miller (1989) avoid the dilemma by concluding, "Therefore, we will refer to the entire range of approaches as *whole language/language experience approaches*" [emphasis in original], for the reasons that they are "based on the premise that speaking, listening, writing and reading are interrelated and interdependent" (p. 89). However, Edelsky (1990a) concluded that such a definition "could not distinguish whole language from language experience approaches from activity approaches of the 1950's" (p. 8).

Additionally, whole language has been the subject of considerable debate, and sometimes intense acrimony, as many individuals have focused on what they view as a weakness in the research base. McKenna et al. (1993) noted, "Regarding this translation of philosophy into method, whole language inherits respectable research bases underlying some of the practices that its adherents espouse" (p. 146). McKenna et al. (1993) complained that "Mainstream researchers are often frustrated by the lack of coherent, universally applicable definitions" (p. 141) and "If whole language varies from teacher to teacher, general definitions and generalizeable conclusions are difficult to make precise" (p. 142). McKenna et al. (1993), Palmer, Gambrell, and Almassi, (1991), Stahl and Miller (1989), and Shapiro (1994), among others, have reviewed whole language research generally, finding that the studies produced different results. Palmer, Gambrell, and Almassi (1991) reviewed whole language research they judged to be well designed, both quantitative and qualitative, and concluded that whole language has not been rigorously assessed. Stahl and Miller (1989) stated, "From the data reviewed, it appears that whole language approaches may have an important function early in the process of learning to read, but that as the child's needs shift, they become less effective" (p. 111). Edelsky (1990a) criticized their study, however, because it included language experience programs. Carrigan (1986) observed differences in a standardized reading test related to whole language versus basal classes and found that his students, including Punjabi-speaking South Asians, in the basal-reading classes outscored the whole language classes at the end of first grade, both in writing development and in standardized reading scores.

Carrigan analyzed the basal workbooks and the standardized reading tests and observed that students in the basal groups had, in effect, practiced test skills over the course of the year. In addition, he noted that their writing was judged to be better because it contained more complete sentences and correct spellings. The sentences were written in basalese; they were short, repetitive sentences that were modeled after the language of the basals. Carrigan concluded that the skills-based program taught test-taking skills and basal language to students whose first language was not English. The language experience students, on the other hand, had not practiced test-taking skills. Their writing contained many more invented spellings, fewer complete sentences, and was less well structured. Carrigan noted, however, that their writing was more interesting and revealed students' developing knowledge of English more realistically than the basal students' writing.

McKenna, Robinson, and Miller's (1993) review identified what they suggest are four major problems in research comparing whole language and basal instruction: (a) Whole language is not well defined; (b) the methods and procedures for researching whole language are deemed by critics to be inadequate or inappropriate; (c) whole language research is selectively reviewed by its advocates, thereby placing interpreters between teachers and researchers; and (d) whole language advocates reject research in favor of politics and rhetoric. Gunderson (1997) concluded, however, that whole language is based on individually developed propositional intertexts that vary from teacher to teacher, views of teaching and learning that contain a set of core propositions, which are not appropriately studied by traditional comparative research. Whole language approaches have been criticized because they do not include direct, systematic instruction in phonics or phonemic awareness.

The learning of skills such as phonics and spelling in the whole language classroom occurs during meaningful interactions with language, both oral and written. Specific phonics instruction generally occurs in an inductive fashion as students demonstrate their needs (see Gunderson & Shapiro, 1988). However, many individuals, particularly politicians, believe that direct, systematic phonics instruction is central to early literacy instruction.

Phonemic Awareness and Phonological Development

Phonemic awareness, the ability to identify individual sounds or phonemes in words, has been shown to be a predictor of literacy development (Juel, 1988; Rego, 1991). In addition, it is related to a student's concept of word (Morris, 1981). Winsor and Pearson (1992) observed that phonemic awareness was an important variable in their study of at-risk first graders. It is generally acknowledged that phonemic awareness should have developed to the point that by the end of kindergarten students should be able to rhyme words or syllables, identify words that begin with the same sound, be able to identify the number of syllables in a word, and know the names of the letters of the alphabet and that they represent sounds or phonemes (Adams, 1990; Cunningham, 1990; Yopp, 1992). These skills are central to a student being able to learn phonics. The whole language teacher is convinced these skills will be learned through meaningful interactions with language, and, indeed, they do (Gunderson & Shapiro, 1988; Shapiro & Gunderson,

1988). However, there are those who are convinced that whole language as an approach does not teach basic skills directly and students, therefore, are disadvantaged because they do not learn them.

In 1995, 60% of California's fourth-grade students scored "below basic" in a national reading test (Lucas & Asimov, 1995). The California State Legislature responded by passing bills that mandated certain kinds of instruction. The first bill required that spelling instruction be included that was comprised of textbooks or computer programs. The second bill required instructional materials in reading to contain fundamental skills including phonics and spelling (Lucas & Asimov, 1995). In 1996 the California State Board of Education rejected two series because they reportedly did not include spelling or phonics instruction (Gunnison, 1996). California is not the only state where there have been back-to-basics campaigns that have resulted in similar phonics laws (see, e.g., Genisio, 1996). Gunderson (1997) concludes that "Research also seems to suggest that systematic phonics instruction is detrimental to performance on standardized reading-comprehension tests in the long term (Korkeamäki and Dreher, 1993), and that whole language results in superior performance on standardized comprehension tests in the long term (McCallum, Whitlow, and Moore, 1991)" (p. 240).

Bottom-up, top-down, interactive, schema-theoretic, and whole language models have been developed to help teachers and researchers to understand the processes related to reading. Teachers develop literacy programs based on models of reading, often implicit views of teaching and learning that are most often bottom-up models. Researchers design studies to observe whether the hypothesized relationships in their models exist. Models have been developed primarily to explore the variables related to reading processes in English because it has been the primary language in schools in the United States, where these models were developed. Over the last 20 years, however, the number of students whose first language is English has declined, whereas the number of students whose first language is not English has risen. There are compelling pragmatic and theoretical reasons to develop second-language models.

SECOND-LANGUAGE READING

In referring to English as a second language (ESL), Grabe (1991) notes that "Most of our current views of second-language reading are shaped by research on first language learners" (p. 378). He also suggests that "A primary goal for ESL reading theory and instruction is to understand what fluent L1 readers do, then decide how best to move ESL students in that developmental direction" (p. 378). Grabe suggests there are six component skills in reading: automatic recognition skills, knowledge of vocabulary and structure, knowledge of formal discourse structures, content and world background knowledge, synthesis and evaluation skills and strategies, and metacognitive knowledge and skills monitoring.

Although L2 learners appear to have some difficulty using spelling patterns to recognize words (Favreau, Komodo, & Segalowitz, 1980; Favreau & Segalowitz, 1983; Mes-Prat & Edwards, 1981), some researchers conclude that both L1 and L2 learners use the same basic word recognition strategies (Connor, 1981; Dank & McEachern, 1979; Goodman & Goodman, 1978; Haddad, 1981; Rigg, 1977). Verhoeven (1990) concludes that second-language readers rely on L1 strategies as they learn to read a L2.

Gunderson (1991b) argues that issues related to reading in a second language are considerably more complex than reading in a first language. Second-language reading, and research into second-language literacy, are more complex because there are significant differences in background. First, second-language learners usually begin to learn to read before they have acquired the vocabulary normally associated with beginning readers. That is, first-language learners, who typically begin formal reading instruction at about 6 years of age, have good-sized speaking vocabularies. Second-language learners often do not. In addition, L1 beginning readers have a well-ingrained working knowledge of grammar, whereas L2 learners often do not.

Some L2 learners have an advantage because they can transfer their knowledge of the world, their sophisticated concepts, and their ability to make inferences from text to the L2 reading task. In addition, they have learned about concepts related to particular academic studies. Grabe (1991) concludes that because of their backgrounds, good L1 readers face a different kind of task, one that focuses on vocabulary. He states, "As a consequence, vocabulary becomes largely a matter of remembering a second label for a well-understood concept" (p. 387). A second-language literacy model should account for learners' L1 literacy backgrounds.

The L2 reading process may also be affected by a number of different kinds of transfer. Syntactic transfer based on differences between L1 and L2 can affect the L2 reader. The kind of literacy instruction an L2 learner has received in L1 can affect L2 processes. As noted at the beginning of this chapter, beliefs about teaching and learning are powerful influences on the L2 learner.

Orthographic differences should be accounted for in a second-language model. Students who have learned to read in a nonalphabetic language may find it difficult to learn to read an alphabetic language, especially a language like English, which is said to have a deep orthographic structure. Orthographies have been characterized by the degree to which they represent phonology. A shallow orthography is one in which there is a one-to-one relationship between a grapheme and a phoneme, whereas a deep orthography consists of more complex relationships (Frost & Bentin, 1992; Katz & Frost, 1992; Perreman, 1992; Turvey, Feldman, & Lukatela, 1984). Orthographies also vary in the way they represent language. Graphemes, depending on the orthography, may represent phonemes (Hebrew), syllables (Kurdish), morphemes (Chinese), words (Japanese), phonemes and morphemes (English), or a combination of these elements (Chinese, Japanese). English is said to be a deep orthography because its alphabet does not simply represent phonemes. The words "kids" and "lids", for instance, end with a grapheme "s" that is morphophonemic in that it represents a voiced alveolar fricative /z/ and is also a lexical marker for "plural." Haynes and Carr (1990), among others, conclude, "Thus, it seems reasonable to suppose that readers practiced in one writing system might experience, when attempting to master a new system, positive or negative interference from lower level L1 reading skills, depending on the similarities and differences between the skills fostered by each of the two systems" (p. 379). Koda (1995) concludes that "These results suggest that specific skills and strategies are developed through initial literacy acquisition to deal with a particular orthographic system used in the language" (p. 311). There is support for the contention that the underlying processing of text differs across languages (Geva, 1995; Koda, 1995; Paradis, Hagiwara, & Hildebrandt, 1985; Turvey et al., 1984; Tzeng & Wang, 1983). Hung and Tzeng (1981) argue that all orthographies "attempt to transcribe sentences at the word level" (p. 408), but that such transcriptions vary in the way they lead to meaning, via either a phonological or a visual pathway. The authors suggest that research should seek to discover the role of orthography in differences in reading processes across languages. Ho and Bryant (1997) conclude, "Chinese children do rely on phonetics for phonological cues in reading Chinese characters after the initial reading phase" (p. 286). In addition, they note that "script–sound regularities in Chinese, though they appear not to be very regular, do help children learn to read Chinese" (p. 286). The students in their study learned to read in Hong Kong, where the "children naturally pick up script–sound regularities by learning to read enough characters" (p. 287). These authors suggest that "enough characters" may have been learned by the second grade for students to begin to make phonic generalizations to apply in new characters. The effects of L1 orthography on the learning of L2 literacy should be a feature of a second-language model.

Second-language educators have developed views of reading instruction based on many different first-language models, for example, the psycholinguistic model (Clarke & Silberstein, 1977; Coady, 1979; Eskey, 1973); the interactive model (Carrell, 1988a, 1988b; Eskey & Grabe, 1988); the schema-theoretic model (Carrell, 1984, 1987a; Carrell & Eisterhold, 1983; Floyd & Carrell, 1987; Hudson, 1982); and the whole language (Freeman & Freeman, 1992; Heald-Taylor, 1986, 1989; Hudelson, 1984; Rigg,

1986, 1991) or whole literacy model (Au, 1993). In many cases, however, the research base involves first-language studies.

SECOND LANGUAGE MODELS

Cummins (1979, 1984) and Cummins and Swain (1986) proposed a "Common Underlying Proficiency" (CUP) model based on the notion that "literacy-related aspects of a bilingual's proficiency in L1 and L2 are seen as common or interdependent across languages" (p. 82). Literacy experience in either language promotes the underlying interdependent proficiency base. This view suggests that "common cross-lingual proficiencies underlie the obviously different surface manifestations of each language" (p. 82).

There is evidence to support CUP (cf. Baker & de Kanter, 1981; Cummins, 1983a, 1983b). Hakuta (1986), on the other hand, noted, "What is remarkable about the issue of transfer of skills is that despite its fundamental importance, almost no empirical studies have been conducted to understand the characteristics or even to demonstrate the existence of the transfer of skills" (p. 218). However, Hakuta, Butler, and Witt (2000) have shown more recent evidence that transfer does occur. Common underlying proficiency has also been referred to as the interdependence principle. Cummins (2000) defines interdependence as:

> To the extent that instruction in Lx is effective in promoting proficiency in Lx, transfer of this proficiency to Ly will occur provided there is adequate exposure to Ly (either in school or environment) and adequate motivation to learn Ly. (p. 38)

Cummins (2000) reviews considerable evidence to support the notion of common underlying proficiency or interdependence. In general, however, the role of English proficiency in ESL students' success at school, including reading, has been viewed as pivotal. "Language is the focus of every content-area task, with all meaning and all demonstration of knowledge expressed through oral and written forms of language" (Collier, 1987). ESL students must learn to communicate in English and to learn in English. Research suggests that older students acquire many features of L2 faster than younger students (Krashen, Long, & Scarcella, 1979; Krashen, Scarcella, & Long, 1982), even though they often have more difficulty with pronunciation and the socioaffective filter. Younger students acquire higher proficiency than those who begin at older ages (Krashen, 1982). ESL students take longer to acquire academic language than social language (Collier, 1987, 1994; Cummins, 1981a; Saville-Troike, 1984).

Cummins (1979, 1980, 1981a, 1981b) proposed that there were two kinds of language proficiencies to be learned, "basic interpersonal communicative skill" (BICS), the language of ordinary conversation or "the manifestation of language proficiency in everyday communicative contexts" (Cummins, 1984, p. 137), and "cognitive academic language proficiency" (CALP), the language of instruction and academic texts, which has come to be known as *academic language proficiency*. It has been suggested that these labels might lead to a misinterpretation of the complexities they seek to describe (Edelsky et al., 1983; Rivera, 1984) and imply a deficit model of language. Edelsky (1990b) likens CALP to "test-wiseness" and develops an additional acronym: SIN, "skill in instructional nonsense" (p. 65). Cummins (2000) addresses this issue in his book and his arguments are not reviewed here. Cummins also discusses the notion of threshold that will be described later.

The two labels have generally, however, come to represent two categories of proficiency: that associated with face-to-face conversation (BICS) and that associated with learning in the context-reduced, cognitively demanding oral and written environment of the classroom (CALP) (Cummins, 1981b, 1982; Swain 1981; Cummins & Swain, 1983). Older students use knowledge of academic material and concepts gained studying L1 to help them in L2 and the acquisition of L2 occurs faster.

Collier (1987) confirmed these findings in her study of 1,548 "advantaged" limited English proficient (LEP) students from upper- or upper-middle-class families. LEP students arriving between the ages of 8 and 11 were the quickest to acquire CALP, and 7-year-old students were slightly behind their rate, whereas students who arrived at ages 5–6 required 2 to 3 more years of schooling to reach the level attained by the 8- to 11-year-olds. Those who had arrived at ages 12–15 were the lowest achievers in all areas except math. Collier projected they would need 2 to 3 additional years to reach the 50th percentile in all subject areas. Collier (1994) proposed that there is a relationship among academic, cognitive, and language development related to ESL students' success in school. She found that students with the greatest amount of academic and cognitive development in L1 have the greatest gains in English and perform significantly above the national average, evidence suggesting interdependence or common underlying proficiencies.

The Cummins (1981a) and Collier (1987) studies are among the most cited. Over the years individual researchers have cited them broadly, but have not noted their limitations. Cummins's (1981a) study titled "Age on Arrival and Immigrant Second-Language Learning in Canada: A Reassessment" was a reanalysis of a study by Wright and Ramsey (1970), who investigated the achievement of approximately 1,200 students in the Toronto (Ontario, Canada) school district. These studies included a group administered Picture Vocabulary Test and an English Competency test that had six subsections. The English Competency Test, according to Cummins, was "an experimental test developed by the Toronto Board with the aim of assessing basic 'competence' in a Chomskian sense" (p. 135). He also cautions the reader that "The experimental nature of the ECT should be borne in mind when interpreting the present result" (p. 135). The ECT consisted of subtests of auditory recognition, sound recognition, intonation, vocabulary (contentives), vocabulary (functors), and idioms. Cummins concludes that CALP takes on the average at least 5 years to develop. The standardized tests used in the original study were developed as experimental instruments. He does not present grade-level equivalent scores for native-English speakers so one must trust his results. Another problem, however, is that the two measures Cummins equates with CALP, Vocabulary and Idioms, are not necessarily measures of academic language. The vocabulary tests required students to match a short definition with a vocabulary item and to fill prepositions into slots in various sentences. The vocabulary tests, therefore, appear to measure students' vocabulary and syntactic knowledge. It is not clear that either of these, strictly speaking, is a measure of academic language proficiency. On the other hand, knowledge of idioms has been shown to be late developing in the first language and very late developing in the second language.

Idiomatic language contains metaphors, similes, and conventionalized usages, items that contain expressions whose meanings cannot necessarily be determined by the meaning of the constituent words. Idiomatic language contains conventionalized expressions such as "He's blue," metaphors such as "he bulled his way through the crowded room," and similes such as "she's thin as a rail." A substantial portion of the idiomatic language we use in English consists of metaphors. Indeed, the term *metaphor* also often refers to similes because both share a common function and a common comprehension process (Kintsch, 1974; Ortony, 1975).

A metaphor is the application of a word or phrase that belongs in one context to another context in order to express meaning through some real or implied similarity in referents (Anderson, 1964; Gambrell and McFeteridge, 1981). The vehicle of a metaphor is the term being use metaphorically. For instance, the term *bulled* is used in a nonfarm setting to indicate that a person has forced his way through a group of people. It is the vehicle of the metaphor. Often one can understand the metaphor because the vehicle is obvious, as in "he moved through the room like a bull in a china shop," but in many cases it is not; the vehicle has become frozen and the term has simply become an idiomatic expression, as in, "he jacked me up" (meaning, "he made me believe he was going to do something and he didn't"). ESL students find idiomatic language difficult to acquire and are hesitant to use it (Irujo, 1986), often translating it incorrectly—for example, instead of "he went out on a limb," "he went out on a stick."

Research in L1 has been directed toward discovering when, how, and why idiomatic language is used (Johnson & Malgrady, 1980; Ortony,

Reynolds, & Arter, 1978; Pearson, Raphael, Tepaske, & Hyser, 1979). Pollio and Pollio (1974) found that the production of figurative language increased over Grades 3, 4, and 5 and that students could use idiomatic language before they could explain the nature of the parts of an item. Gardner, Kircher, Winner, and Perkins (1974) concurred that age was associated with the ability to produce appropriate metaphors. Winner, Rosentiel, and Gardner (1976) studied students from 6 to 14 years of age and concluded that there were four stages of metaphorical comprehension development: magical (accepted at face value); primitive (focus on incidental aspects of terms); metonymic (inappropriate juxtaposition of terms); and genuine (focus on the appropriate aspect of the terms). They found there was a developmental sequence in the acquisition of metaphor: spontaneous production, comprehension, and finally production, comprehension, and the ability to explain the rationale of an idiomatic phrase requiring "metalinguistic awareness" that only emerges in preadolescence. Youngsters are able to produce idiomatic language, including metaphor, by the time they are 5 or 6 years old (Winner et al., 1976) and their use of novel metaphors increases with age (Gardner et al., 1974; Pollio & Pollio, 1974). It has been suggested that this increasing ability is related to students' growing cognitive ability and the acquisition of world knowledge. Arlin (1978), however, concluded that the ability to understand metaphoric language is dependent on cognitive development. Billow (1975) showed that "rudimentary forms of metaphor comprehension occur early in a child's life" (p. 420). Students' perceptions of metaphoric language decrease in quantity with age, and the majority of items they produce consists of frozen or conventional idioms (Gardner et al., 1974; Pollio & Pollio, 1974). However, Ortony, Schallert, Reynolds, and Antos (1978) suggest that the difficulty of the idiom was not as significant in understanding as was the degree to which the item was related to context of the item, whereas Winner, Engel, and Gardner (1980) found that the form of the idiomatic expression was related to its difficulty.

Generally, students' abilities to function with idiomatic language, including metaphors and similes, develop at any early age, and mature through a developmental sequence that seems to match their cognitive development and experience with the world (Grindstaff & Muller, 1975). Metaphor makes text more difficult to read in some cases (Cunningham, 1976; Winkeljohann, 1979). If the text is unfamiliar, however, it may increase students' comprehension (Pearson et al., 1979), which may also take place if the metaphors are concluding statements (Reynolds & Schwartz, 1979) or students are of low ability (Arter, 1976). Baldwin, Luce, and Readence (1982) concluded that students have difficulty with idiomatic language because they lack background knowledge, not because they are unable to cope with the form of the idiom. These authors conclude that instructional programs should focus on increasing students' knowledge rather than on the analysis and interpretation of language forms.

Jordans (1979) and Kellerman (1977) both concluded that ESL learners were reluctant to transfer language-specific items to the second language. Iruju (1986) found that ESL students produced and understood idioms best when they were related to items found in their first language. However, there was a negative transfer if they were similar in both languages. She suggested that similarity caused interference. She also suggested that idioms be taught as lexical items. Gunderson, Slade, and Rosenke (1988) showed that idiomatic language increased native-English-speaking (NES) students' reading comprehension whereas it decreased ESL adult students' comprehension. They suggested there was a developmental sequence in ESL students' acquisition of idiomatic language.

A large part of the native-English-speaking (NES) student's background knowledge is an understanding of idiomatic language. Competence in idiomatic language is a late-developing skill in NES students (Gardner, 1974). Metaphor, a major component of idiomatic language, appears to facilitate understanding because it serves as the link between the known and the unknown (Ortony, 1975; Petrie, 1979). Idiomatic language results in higher NES students' reading comprehension than does literal language, whereas ESL students' literal comprehension is higher than their idiomatic comprehension (Gunderson et al., 1988). When two passages of comparable readability level are read, the one containing idiomatic language is comprehended at a higher level than the one containing literal language by NES students, but not by ESL students. One thing that is clear from the Cummins research is that the test of metaphors was difficult for the native English speakers, shown in that their scores (combined with the ESL scores, unfortunately) increased from a mean of 4.7 out of 10 at Grade 5 (10-year-olds) to 7.8 at Grade 9 (14-year-olds). There is a developmental difference in native English speakers' ability to deal with idiomatic language. It is not clear that idioms represent academic language.

It is not clear that the measures used in the Cummins (1981a) study reliably measured academic language proficiency. Cummins notes that "Finally, it should be noted that the present findings are not necessarily generalizeable outside of the Canadian social context, and even within that context may not hold for particular immigrant groups" (p. 148). It is fair to say that many authors have, in fact, grossly overgeneralized the findings of this study. Collier (1987), for instance, notes that "Analyzing rate of attainment of CALP in the second language Cummins (1981a) found that whereas it generally takes students 2 years to master BICS in the L2, young children with little or no formal schooling in the L1 require approximately 5–7 years to reach the level of native speaker in CALP in the second language, as measured on standardized tests" (p. 619). This generalization is unfounded and entirely too broad. It is not clear that Cummins measured CALP. His findings cannot be generalized to whole populations, to "students" or "young children" in general. Unfortunately, over the years these overgeneralizations have come to be viewed as representing the truth.

The Collier (1987) study, "Age and Rate of Acquisition of Second Language for Academic Purposes," was, broadly, a follow-up study of the Cummins (1981) study. Collier selected her subjects from several databases. From 14,000 possible students who had registered for ESL classes, "only those students who entered at the beginning level of ESL proficiency and who were at grade level in L1 literacy and math skills had been selected and those who had not remained in the school system had been eliminated" (p. 623). It is important to note that Collier states these students were "at grade level in L1 literacy."

The resulting data set contained 1,548 limited English proficiency students. The sample was convenient, not randomly selected, and generalizations are not possible. Indeed, the group is unique in that it was stable relative to the large number of students who appeared to have left the school district. The study appears to show rather a large disappearance rate for the second-language students. It seems that only slightly more than 10% remained. The basic problem with Collier's (1987) findings are that they are misinterpreted. She notes:

> Although some groups of LEP students at all grade levels had reached the 50th NCE (the national average) on some subject-area tests within the 4–5 years measured in this study, when compared with the achievement levels of native speakers in their local school district, LEP students had not yet begun to reach the school system means across grade levels of 62–64 NCEs in reading, 62–64 NCEs in language arts, 60–65 NCEs in social studies, and 69–64 NCEs in science. They had for the most part, met and excelled native speakers' achievement in mathematics, in which the school system mean ranged from 62 to 71 NCEs across all grade levels. (p. 627)

Collier reports mean scores, average normal curve equivalents (NCEs). If a particular sample of students is "normal" or "average," its NCE should be 50. Collier produces four figures showing students' average NCEs. Inspection of the graphs reveal that the LEP Grade 4, 6, and 8 students' scores for reading, language arts, and social science were all near the 50 NCE point, all of them in the 1–2 year range. This pattern does not follow for the 11th graders. Collier (1987) concludes:

> Given that the 5-year-old arrivals performed less well than their *peers in 4th grade* [emphasis added], that the 6- and 7-year-old arrivals did less well than *their peers in 6th grade* [emphasis added], and that the 12- to 15-year-old arrivals tested in 11th grade achieved significantly lower that the national average even after 4–5 years of all-English schooling, then it would appear that the 8-

to 11-year-old arrivals experienced the shortest length of time for reaching the aspects of CALP development in the L2 measured by the SRA tests. (p. 635)

This is simply wrong. If the tests measured CALP and the norm group is representative of all learners in the United States, then their scores should be 50. And they generally appear to be, except for reading. Collier compares LEP scores to local means for two groups and to national means for the other two. This is wrong. The interesting finding is that her subjects' reading scores were generally lower, yet they scored higher on tests requiring reading skills that focused on academic content. Based on Collier's figures it appears that it takes about 1–2 years to develop CALP for younger students. Another interesting finding is that 8th graders who arrived at 12 years of age and who were in the United States for only 1–2 years scored significantly higher than 11th-grade students who arrived when they were 12 and were in the United States for 4–5 years. Most interesting, however, were Collier's 11th-grade students who scored significantly lower on all measures than the 4th, 6th, and 8th graders in her study and, except in mathematics, significantly lower than the 50th NCE. Although Collier suggests these results are related to differences in test instruments, it seems equally as probable that it was due to differences in the sample of 11th graders. This is a possibility, considering subjects were convenient not randomly chosen.

Gunderson (1995) found that immigrant students required about 5 to 7 years to develop academic language. However, he also found that 90% of the 9,579 immigrants he studied were 3 or more years behind in reading comprehension as measured by the Gates–MacGinitie test after 3 years of instruction in Canada. Gunderson's study suffers because it used only the comprehension section of the Gates–MacGinitie test to measure CALP and a locally developed oral language test to measure BICS. Generally, it would appear that the skill measured by standardized reading tests does take some time to develop in ESL students. These students represent a serious problem for schools, particularly the secondary-level students.

Harley, Cummins, Swain, and Allen (1990) integrated the Cummins model with Canale's (1983) refinement of the communicative competence framework developed by Canale and Swain (1980) to create a framework of grammatical, discourse, and sociolinguistic competence measured by oral and written modes and by multiple-choice tests within a 3 × 3 matrix operationalizing three traits—grammar, discourse, and sociolinguistic—to guide their study of students in French immersion and francophone schools. Their main goal was to measure empirically the traits hypothesized to form communicative competence. Although findings did not clearly support their model, it was concluded that "language proficiency must be conceptualized within a developmental context as a function of the interactions that students or learners experience in their languages" (p. 25).

Robson (1981), in a study of Hmong refugees, observes that "The ability to read helped the subjects in their efforts to learn another language" (p. 12). She also concludes that L1 literacy was a more important factor in learning a second language than schooling. Olson (1992) emphasizes that "Children or adults learning to read a second language, therefore, may be expected to benefit enormously from the ability to read their first language" (p. 20). First-language literacy background is viewed as being significant in learning to read in a second language and predictive of L2 reading achievement (Gunderson, 1991a).

Royer and Carlo's (1991) study revealed that L1 reading and listening skills transferred to L2, whereas general linguistic ability did not. That is, CALP transferred whereas BICS did not. Collier's (1994) more recent studies have supported the notion that CALP does transfer from L1 to L2 and that L1 background is significant in learning L2. Hornberger (1989) notes that the relationship between first- and second-language literacy is complex. She suggests that, as a result of the complexity, not all aspects of the L1 necessarily aid the development of the L2. Bell (1995) concludes, in referring to research, that "Most suggest that a high level of fluency in the native language aids progress in both L1 and L2, and that linguistic transfer thus does occur" (pp. 688–689). She also concludes that "minority children can have difficulty developing target language literacy in the absence of adequate initial literacy developing in the native language" (p. 689). Cummins concludes in 2000 that "the results of virtually all evaluations of bilingual and second language immersion programs are consistent with predictions derived from the interdependence hypothesis insofar as instruction through a minority language appears to result in no adverse consequences for students' academic development in the majority language" (p. 186).

Cummins (1978) suggested that there may be a threshold of linguistic ability required before transfer is possible. The issue of threshold has also received considerable criticism. Cummins (2000) notes, "I have used the term *common underlying proficiency* [emphasis in original] to refer to the interdependence of concepts, skills, and linguistic knowledge that makes transfer possible" (p. 191). Cummins (2000) also notes that "it was hypothesized that continued academic development of both languages conferred cognitive/linguistic benefits whereas less well-developed academic proficiency in both languages limited children's ability to benefit cognitively and academically from interaction with their environment through those languages (e.g. in school)" (p. 175). Cummins notes that threshold has also come to be known as the "short-circuit" hypothesis. In this view, researchers suggest that correlations between first and second language are only possible after students have obtained a threshold of L2 reading ability. Cummins rejects this view, but it is one that many second-language reading researchers appear to hold. Bernhardt and Kamil (1995) succinctly frame this second view of threshold by stating, "In other words, a given amount of second-language grammar/linguistic knowledge was necessary in order to get first-language reading knowledge to engage" (p. 17).

BICS and CALP have become commonly accepted notions. Research also shows reliably that they take different amounts of time to develop, (see, e.g., Hakuta et al., 2000). The common underlying proficiency model postulates that L1 processes or strategies transfer to the L2. However, it is not clear what the L1 processes actually are. Indeed, the processes that are said to underlie reading vary relative to a researcher's model. Hypothetically, if a researcher is convinced that L1 reading is bottom-up, then the proficiency features to be applied to second language are most likely to be hypothesized as bottom-up skills. Second-language researchers have adopted different first-languages models.

ESL Bottom-Up Models

Thonis in 1970 produced one of the first books written specifically to describe the systematic teaching of reading to ESL students, *Teaching Reading to Non-English Speakers*, a book that became a classic. Thonis focused on the sequential development of reading skills through use of the linguistic approach, language experience approach, and basal reading instruction. Her orientation to reading and reading instruction was skills based. Her model was a bottom-up model. Indeed, she notes, "The teaching of reading demands that the teacher order the learning sequence from the simple to the complex, from the known to the unknown, and from the nonmeaningful to the meaningful" (pp. 64–65). In many respects the bottom-up model of reading is similar to the audiolingual approach in second-language instruction, which also posits a skills hierarchy (see Larsen-Freeman, 1986, for a description of the audiolingual approach). Thonis's general conclusion about reading sounds very much like the audiolingual approach:

> All approaches to beginning reading instruction are based upon certain learning principles derived from theories of learning. The reading process is one that requires the learner, if he is to be successful, to develop habits, to be motivated, to have practice, and to *overlearn* [emphasis in original] so that his responses to written language may become as automatic as his responses to oral language. (p. 64)

ESL teachers, as evidenced by their instruction, continue to view reading and reading instruction within a bottom-up framework (Gunderson, 1985b, 1991a). It is also clear that such individuals would posit a particular set of underlying proficiencies, bottom-up processes, as the ones that are transferred to the second language. On the other hand, the ESL research community appears to have adopted on a fairly large scale the notion that L2 reading is represented better by a top-down or psycholinguistic model.

The predominant second-language instructional reading model has been the bottom-up model, a view that still drives second-language instruction in literacy today. It is also clear that first-language models are adopted and adapted to account for second-language reading. This approach is quite evident when one reads second-language journals and textbooks. For example, Carrell, Devine, and Eskey's edited volume first published in 1988, entitled *Interactive Approaches to Second Language Reading*, involves three chapters written by well-known first-language researchers who describe and discuss first-language reading models. The focus of the book is applying first-language reading models to second-language reading.

Second-Language Psycholinguistic Models

A change in view from the predominant bottom-up notion of second-language reading to a psycholinguistic view began early in the 1970s. Eskey (1973), for instance, concluded that the skills-based model, one that focused on decoding, was inadequate to account for the contributions of readers. Specifically, the role of prediction on the part of readers based on their knowledge of the syntax, semantics, and pragmatics of language was not acknowledged in the bottom-up model. Second-language researchers began to view reading within the psycholinguistic model and posited that second-language readers are active information processors who use graphophonic, syntactic, semantic, and pragmatic knowledge to sample parts of text to make predictions (e.g., Clarke, 1979; Clarke & Silberstein, 1977; Mackay & Mountford, 1979; Saville-Troike, 1984; Widdowson, 1978).

In 1979 Coady published an influential second-language model that extended the psycholinguistic model. Coady's model included conceptual abilities, general intellectual capacity, processing strategies, reading and language subskills, and background knowledge. Although he did not elaborate on background factors, Coady did note that "The interest and background knowledge will enable the student to comprehend at a reasonable rate and keep him involved in the material in spite of its syntactic difficulty" (Coady, 1979, p. 12). As Bernhardt (1991) notes, the psycholinguistic model has been the most influential model in second-language, at least as far as researchers have been concerned. However, it is criticized because the role of background knowledge is not given the emphasis many believe it should have. Clarke and Silberstein (1977), for instance, conclude:

> The reader brings to the task a formidable amount of information and ideas, attitudes and beliefs. This knowledge, coupled with the ability to make linguistic predictions, determines the expectations the reader will develop as he reads. Skill in reading depends on the efficient interaction between linguistic knowledge and knowledge of the world. (pp. 136–137)

The psycholinguistic model inadequately accounts for background knowledge, particularly for second-language learners who have backgrounds that often differ from mainstream students in their culturally related contents. Schema theory, as noted earlier, focuses on readers' background knowledge. Second-language theorists found it to be an attractive alternative to the psycholinguistic model.

Second-Language Schema-Theoretic Models

Carrell (1983), a well-respected and influential second-language reading expert, added to schema theory by making the distinction between *formal schemata*, background knowledge related to the formal, rhetorical structures of different kinds of texts, and *content schemata*, the background knowledge related to the academic content of texts. Authors have found schema theory to be particularly appropriate for second-language learners because differences in schema are often related to differences in culture and the model can account for them. When ESL readers encounter culturally familiar texts their comprehension is higher than when they encounter texts of equal difficulty but culturally unfamiliar (Carrell, 1981; Johnson, 1982). Johnson's (1982) classic study showed that a passage containing familiar content was comprehended better than a text on the same subject, but with unfamiliar content.

Johnson studied 72 advanced-level students in reading classes at an American university. She asked students who had participated in Halloween activities to read a passage about Halloween containing an introductory "familiar" section and a concluding "unfamiliar" section under four conditions: reading without a vocabulary list; studying target words before reading; reading the passage with words glossed; and studying the words before reading with vocabulary words glossed in the passage. She notes, "Results of the statistical analysis seem to indicate that real experiences within the culture context provided background information for more effective reading comprehension" (p. 511). Johnson does not adequately explain, however, why the group that received glossed vocabulary did not score significantly lower in the unfamiliar passage than in the familiar passage, as the other groups did. She concludes that because of the redundancy in English it may take a great deal of difficult vocabulary to decrease comprehension. Steffensen, Joag-dev, and Anderson (1979) showed that texts from a student's own culture are easier to understand than equivalent texts from different cultures. Because language is a reflection of culture, understanding the cultural content of text is a significant factor in comprehension (Lono, 1987; Nelson, 1987). There is related second-language research that suggests that teaching background knowledge, including in some cases cultural knowledge, increases students' comprehension of the texts they read (Carrell, 1984; Chen & Graves, 1995; Floyd & Carrell, 1987; Gatbonton & Tucker, 1971; Johnson, 1982; Taglieber, Johnson, & Yarbough, 1988). Parry (1996) concludes that "cultural background is an important factor in the formation of individual reading strategies but that this fact should not lead to a simple cultural determinism; individual variation must always be acknowledged, and so must the fact that both individuals and cultures may change in the very process of L2 learning" (p. 665). Generally, schema-theoretic models are considered by second-language researchers to be interactive models because they view reading as the interaction of background information and text (Grabe, 1988). Grabe concludes:

> While this analysis of textual interaction is admittedly exploratory, it nevertheless points out that the product within which reading occurs, the text itself, involves a sort of complex form–function interaction that is not simply the interactive process of reading (i.e., text–reader relations) as usually discussed, nor can it be simply represented by interactive models of reading (i.e., interaction of various component skills), which are essentially process oriented. (p. 65)

Second-Language Whole Language Models

Whole language models have been developed to focus on second-language learners. However, in most cases the approach is to infer teaching and learning strategies from general language studies or philosophical observations, not empirical studies of second-language literacy learning. Miller (1990) suggests that whole language is grounded on the beliefs and views developed by philosophers and educators such as Dewey, Montessori, and Rouseau. Freeman and Freeman (1992) base their whole language approach on seven tenets, drawn broadly from research, that are untested in a broad sense. In general they seem like common sense notions of learning. They are:

> 1. Lessons should proceed from whole to part; 2. Lessons should be learner centered because learning is the active construction of knowledge by students; 3. Lessons should have meaning and purpose for students now; 4. Lessons should engage groups of students in social interaction; 5. Lessons should develop both oral and written language; 6. Learning should take place in the first language to build concepts and facilitate the acquisition of English; and 7. Lessons that show faith in the learner expand students' potential. (pp. 7–8)

The difficulty with whole language as applied to second-language students is that it is an instructional model of literacy, one that focuses on critical thinking, learner independence, and creative involvement with literature; features that do not necessarily represent the view of literacy held by students from different cultures (Anderson & Gunderson, 1997, 2001; Gunderson, 1997). The difficulty a number of researchers have with whole language is that they believe it has not been tested empirically to any degree.

Most second-language models have been borrowed or adapted from first-language research. One notable exception is the Bernhardt model.

The Bernhardt Model

Bernhardt (1991) bases her model, "an interactive, multidimensional dynamic of literacy," on the notions that second-language literacy is developmental, literacy abilities develop over time, different facets are apparent at different times, miscues can reveal literacy development, there are commonalities in the processing of text "between and among literate learners and languages," and 100% proficient readers do not exist. She calls her model "a multifactor theory of second-language literacy" (p. 169). This model is shown in Figure 2.1.

Proficiency in the model varies from low to high and is graphed against error rate. The curves represent Bernhardt's hypothesized relationships. So, for instance, word recognition errors are high in the beginning, but decrease rapidly as learners become more proficient. She notes, for example, "In like manner, the phonemic/graphemic confusions' curve starts in a similar area, but drops much more quickly and sooner than the word recognition curve" because "problems in understanding related to sound and word-shape features quickly diminish as proficiency increases" (p. 170). The Bernhardt model is a noteworthy endeavor in that it does not simply borrow from an existing first-language model of literacy.

Bernhardt (2000) developed a second model she refers to as the "Revised statement of a theoretical distribution of reading factors." The *x* axis represents proficiency, whereas the *y* axis represents comprehension (Fig. 2.2).

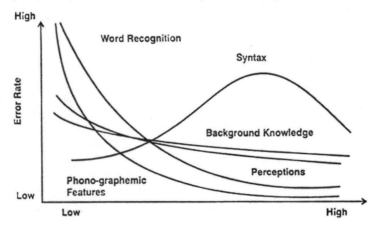

FIG. 2.1.   Theoretical distribution of reading factors. From *Reading development in a second language: Theoretical, empirical, and classroom perspectives* (p. 169), by E. B. Bernhardt, 1991, Norwood, NJ: Ablex Publishing. Copyright © 1991 by Ablex Publishing. Reprinted with permission of the author.

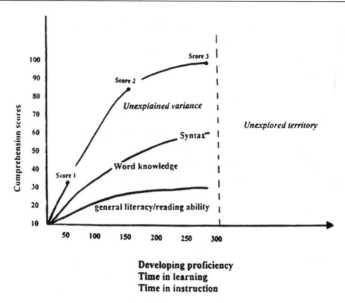

FIG. 2.2. Revised theoretical distribution of reading factors. From "Second language reading as a case study of reading scholarship in the 20th century" (p. 803), by E. B. Bernhardt, 2000. In M. L. Kamil, P. B. Mosenthal, P. D. Pearson, and R. Barr (Eds.), *Handbook of Reading Research*: Vol. 2 (pp. 791–811). Mahwah, NJ: Lawrence Erlbaum Associates. Copyright © 2000 by Lawrence Erlbaum Associates. Reprinted with permission.

Bernhardt acknowledges that there are advantages and disadvantages to her model. She notes that her review finds that "general literacy ability (about 20% of any given score), grammar (about an additional 30% of any given score, 27% of which is word knowledge and 3% syntax), and 50% of any given score at any particular point in time is unexplained" (p. 804) are the relative contributions made to comprehension scores.

Joshi and Aaron (2006) edited a book that contains a collection of studies that explores the acquisition of reading in different orthographies. There are a number of studies that involve comparisons of reading development in English and other languages such as Japanese. These studies are not reviewed here because they involved measures such as phonemic segmentation, a lexical decisions task involving pseudohomophones, and the recognition of nonwords. None of these measures were available or possible in the present study so their findings are of limited application. However, the chapters in the Joshi and Aaron (2006) book are highly valuable contributions to the literature related to reading in different languages.

Language Socialization

Learning a second language is complex. The models discussed so far have been simplistic, however, in that they have accounted for only a very few of the complex variables involved. Indeed, the models are based on results of standardized tests and measures of reading. Developmental differences are generally ignored. Bernhardt (2000) proposes that development is measured by differences in comprehension scores over time, but this is a limited view. Models also do not account for features of the learning environment. A second-language learner must learn features of the culture if he or she is going to become communicatively competent.

Schieffelin and Ochs's (1986a, 1986b) language socialization model has been applied to various English-as-a-second-language contexts in recent years, relating the developmental nature of L2 acquisition to sociocultural competence that L2 learners acquire over time in a target speech community (e.g., Crago, 1992; Poole, 1992; Schecter & Bayley, 1997; Willett, 1995). ESL is defined as learning a second language in a second-language community (Gunderson, 1994). English as a foreign language (EFL) generally refers to situations in which students learn a second language in a non-second-language community. Students in Japan, for instance, study EFL because the language of the community is Japanese, not English. ESL methodology differs from that of EFL because of the difference in the availability of models of the second or target language (Gunderson, 1994).

CULTURE AS A READING VARIABLE

There has been considerable debate and controversy related to defining the term *culture*. Fifty years ago Kroeber and Kluckhohn (1954) identified 160 different definitions of culture. Larson and Smalley (1972) argued that culture was somewhat like a map or a blueprint that

> guides the behavior of people in a community and is incubated in family life. It governs our behavior in groups, makes us sensitive to matters of status, and helps us know what others expect of us and what will happen if we do not live up to their expectations. Culture helps us to know how far we can go as individuals and what our responsibility is to the group. Different cultures are the underlying structures which make Round community round and Square community square. (p. 39)

Vontress (1976) concluded that each of us lives in five cultures that intermingle: the universal, the ecological, the national, the regional, and the racio-ethnic. Culture is more than a sum of its constituent parts and each of us is more culturally complex than we know or can describe. Culture allows human beings to survive by providing the mental constructs to categorize the world. Murdock (1945) describes seven characteristics of cultural patterns: (a) They originate in the human mind; (b) they facilitate human and environmental interactions; (c) they satisfy basic human needs; (d) they are cumulative and adjust to changes in external and internal conditions; (e) they tend to form a consistent structure; (f) they are learned and shared by all the members of a society; and (g) they are transmitted to new generations. Culture can be viewed at a "macro level," a broad generalization consisting of shared features across a group, and a "micro level," with particular features related to an individual or a very small group of individuals.

A discussion of culture often includes descriptions, discussions, and arguments for and against including such issues as race, ethnicity, socioeconomic status, economy, gender, religion, and political philosophy. Often culture is defined relative to the discipline of the individual doing the defining. In essence, culture is defined within the parameters of a particular academic culture. Sociolinguistic definitions differ from anthropological definitions, which differ in turn from ethnolinguistic definitions and so on. Sociolinguists, for instance, focus on the language use that distinguishes communities. An individual, in this view, is a member of multiple cultural groups that can be identified by language and language use. Individuals are able to "code switch" as they move from one community to another. Subgroups or subcultures can be identified by their use of jargon or "restricted codes." Individuals are "marked" by their membership in groups, so that an individual's language signals social status, gender, age, and so on. Culture affects the way an individual perceives the world, both on a macro and on a micro level. In particular, culture has a direct relationship to one's beliefs about, attitudes toward, expectations for, and views of teaching and learning and the importance of learning.

The notion of culture developed in this book is that culture is the ideas, customs, language, arts, skills, and tools that generally characterize a given group of individuals in a given period of time, particularly as they relate to its members' learning in North American schools. Students do not simply adopt or adapt a new culture or become bicultural; rather, they acquire and reject some features of the new culture, retain and reject some features of their first culture, adapt some features of first culture to second culture, and become socialized into a system that is uniquely individual, imbued with first- and second-cultural features that are often predictable.

Culture is a social phenomenon, but so is language. When individuals move from one culture to another there are both micro- and macro-level consequences. There are a number of views concerning the consequences of entering a new culture. Micro-level features according to Schumann (1978a) may include such phenomena as culture shock, motivation, and ego permeability. In 1986 Schumann categorized acculturation relative to the group of individuals involved: those who wish to assimilate fully into a culture and those who do not wish to assimilate.

Schumann (1978a, 1978b) proposed that two factors affect the degree to which an individual learner acculturates: social distance and psychological distance. Social distance represents how well learners become members of the target-language community—that is, how well they are able to achieve contact with them. Psychological distance represents the degree to which a particular learner is comfortable learning the second language. Variables related to social distance include social dominance, integration pattern, enclosure, cohesiveness, size, cultural congruence, attitude, and a learner's intended length of residence. Psychological distance is related to language shock, culture shock, motivation, and ego permeability.

In Schumann's view, culture shock is often one of the most difficult experiences immigrants encounter. An individual new to a culture begins to go through a process called *acculturation,* according to Shumann and others, during which there are "stages" that represent the degree to which one has become part of or adapted to the new culture. This is a view that suggests immigrants or nonmainstream individuals must adapt to North American culture.

Culture Shock

Acculturation is a term that refers to the notion that an individual from one culture must adapt to a new culture. The term assimilation refers to the case in which an individual's first culture is submerged in the new culture and there is often a loss of first cultural values, beliefs, and behavior patterns. Acculturation is often associated with an individual's success in learning a new language. Indeed, many authors have suggested that failing to acculturate often is associated with failure to learn a second language (Ellis, 1994; Schumann, 1978a, 1978b, 1986). It has been observed by some that "normal" acculturation occurs in four stages: euphoria, culture shock, recovery, and acculturation. It is important to emphasize that these so-called stages are not particularly precise or accurate. "Under normal circumstances, people who become acculturated pass through all the stages at varying rates, though they do not progress smoothly from one stage to the next and may regress to previous stages" (Richard-Amato, 1988, p. 6). There is variation in acculturation both between and within cultural groups. The degree to which students are successful in school, especially related to second-language acquisition, will be related to the degree to which they become acculturated, according to this model. The degree to which they will become acculturated is related to their backgrounds. Schumann's (1978) model "seeks to explain differences in learners' rate of development and also in their ultimate level of achievement in terms of the extent to which they adapt to the target-language culture" (Ellis, 1994, p. 230). Schumann (1986) observes:

> We are concerned with variables, which involve the relationship between two social groups who are in a contact situation, but who speak different languages. One group is considered the second-language learning (2LL) group and the other the target language (TL) group. (p. 380)

Acculturation, according to Schumann, means, "the social and psycho-logical integration of the learner with the target language (TL) group" (Schumann, 1986, p. 379). Second-language researchers have suggested that this view is a negative one (see, e.g., Duff & Uchida, 1997) because it characterizes the second-language learner as one who must give up a first culture. Socialization theorists have a more positive view.

A central notion of language socialization theory is that children and other novices learn to function communicatively with members of a com-munity by organizing and reorganizing sociocultural information that is conveyed through the form and content of the actions of others (Schieffelin & Ochs, 1986a, 1986b). This theoretical framework views the acquisition of linguistic and sociocultural competence as interdependent. Schieffelin and Ochs (1986b) conclude that as children learn to become competent mem-bers of their society they also learn to become competent speakers of their language. Acquiring pragmatic competence, that is, the ability to use and interpret language appropriately in contexts, is an essential part of the lan-guage socialization process, because without pragmatic competence it is extremely difficult to participate in ordinary social life. In many respects, what is appropriate in a particular context is related to pragmatic cultural features. The language competence for giving advice, for instance, varies culturally (Matsumura, 2001). It is important to understand that cultural features contribute to one's ability to communicate.

There are a number of important cultural variables that affect a student's learning of reading and writing in a second language. Indeed, the defini-tion of what constitutes reading varies in significant ways across cultures. The production of a perfect oral model in response to writing has been the predominant view of reading over the last 2,000 years or so (Gunderson, 2000). A focus on reading comprehension is a relatively recent develop-ment (cf. Diringer, 1968; Mathews, 1966). There are cultures that continue to view reading within this perspective. Gunderson (2004) reports on the views of Punjabi-speaking immigrants who learned to read using the Ko-ran. Their purpose was to produce perfectly the words on the text, not to question them or to be asked questions about them. Anderson and Gunderson (2001) found that Chinese immigrants had different views of reading. The individuals they observed separated "reading" (for pleasure) and "reading" (for study). This distinction is mirrored in their orthography, where separate logographs distinguish reading and studying. Rosowsky (2001) concluded that decoding, or translating the printed word into its oral form, is the view of reading of some cultures. Historically it was the view of many in Western cultures until about 100 years or so ago (Mathews, 1966).

Teaching and learning strategies often reflect cultural features. Teaching students to read in Hong Kong is through rote memorization of symbols. Immigrant students and parents often see Western teachers' focus on process as poorly informed at best and wrong at worst. Their learning of the second language in this case is affected by the views they have about teaching and learning that they acquired as students in their home countries (Anderson & Gunderson, 1997, 2001; Gunderson & Anderson, 2003). Their views of themselves as students are derived from the interactions they have had with their teachers, friends, families, and others in their social environments. In many respects, how they view themselves, their notions of identity, are products of their culture, nationality, ethnicity, social class, community, gender, and sexuality (Woodward, 1997).

A second-language model should account for a very large number of variables. Indeed, it should also represent the dynamic nature of change represented by student development, by first-language literacy history, and by differences related to first-language orthography.

THE DIFFERENTIAL BASE MODEL

Gunderson (1991a) developed a second-language instructional model based on the notion that two variables, representing complex combinations of background factors, predict broadly the probability that a student will be able to read and to benefit from instruction. It is based on Cummins's notion that portrays language proficiency as developing in situations that vary from "context-embedded," in which participants interact by questioning, negotiating meaning, and providing feedback, to "context-reduced" communication in which interpretation of the message depends on knowledge of the language itself (Cummins & Swain, 1983). The basic notion is that reading, specifically understanding or comprehension, occurs only when input is comprehensible (Krashen, 1982). In essence, the model operationalizes the notion of comprehensibility. The vertical axis represents the degree to which a learner must apply "active cognitive involvement." Many activities when first learned demand a great deal of cognitive energy to master. After a time, they become automatic. In reading, for example, LaBerge and Samuels (1974) suggest word recognition activities become automatic and require little cognitive energy after a reader has developed.

Cummins and Swain (1986) Model

The problem with this model is that it is static; it was designed to be representative of all situations. It does not provide a way to predict such interactions as the difficulty some face in context-embedded, low-cognitive-demand situations; the ease some have in learning in context-reduced, high-cognitive-demand situations; the differential effects of curriculum on cognitive demand; and the differential effects of multiple background vari-

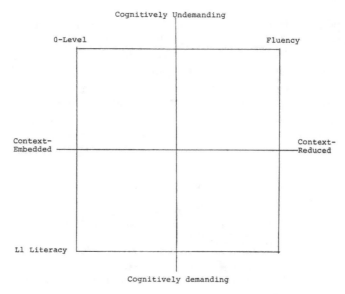

FIG. 2.3. Cognitive demand, embeddedness, L1 literacy, and L2 fluency.

ables on the degree of informativeness of context conditions and cognitive requirements (see Fig. 2.3). It is amazing to see students with reading difficulties attack, often in a word-by-word fashion, texts like a driver's license manual with great drive and interest.

The Differential Base (DB) model extends the Cummins's model by hypothesizing that there are sets of variables that affect learning by increasing the informativeness of embeddedness and/or decreasing the cognitive demands of individual learning situations. That is, comprehensibility varies in relationship to various complex background variables. A student, for instance, who comes from a background in which the instructional focus has been on memorization will often find a Western focus on independent critical comprehension difficult to understand. A student who has learned to read a first language that utilizes a modified Roman alphabet, all else being equal, will likely have an advantage learning to read English compared to a student who has learned to read a language that utilizes a non-Roman orthography, all else being equal.

L2 literacy occurs in different context situations and requires different levels of cognitive energy, which are relative, not absolute. Variables that interact in the learning of second-language literacy include individual developmental, affective, and achievement variables; group variables such as L1 literacy, cultural, and political features; and instructional variables such as teaching approach, teacher factors, and philosophy.

Although the matrix of Figure 2.4 represents a general state, the axes are relative not fixed and move depending on individual backgrounds. L1 literacy background and oral proficiency are two powerful variables that generally predict literacy processes and appropriate instructional strategies.

L1 literacy background and English proficiency are powerful variables that map out generally what will be comprehensible for a particular L2 learner. Gunderson (1991a) produced instructional decision heuristics for elementary, secondary, and adult ESL students. L1 literacy background, for instance, is canonical in the sense that it represents variables such as students' knowledge of print, purpose of reading, and processing of text. The matrix maps out what will be comprehensible for a particular individual and is useful in planning instructional strategies.

Learning to read using basal readers, for instance, is less cognitively demanding and is context reduced for L2-fluent, L1-literate individuals than it is for 0-level-L2, 0-L1 literate individuals. L2 reading acquisition occurs in school settings in instructional episodes that have different levels of context-embeddedness and require different levels of cognitive demand. The 6-year-old child who has 0-level L2 oral proficiency and is L1 illiterate finds the learning of L2 reading extremely cognitively demanding and context reduced. The individual with a long L1 literacy history and a high L2 oral proficiency level finds L2 reading activities, depending on the instructional program, generally less cognitively demanding and more contextualized. A major limitation of previous models has been that they are nearly all designed to represent mature reading and do not include developmental features. Gunderson (1991a) produced the instructional strategies heuristic shown in Figure 2.5.

The heuristic is useful in planning instructional programs. However, the underlying relationships among related variables are more complex than

	Non-English	Very Limited	Limited	Limited Fluency
L1 Literacy				
None				
1-2 Years				
3+ Years				

FIG. 2.4.   Reading heuristic. From *ESL literacy instruction: A guidebook to theory and practice*, by L. Gunderson, 1991, p. 23. Copyright © 1991 by Pearson Education, Inc. Reprinted with permission of the author and Pearson Education, Inc.

	0-Level	Very Limited	Limited	Limited Fluency
L1 History None	Oral Lang. dev.*	Oral Lang. Dev.*	Oral Lang. Dev. a) Printed Voc. b) Word Banks c) Sentence Strps.	Oral Lang. Dev. a) Printed voc. b) Word Banks c) Sentence Strps. d) Pers. Dicts. e) Active Listen. f) cloze² g) LEA h) Immersion³
1-2 Years	Oral Lang. Dev*	Oral Lang. dev.* a) Printed voc. b) Word Banks	Oral Lang. Dev. a) Printed voc. b) Word Banks c) Sentence Strps. d) Active Listen	Oral Lang. Dev. a) Printed voc. b) Word Banks c) Sentence Strps. d) Pers. Dicts. e) Active Listen. f) cloze² g) LEA h) Immersion³ i) Basal DRA (L2)
3+ Years	Oral Lang. Dev.* a) Printed Voc. b) Word Banks	Oral Lang. Dev.* a) Printed Voc. b) Word Banks c) Sentence Strps.	Oral Lang. Dev. a) Printed voc. b) Word Banks c) Sentence Strps d) cloze² e) Active Listen. f) LEA g) Immersion³	Oral Lang. Dev. a) Printed Voc. b) Word Banks c) Sentence Strps. d) Pers. Dicts. e) Active Listen f)cloze² g)LEA h) Immersion³ i) Basal DRA(L2)

*L1 Instruction recommended
²cloze instruction beginning with sentences and progressing to passages.
³D.R.T.A, L1 & L2 U.S.S.R., Hearing L1 and L2 Reading, etc.

FIG. 2.5. Reading heuristic with instructional activities. From *ESL literacy instruction: A guidebook to theory and practice*, by L. Gunderson, 1991, p. 58. Copyright © 1991 by Pearson Education, Inc. Reprinted with permission of the author and Pearson Education, Inc.

can be represented by such a graphic. Second-language literacy reflects the influences of background variables that include L1 reading and writing processes; L1 orthography; L1 syntactic, semantic, and pragmatic systems; L1 teaching and learning practices; L1 literacy proficiency; individual differences in cognitive and perceptual processing; individual and cultural attitudes toward literacy; affect; and individual developmental features. L2 literacy can be thought of as a cluster of features that shares some of the same features as L1. Learning that the graphic images represent language, for instance, is a shared, common underlying proficiency. Generally, reading and writing can be considered to be a part of a larger language complex. Reading, for instance, can be characterized by "the product," as Leu (1981) suggests. In English the product can be "production," a reader producing the oral equivalent of the graphic form, "comprehension," a reader understanding the lexical features associated with the graphic form, or both production and comprehension. The case of writing is roughly equivalent in that it is possible to write, to make the appropriate squiggles, and to compose material that has meaning. The model is shown in Figure 2.6.

The model is dynamic in that the links between background features and L1 literacy vary from individual to individual. The shorter the link, the more powerful is the connection. The links can vary as the individual develops and different literacy tasks are learned, hence the name Differential Base. A great deal of research and debate, for instance, has centered on the role of phonological awareness in success in learning to read (e.g., Bradley & Bryant, 1985; Brown & Felton, 1990; Cunningham, 1990; Evans & Carr, 1985; Hatcher, Hulme, & Ellis, 1994; Iverson & Tunmer, 1993; Juel, 1994; Lie, 1991; Olofsson, 1993; Pflaum, Walberg, Karegianes, & Rasher, 1980; Tunmer & Nesdale, 1985). Bernhardt (1991) concludes her extensive review of second-language reading studies by noting, "The variability from study to study makes comparisons in reading development across readers, languages, and proficiency levels tantamount to impossible" (p. 68). The second-language literature, however, appears currently to focus on a number of hot issues.

There is a popular notion that extensive reading, especially free voluntary reading, promotes literacy development in both first and second languages (Cho & Krashen, 1994; Elley, 1991; Elley & Mangubhai, 1983; Hafiz & Tudor, 1989; Krashen, 1993). Krashen (1993) makes the case that free voluntary reading provides the foundation for second-language learners to acquire higher levels of competence. He suggests that free voluntary reading is beneficial to ESL students' overall language development. There is no large-scale research to support the contention that voluntary reading raises ESL students' reading achievement scores. However, Gradman and Hanania's (1991) study of the background factors that predicted adult ESL learners' proficiency found that extracurricular reading, reading outside of class, had the strongest effect on English proficiency. The authors conclude,

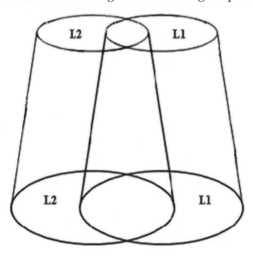

FIG. 2.6.   Differential base model.

"Our results demonstrate that, out of a large number of background factors which might contribute to success in language learning, a few stand out as particularly important. Foremost among these is the extent of active exposure to the language through individual outside reading" (p. 48).

Although L2 learners appear to have some difficulty using spelling patterns to recognize words (Favreau et al., 1980; Favreau & Segalowitz, 1983; Mes-Prat & Edwards, 1981), some researchers conclude that both L1 and L2 learners use the same basic word recognition strategies (Connor, 1981; Dank & McEachern, 1979; Goodman & Goodman, 1978; Haddad, 1981; Rigg, 1977). Verhoeven (1990) concludes that second-language readers rely on L1 strategies as they learn to read an L2. Hung and Tzeng (1981) argue that all orthographies "attempt to transcribe sentences at the word level" (p. 408), but that such transcriptions vary in the way they lead to meaning, via either a phonological or a visual pathway.

Many have recommended that the learning of English and academic content should be integrated (see, e.g., Brinton, Snow, & Wesche, 2003; Early, 1989; Gaffield-Vile, 1996; Swain, 1996). Mohan (1986) developed a knowledge framework consisting of six knowledge structures to guide secondary teachers' instruction. As second-language students learn the language of an academic discipline, both L1 and L2 links can change. A student with a deep knowledge of a particular subject, a graduate student in an academic discipline, for instance, will have powerful L1 links to the L2 academic task. A second-language model needs to account for L1 and L2 processes that are both separate and shared.

Two systems overlap and have areas that are separate and areas that are coterminous. Again, the connections can be short, high relationships between the two systems, or long, low relationships. A literate Spanish speaker learning literacy skills in Portuguese would represent a case in which the two systems may be close and the connections short, whereas the same speaker learning Kurdish would have some connections that are long. The power or strength of a L1 variable, or factor, is inversely proportional to the distance between the two systems.

L2 Writing

The focus in this discussion, with the exception of whole language models, has been on L2 reading. The DB model includes writing. The difficulty with observing the relationships existing between L1 and L2 writing is the difficulty of assessing L1 writing, particularly when many L1s are involved. Generally, Silva (1993) concludes, "There is evidence to suggest that L1 and L2 writing are similar in their broad outlines: that is, it has been shown that both L1 and L2 writers employ a recursive composing process, involving planning, writing, and revising, to develop their ideas and find the appropriate rhetorical and linguistic means to express them" (p. 765).

The DB model attempts to capture the dynamic nature of the learning of literacy in a second language. One of the purposes of this book is to explore the links between first language and the language and academic learning of immigrant students.

SUMMARY AND CONCLUSIONS

Gunderson (1991a) concluded that "ESL reading instruction is, in many respects, a more complicated concern than reading instruction for native English speakers" (p. 21). He noted:

> There are several factors to consider: 1) students' first-language (L1) literacy background, 2) their second-language (L2) proficiency, 3) their L2 reading ability, 4) the cultural and age appropriateness of the L2 materials, 5) students' reasons for learning to read English relative to their age, 6) their purposes for reading, and 7) the difficulty level of the material to be read. (p. 21)

It is an unfortunate reality, however, that L2 educators and researchers most often adopt L1 reading models to represent L2 processes, both reading and writing. The major L1 models, bottom-up, top-down, interactive, schema-theoretic, emergent literacy, and whole language, have been used to infer L2 literacy processes and to prescribe teaching and learning strategies. Bernhardt's (1991) model is a refreshing departure. Although it is based on notions from first-language research, her model was developed from her interpretations of second-language research. She suggests:

> If research in second-language reading is in a very real sense "unprincipled" and directionless, the same comment can be made regarding instruction and assessment. (p. 69)

Various models have been developed to represent the theoretical relationships among the various cognitive, perceptual, educational, developmental, and social variables involved in reading and learning to read. First-language models have been applied to second-language learners. Unfortunately, the models do not account for the complexities associated with second-language learning, for example, fully L1 literate medical doctors learning initial L2 reading skills or 65-year-old L1 illiterates learning initial L2 reading and writing skills (Gunderson, 1991a). The model is based on the hypothesis that first-language proficiency represents a knowledge base that second-language learners apply in various ways to learn second-language literacy skills. As L2 literacy develops, an underlying proficiency base evolves. Second-language development is affected by and affects L1 processes. Hayashi (1994), for instance, observed that students' written Japanese increasingly showed features of English syntax over the course of the year they were enrolled in an undergraduate university-level English and academic program.

The case of the fully biliterate person is one in which the underlying proficiency base has both L1 and L2 features, whereas the construct "literacy," production, comprehension, and production and comprehension, and the processing related to them also have shared and separate features. It is hypothesized that L1 literacy background is involved in the learning of L2 reading in various complex and interactive ways.

Various models are explored in this book. The exploration investigates the relationships existing among L1 literacy variables, personal developmental variables, health variables, L2 proficiency variables, and L2 achievement variables in order to test the DB model and the other models described in this chapter.

3

The Setting, the Population, and the Measures

No one know me, mother, father, sister, no one.
The school filled with stranger, they not look.
I gone to nothing, disappear,
No one care.[1]

Life in the primary grades (kindergarten to Grade 3) is extremely difficult for immigrant students. More than 20 years ago Gunderson (1983) found that young immigrant students suffer from isolation, loneliness, and difficulties in literacy learning in mainstream classrooms. In many cases, immigrant students were placed in reading groups with the poorest English readers in their classes. They were asked to listen to the worst possible oral reading. They were also observed to be isolated on the playground. The difficulty for primary students is that they are most often simply immersed without support in an English-speaking environment because educators assume they will acquire English quickly. The difficulty is that many primary classrooms have become non-English environments where the majority of students speak languages other than English. In some primary classrooms the only English speaker is the teacher. Students are not immersed in English.

High schools, despite the surface-level chaos, are planned communities of administrators, teachers, staff, and students. Schools are organized to teach students the knowledge deemed important by educators or, in many cases, by politicians. The buildings are designed to house as many individuals as possible within fairly limited spaces. They are efficient in moving groups of students from room to room and making certain there are teach-

[1]Male, 16 years, Grade 9, Vietnam.

ers there to meet them. Courses and course content are warehoused, stratified, codified, and planned as curriculum. But the lived life of a secondary student is different from the planned life of the curriculum guides. The purpose of this book is to explore immigrant students' views of their lived lives, their identities, and their school successes and failures and to provide evidence from multiple sources on how well they have succeeded in learning language and the academics that are so important in the planned curriculum of the high school. The lived life of a secondary student is complex; it requires the ability to struggle with multiple identities. The most difficult identity to deal with is the one called "immigrant," an identity filled with negative features, often of "failure."

Gunderson (2000) notes, "The foundation of an individual's sense of self-worth is an aggregate of success, acceptance, belonging, acknowledgement, recognition, and encouragement. To have such a sense, however, one must have a fairly clear awareness of self. Human beings define what they perceive of as self by those criteria that are culturally appropriate" (p. 619). Norton-Peirce (1997) concludes that "identity relates to desire—the desire for recognition, the desire for affiliation, and the desire for security and safety" (p. 410).

Most studies of immigrant achievement focus on measures that describe their responses to standardized test instruments. Such measures define groups in decontextualized terms that often marginalize individuals. Indeed, such measures often identify immigrant students as low achievers or poor learners. Standardized measures are used in this study to provide general information about how immigrant students are succeeding in reference to established norms. Students' notions about identity are also explored in this book. Their views help to present them in ways that standardized scores cannot. So, for instance, statistical methods are used to explore which variables predict students' success. This is a fairly standard approach. In addition, students' own views of their success are explored. In a way, students' voices are sought in order to "triangulate" and confirm the more traditional statistical findings. In essence, the studies in this book were designed to provide both qualitative and quantitative data about individuals and groups of students. In total, about 25,000 immigrant students have contributed in some way to these studies. What they all have in common is a visit to the Oakridge Reception Center.

THE OAKRIDGE RECEPTION AND ORIENTATION CENTER

The Vancouver, British Columbia, school district enrolls approximately 58,000 students in 18 secondary and 90 elementary schools and annexes. In June 2005 Vancouver had a 55.5% ESL population in its elementary schools and a 47% ESL population in its secondary schools. In 1988 a team was invited to the school district to review its ESL programs. Ashworth, Cummins, and Handscomb (1989) made a number of recommendations; the most significant one was that the school district should establish a centralized ESL reception and orientation center. The Oakridge Reception and Orientation Center (OROC) was established and first began operation in August 1989 with Catherine Eddy as supervisor. It has since been renamed the Vancouver Reception and Placement Center.

The OROC Mandate

OROC was designed to serve as a center that immigrants, regardless of first language, would find inviting and hospitable. The physical plant was originally a school for the physically disabled. It contained classrooms, a gym, a general office, and a variety of rooms of various sizes. The original school had a swimming pool, which did not find use at OROC. Two rooms were set up as waiting rooms for parents and students; they contained coffee or tea for parents, a variety of published information about schools and teaching and learning in British Columbia in 36 different languages, and a playroom for small children. They contained bookshelves with many different first-language children's books.

Catherine Eddy, the founding supervisor of OROC, designed the center to serve various functions: to provide health and dental screening, to conduct language and math assessments, to collect developmental and family background information, to ascertain students' literacy backgrounds, to assign students to appropriate grade levels, programs, and schools, and to serve as a research center to provide information for the school board and for teachers and researchers interested in ESL and immigrant students. One of the most important mandates was that students and their families would be interviewed in their first languages, a monumental task.

The OROC Interview

An interview protocol was developed by OROC staff after consultation with various interested individuals that included items concerning such issues as development, literacy learning background, first- and second-language interactions, school history, English study, and health history.

During the interview both children and parents are encouraged to respond. Interviews are conducted in English when possible. However, for families unable to be interviewed in English, special interpreters are hired who are native speakers of the family's first language and generally know the customs and cultural background of the families. Following the interviews, students' English skills are assessed using various standardized and holistic instruments, beginning with an individual oral language assessment.

The oral assessment begins with the assessor asking simple questions in an effort to begin to understand the student's English ability. Items include:

1. What's your name?
2. How old are you?
3. Where are you from?
4. What did your mother do in _____?
5. What did your father do in _____?
6. Do you have any brothers or sisters? Tell me about them.
7. What is your favorite food?

Students' responses begin to inform the assessor about the student's English ability. The following items were designed to discover specific information about different kinds of English knowledge.

1. Tell me the days of the week.
2. What day was yesterday?
3. What day will tomorrow be?

The child is asked to count from one to as high as possible, followed by naming numbers shown in random order. Eleven basic colors are shown and students are asked to name them. Reciting the alphabet is followed by the recognition and naming of letters at random. Nineteen different body parts are shown in pictures and students are asked to name them, followed by the naming of six different school items such as a pencil and crayons. These items generally require students to have a basic English vocabulary.

The second portion of the oral assessment focuses on English structure. The student is asked:

1. Tell me two things you did yesterday.
2. Tell me two things you are going to do tomorrow.
3. Tell me one thing you would like to do when you grow up.

The child is shown a series of pictures containing objects that are in different positions relative to each other. The teacher demonstrates the process by showing a picture and saying "The ball is on the table." The subsequent pictures are each prompted by the assessor saying, "The ball is _____." The student is asked to fill in the correct preposition.

The student's ability to formulate questions is assessed by the teacher saying, "Now it's your turn to ask me some questions."

1. Ask me my name.
2. Ask me where I live.

3. Ask me what I did yesterday.
4. Ask me what I am going to do tomorrow.

Performance on these items is informative and helps to guide the assessor in selecting further appropriate reading assessment instruments. Elementary students who have some English ability are administered the word recognition and comprehension sections of the Woodcock Reading Mastery test. Older students are administered the "New Gap" test (McLeod & McLeod, 1990) the "Gap" (McLeod & McLeod, 1977), or the Comprehensive English Language Test (CELT; Harris & Palmer, 1986). All students are administered a math skills test developed by local curriculum consultants. Occasionally a student is seen at the center who appears to have special needs. These students are administered different tests depending on their perceived needs, such as the Test of Nonverbal Intelligence.

Assignment to Schools and Support Levels

The information gained from the interviews and assessments is outlined and included as part of enrollment packages sent to schools to be part of the records seen by students' teachers as they begin to plan programs. Students are assigned to schools and to support levels, ESL classes, depending on their performance on the various instruments. Students in Grades 4 to 8 may be assigned to full-time ESL classrooms or to various kinds of ESL support, varying from one 40-min session per day to one 40-min session per week. Secondary students may be assigned to English Language Centers where they receive instruction in English or to special ESL academic classes, where students study academic disciplines but with individuals especially trained as ESL teachers. Students who are enrolled in kindergarten through third grades are placed in regular mainstream classrooms where instruction is in English.

All students are involved in English-only instruction. The study of languages other than English is possible, but occurs in foreign-language contexts. It is possible, for instance, to study Punjabi in some schools beginning at fifth grade and extending to 12th grade.

The interviews also include sessions with parents and students where they are told about homework policies, school supply fees, available school services, and other related information, which is also available in published booklets written in various languages.

Immigrants often come from countries or regions in which serious, often fatal, diseases are endemic. A public health nurse has an office at OROC and individuals are referred to her if there are concerns about a student's health. Immigration to Canada normally includes a physical examination prior to entry. However, refugees normally enter the country without such medical screening. In addition to medical screening, dental screening also takes place at OROC.

The Oakridge Reception and Orientation Center is an extraordinary institution that serves the students and families new to British Columbia. It serves as a research and evaluation center. During the summer it is not unusual for the center to interview and evaluate 300 families. Indeed, the number of new immigrants has increased steadily since 1989 when the center opened its doors.

DATA COLLECTION AND ANALYSES

Data Collection

Three sources of data were available: the Oakridge Center, achievement data from the schools, and data from structured interview and follow-up assessment sessions. The Oakridge data have been collected since 1990 and collection continues today. However, only students who entered Canada between January 1, 1991, and December 31, 2001, were included in the analyses reported here.

Oakridge Data

From the assessment and interview records the following data were coded and recorded into computer files for analysis: L1, age, gender, birth status, health, health history, hearing and vision status, immigration status, age of first single-word utterances (what language), first simple sentences (what language), age beginning to read (what language), age beginning to walk, language spoken at home, dominant language, second or additional languages if any, parents' ability to communicate in English, language spoken with playmates, independent reading habits, age first enrolled in school, type of school, country, language of instruction, hours of instruction per day, number of days per week, class size, home study facilities, favorite school subjects, least favorite school subjects, number of hours and years of English study, and school placement, country of birth, years of instruction in L1, years of study of L2 in home country (if any), L1 writing quality, sex, age, L2 oral proficiency, L2 structural knowledge (Gap, Gapadol [McLeod & McLeod, 1990] and Comprehensive English Language Test, 1989), L2 written grammar assessment, L2 word recognition and comprehension (Woodcock Reading Mastery Test; Woodcock, 1973), mathematics ability, and L1 and L2 composition holistically scored. Data were coded and recorded beginning in September 1990 by six different trained research assistants at different times in the course of the study. Raters included two Mandarin-speaking–English bilinguals, one native-English-speaking–Japanese bilingual, one native English speaker, two Japanese-speaking–English bilinguals, and one na-tive-English-speaking–Spanish-fluent speaker. Interrater reliability was measured for all of the variables over the six raters by having each rater code the same 150 records. The codings of one research assistant, a Japanese–English bilingual, were not used in the study because he was unable to score data reliably. Reliability coefficients varied from .91 to .99 over the six raters and 75 variables coded. The lowest coefficients were associated with "type of school" in home country and number of hours of schooling per day, .91 and .92 in the case of two raters. Some variables had virtually 100% agreement, for example, year of birth, number of siblings, and raw scores, after the data were cleaned to eliminate errors of coding and recording. Such errors were found by running descriptive statistics and locating obvious errors, for ex-ample, students born in 1909, students older than 20 years, or students who had a gender coded other than female or male. Approximately 300 cases had incorrect data because one data input technician put data in a column that was meant to be empty. These cases were all easily corrected. In addition, a hard copy of the database was visually scanned to check for obvious errors of omission or commission. A few errors were located in this manner; most were found in the process of producing descriptive statistics and looking for obvious outliers. Because the database is large it is clear that there may be some errors still included.

Coding

Data representing such variables as L1, immigration status, type of school, country of origin, home language, favorite school subject, ESL level assign-ment, and least favorite school subject were coded using a scheme devel-oped over the course of the study. L1, for instance, ranges from 001 (Amharic) to 143 (Chaldean). As new L1s were encountered, the next avail-able numbers were used to code them.

A number of variables were dichotomous, such as gender, English study before immigration, communicates in English, and communicates in L1, whereas some had three-levels, such as Uses L1 at home (1) most of the time, (2) about half of the time, and (3) seldom. One difficult variable to code turned out to be whether a child had suffered a serious disease. One Mandarin-speaking research assistant had been a medical doctor before she came to Canada to enter the doctoral program in Educational Psychol-ogy. Her view of what constituted a serious disease differed from the view held by the other raters, especially those born in North America. After con-siderable discussion, consensus was reached on what constituted a serious childhood disease; for example. measles was not considered for purposes of the study to be a serious childhood disease, whereas malaria and cholera were considered serious.

Dichotomous variables:

Gender.

Were the pregnancy and birth normal? Describe it.

Has your child had any contagious disease such as tuberculosis, hepatitis, typhus, meningitis, malaria?

Does your child have allergies?

Does your child take any special medications or remedies?

Do you have any concerns about your child's hearing?

Do you have any concerns about your child's vision?

Has your child's hearing been checked?

Has your child's vision been checked?

Has you child ever been to the dentist?

Does your child have any fears or worries? What are they?

Has your child studied English?

Do you have books and/or magazines in your home?

Are you able to help you child with homework?

Is there a place to do school work at home?

Three-, four-, and five-level variables:

How often does your child use his/her native language? Most of the time? Half of the time? Seldom?

Can you communicate with your child in your native language? In English?

Does your child like to have stories read aloud to him/her?

Does your child like to read alone?

Does your child have a learning problem?

Does your child have a special skill or talent?

Has your child ever repeated a grade?

Has your child ever skipped a grade?

Alphabet.

Numbers.

Question formulation.

English structural knowledge.

L1 writing.

L2 writing.

ESL support level.

Multiple-level categorical variables:

What is country of origin?
What is immigration status?
What is the language used at home?
What other languages are used at home? Spoken? Written? Read?
What languages does your child understand, speak, read, write?
What language does your child speak to his friends in?
What kind of school was your child enrolled in?
What was the language of instruction?
What subject is liked the most?
What subject is liked the least?

Chronological variables:

Date of birth.
Date of entry.
At what age did your child begin to:
Say single words? What language?
Say simple sentences? What language?
Begin to read? What language?
Walk?
At what age did your child begin school?
How many days a week?
Years and hours of English study.

Numerical variables:

What were the hours?
How many students were in the classes?
How many hours a week and for how many years?
How many siblings?
Days of the week.
Body parts.
School items.
Prepositions.
Woodcock Reading Mastery test.
Math Skills Test.
Gap.
Gapadol.
Comprehensive English Language Test.

Many variables were put into the database as raw numbers, for example, scores on standardized assessment instruments and scores on individually administered oral language tests. In addition, notes were kept concerning responses. So, for instance, the fear of dogs was noted for many of the students whose parents said they had childhood fears.

Two measures involved the holistic scoring of L1 and L2 compositions. Students were asked to select a prompt and write an essay in both L1 and L2 when possible. L1 essays were assessed by trained L1 interpreters who made written comments about the grade-appropriateness of the L1 essays, including comments about spelling, grammar, usage, and organization. These comments were evaluated by the raters and coded as (1) very poor for the grade level, (2) poor for the grade level, (3) average or appropriate for the grade level, (4) good for the grade level, and (5) outstanding for the grade level. Where possible, raters also evaluated the L1 essay themselves to confirm the interpreters' comments. The same scale was used to assess students' English essays. Interrater reliability for L1 essays varied from .94 to .99 as measured by SPSS Reliability. Interpreters' comments were reliably coded into holistic scores. The validity of interpreters' comments was measured by having bilingual graduate students evaluate L1 essays independently. Again, there was a high degree of reliability varying from .92 to .96. English essays were evaluated by raters and their reliability was high, .94 to .96.

School Achievement Data

Students' secondary-school grades were provided by the school district. Data were collected on the number of years students remained in ESL support classes. Grades were recorded and scored on a 4-point scale:

A = 4.00
A– = 3.75
B+ = 3.50
B = 3.00
B– = 2.75
C+ = 2.50
C = 2.00
C– = 1.75
D+ = 1.50
D = 1.00
D– = .75
F = 0.00

P = 1.00
SG = 1.00

Students' grades were collected for Math, Science, ESL, English, Social Studies, and Communications classes in order to observe possible differences in students' achievement related to differences in course content. Students who wish to graduate and enter a university in British Columbia are required to take English 12, among other courses, whereas those who do not wish university entrance take Communications 12. These data were entered into the database.

Follow-Up Interviews and Assessments

A random sample was taken of students who had entered the Vancouver school district who were at the secondary level. The principals of their schools were contacted and the project was explained. Letters were sent home to parents to seek permission to include their children in the follow-up study. Two sessions were conducted with students whose parents had consented that they be part of the study. Interviews were conducted in all of the 18 secondary schools in the district. In addition, interviews were conducted in the 4 secondary schools in a nearby suburban school district for purposes of validation and confirmation.

This sample of students was selected to ascertain their personal views of the teaching and learning they experienced, their views of their own schooling, and their opinions of various related school issues such as ESL instruction, bilingual teaching and learning, and homework policy. The following interview protocol was developed and pilot tested. It was used during the interviews to elicit students' responses.

Interview Protocol

Name: _____Date: _____

School: _____Grade: _____

Grade on arrival in Canada? _____

Date left ESL: _____ L1 _____ L2_____

1) In which language are you strongest:

(a) speaking   (b) reading   (c) writing

2) How often do you:

use L1:   (a) all the time   L2:   (a) all the time

(b) 1/2 the time   (b) 1/2 the time

(c) seldom   (c) seldom

3) With whom/in what situations do you use L1?

4) With whom/in what situations do you use L2?

5) What languages do you read?

6) Do you enjoy reading:

L1:

L2:

7) For what purposes do you read? (pleasure, study)

L1:

L2:

8) What do you read?

L1:

L2:

9) How many hours/day (week) do you read? L1 _____ L2 _____

10) Do you believe that knowing how to read L1 has helped you learn to read L2? Why/why not? In what ways?

11) When you have trouble in school who helps you? (parent, sibling, peer, teacher)

12) Have ESL classes helped you:

(a) to learn English?

(b) with your course work?

13) What do you think about ESL classes? If negative what suggestions, if positive what would improve ESL services for new students.

14) What has helped you the most in learning English?

15) What has helped you the most doing your school work?

16) How many hours/day do you spend doing homework?

17) Which subjects require the most time? Why?

18) What is your favorite/least liked subjects? Why?

19) Which subjects are easiest? Why?

20) Which subjects are most difficult? Why?

21) How do you learn best?

Math

Science

Social Studies

English

22) On what type of tests do you do:

(a) best - why?

(b) worst - why?

23) Are you able to express yourself adequately on tests and assignments?

24) Do you think you are a good student? Why/why not? Are you happy with your grades?

25) Do your parents think you are a good student? Why/why not? Are they happy with your grades?

26) What were the most difficult things to get used to in school?

27) What advice would you give a new ESL student?

28) What would you do differently if you could start over?

29) What are your plans for the future after graduation?

30) What do your parents want you to do in the future after graduation?

31) How did you get your English name? How do you feel about it?

32) What do your parents think about your English ability?

33) Compared to schools in your home country, schools in Canada are _____ because _____

34) Do you participate in extracurricular activities like after school sports? If yes, why was it valuable? If not, why not? What would have helped you to be able to participate more in such activities?

Primary Students

The original assessment plan for OROC was developed in 1989 and it did not include primary-level immigrant students. The unwritten policy of the Province of British Columbia and of the Vancouver School Board was that instruction for immigrant students was English-only and that they would receive appropriate ESL support. On the other hand, primary-level students were simply immersed in mainstream classrooms and would not be assessed in any formal way. Eddy (2001) concluded that many primary students were failing to learn to read and write and that there was an urgent need to develop an assessment measure for them.

The Primary Assessment was developed by Eddy and her staff. An oral interview including six items was developed. They were:

What's your name?
How old are you?
Where do you live?
Who lives with you in Canada?
What food do you like?
What game do you like to play?

Students were asked to count from 1 to 5 in English and from 1 to 10. They were asked to read eight single-digit numbers and seven different multiple-digit numbers. In addition, they were asked to recite the alphabet aloud. They were shown eight upper-case and eight lower-case letters and asked to read them. They were shown six colors to identify pictures of six body parts, and six school items. Students were asked to follow six different oral directions: Please give me the eraser; put the ruler under the book; open the book; pick up the paper; put the paper in the book; and please close the book and put it on the table. The assessment included items that asked students to print their names, to write numbers from 1 to 20, to print the alphabet, and to copy a sentence. Students were asked to write a story in their L1s if possible and one in English if possible. They were administered the passage comprehension section of the Woodcock Reading Mastery test if they were able to do so and a math skills test.

A Single Immigrant Student

The lived life of a single immigrant student with an apparent reading disability in English is described next. This student attended school in a large urban school district on the coast of California. Data are presented as a case study.

HYPOTHESES

The purpose of the studies was to describe the lived lives of individuals and groups of immigrant students in various ways. One purpose was to explore the use of an English assessment battery designed for primary-level students. It was also the goal of the research to provide multiple perspectives on students' lives in secondary schools where they faced the difficult tasks of learning, living, developing identities, and becoming adults, all within the context of new schools, a new country, a new society, and a new language. The studies are both qualitative and quantitative and therefore necessarily require a variety of analyses. Because various research methodologies were used, there are various hypotheses, questions, and issues to be explored.

The relationship between socioeconomic background and success in schools has been investigated in many ways with many populations. In this respect it was predicted that students' achievement, as measured by grade point average, would be directly related to their socioeconomic backgrounds. It was expected, for instance, that the refugees would have more difficulty in school than those from "entrepreneurial" backgrounds.

It was predicted that students would have identity problems related to their status as immigrant students. It was also predicted that there would be differences in identity problems related to socioeconomic status.

A student's first language and first-language orthography were predicted to have an affect on the way in which the student learned English. It was predicted that the relationship between first language and English could be predicted by the "depth" of the first-language orthography. There were a number of hypotheses related to classical hypothesis testing involving statistical measures.

It was hypothesized, for instance, that there would be a positive relationship between L2 achievement measured in various ways and students' L1 literacy backgrounds. It was hypothesized that:

1. The number of years of schooling in home country would be positively related to English achievement.
2. There would be a positive relationship between home literacy uses and English achievement.
3. There would be a positive relationship between L1 development and L2 achievement.
4. L2 achievement would be related to age and L1 literacy background.
5. There would be a relationship between socioeconomic status and students' achievement.
6. There would be differences in L2 achievement related to students' first languages.

CONCLUSION

Immigrant students represent an ever-increasing proportion of students in schools in the United States and Canada. They come from rich backgrounds and have complex skills and abilities. The chapters that follow examine the complexities of their language abilities, their lives, and their success in schools.

Part II

Findings of the Studies

4

Demographic and Descriptive Findings

*I came from Afghanistan. I went to
Pakistan and then Turkey then Germany
then Quebec Vancouver myself. Don't
know where my family is.[1]*

This chapter details some of the interesting descriptive findings of the study. The report is limited rather than exhaustive because of the size of the database and the thousands of separate analyses that could be made. It focuses on reporting results of the tests, measures, and observations made at the Oakridge Center (OROC). The study was designed to report findings from observations and measurements used in the normal course of events by Vancouver school personnel. In this respect, the study has a high degree of face validity because the measures were developed to represent "readiness" skills for learning in an English-based school system. No interventions were planned, so this is not an intervention study. It is not an experimental study. Rather, it reveals different degrees of reality—dependent, of course, on the validity and reliability of the measures chosen by the assessors at the center.

The findings presented in this chapter are based on data collected when students entered Vancouver schools. Findings represent the state of affairs as students entered the country as measured by various observational and standardized measurements. The following findings represent the foundational data of the studies reported in this book.

---

[1] Male, Afghanistan, 20 years, Grade 12.

THE DATA

Each student interview and assessment record was coded and the data were entered into computer files for analyses. Data were coded and recorded beginning in September 1995 by different trained research assistants at different times in the course of the study. Raters included two Mandarin-speaking–English bilinguals, one native-English–Japanese bilingual, four native English speakers, two Japanese-speaking–English bilinguals, and one native-English-speaking–Spanish-fluent speaker. Interrater reliability was measured for all of the variables by having each code the same 150 records. The coding of one research assistant, a Japanese–English bilingual, was not used in the study because he was unable to score data reliably.

Reliability coefficients varied from .91 to .99 over the raters and 75 variables coded. The lowest coefficient was associated with "type of school" in home country and number of hours of schooling a day, .91 and .92 in the case of two raters. Some variables had virtually 100% agreement, for example, year of birth, number of siblings, and raw scores, after the data were cleaned to eliminate errors of coding and recording. Such errors were found by running descriptive statistics and locating obvious errors, such as students born in 1909, students older than 20 years, or students who had a gender coded other than female or male. Approximately 300 cases had incorrect data because one data input technician put data in a column that was meant to be empty. These cases were all easily corrected. In addition, a hard copy of the database was visually scanned to check for obvious errors of omission or commission. A few errors were located in this manner; however, most were found in the process of producing descriptive statistics and looking for obvious outliers. Because the database is large it is clear that there may be some errors still included.

The database took approximately 8 months to clean. It contains data involving 90 variables and 24,890 students. The potential number of analyses is immense. It is possible, for instance, to compute such findings as the average reading recognition scores for boys and girls, recognition scores for boys and girls across 148 first languages, recognition scores for boys and girls across 148 languages and 128 countries across 4 immigration statuses, and word recognition scores across orthographies. Indeed, the extensive background information contained in the database allows one to norm the instruments used in the study. However, the focus here is limited so extensive findings are not presented. Interested readers may contact the author at lee.gunderson@ubc.ca for further information or specific inquiries.

DEMOGRAPHIC FINDINGS

The database consists of 24,890 school-age immigrant students who entered the Vancouver school district between January 1, 1991, and December 2001. The data in Table 4.1 were collected as part of the family interviews.

Some responses appear to be inaccurate. For instance, Acholi is a language spoken in Uganda not Kenya, but the two siblings reported here were refugees who had traveled to Kenya before immigrating to Canada (also Acoli, Atscholo, Shuli, Gang, Lwo, Lwoo, Akoli, Acooli, Log Acoli, Dok Acoli; see Pittman & Grimes, 2000).

TABLE 4.1
Frequencies of Languages and Countries of Origin

Language	Country	Number of Speakers
Acholi	Kenya	2
Afghani	Afghanistan	5
Afrikaans	South Africa	5
Akan	Ghana	1
Albanian	Albania	3
Algerian	Algeria	1
Amharic	Ethiopia	37
Arabic–Asari	Saudi Arabia/ME[a]	94
Armenian	Armenia	3
Assamese	India	1
Assyrian	Iraq	2
Bahasa	Indonesia	31
Bangla	Bangladesh	1
Bemba	Zambia	2
Bengali	India	43
Bicolono	Philippines	10
Bisaya	Philippines	2
Bosnian–Croatian	Bosnia	23
Brong	Ghana	1
Bulgarian	Bulgaria	40
Burmese	Burma	8
Busanga	Ghana	3
Cambodian	Cambodia	30
Cantonese	Hong Kong, PRC[b]	9,106
Cebuano	Philippines	11

(*continued*)

Table **4.1** (*continued*)

Language	Country	Number of Speakers
Chaldean	Iraq	9
Chiarati	India	1
Chiuchow	Vietnam	5
Creole	Haiti	4
Croatia	Croatia	37
Czech	Czechoslovakia	40
Danish	Denmark	10
Dari	Afghanistan	21
Dutch	The Netherlands	15
Egyptian	Egypt	2
English	United States, United Kingdom, Australia, New Zealand	997
Ewe	Ghana	1
Farsi	Iran/ME	129
Fijian	Fiji	8
Filipino	Philippines	7
Finnish	Finland	18
Foochow	East Central India	17
Fookien/Fukien	China	52
French	France/East Canada	126
Georgian	Indonesia	1
German	Germany	47
Greek	Greece/Greek Isles	29
Gujarati	India	30
Hainanese	Malaysia	12
Hakka	China, Singapore	65
Hausa	Nigeria	1
Harari	Nigeria	2
Hebrew	Israel	61
Henghun	Malaysia	1
Hiligaynon	Philippines	1
Hindi	India	335
Hockchew	China	3

Hokkien	Malaysia	45
Hunan	Taiwan/Vietnam	4
Hungarian	Hungary	9
Icelandic	Iceland	9
Ilocano	Philippines	42
Indonesian	Indonesia	26
Irania	Iran	9
Italian	Italy	22
Japanese	Japan	520
Kajai	Brunei	1
Kanjobal	Central America	1
Kheh	Thailand	27
Khmer	Cambodia	108
Kiswahili	Africa	6
Korean	Korea	605
Kurdish	Iraq/ME	123
Lao	Laos/SEA[c]	8
Lebanese	Lebanon	1
Latvian	Latvia	1
Luganda	Uganda	1
Lukonzo	Uganda	1
Malay	Malaysia	12
Malayalam	India	1
Maltese	Malta	6
Mandarin	Taiwan/China/SEA	3,882
Marathi	India	3
Memon	Unknown	1
Mihahasa	Indonesia	1
Ndebele	Zimbabwe	1
Nepali	Nepal	2
Nuer	Ethiopia	1
Norwegian	Norway	10
Ogandian	Somalia	1
Oromiffa	Ethiopia	3
Oromo	Ethiopia	4
Pampango	Papua New Guinea	4

(continued)

Table 4.1 (*continued*)

Language	Country	Number of Speakers
Pangasian	Phillipines	1
Persian	Iran/ME	134
Pojulu	Sudan	1
Polish	Poland	416
Pongwli	China	2
Portuguese	Portugal	114
Punjabi	India	550
Pushtu	Afghanistan	14
Romanian	Romania	139
Rusanga	Ghana	1
Russian	Russia	245
Saho	Ethiopia	3
Sanish	Saudi Arabia	1
Sena	Mozambique	4
Serbian	Yugoslavia	1
Serbo-Croatian	Yugoslavia	249
Sestho	Lesotho	1
Shanghainese	China	2
Shilluk	Sudan	3
Shona	Simbabwe (Zimbabwe)	2
Sinhala	Sri Lanka	17
Slovak	Czechoslovakia	27
Somali	Somalia	108
Spanish	Spain/Central & South America	1,327
Sunwoo	China	1
Swahili	Kenya	1
Swedish	Sweden	19
Swiss	Switzerland	1
Tagalog	Philippines	1,091
Taiwanese	Taiwan	105
Tamil	Sri Lanka/India	93
Taosai	China	2
Teochew	Singapore	23
Thai	Thailand	21

Tigrinia	Ethiopia	29
Tiv	Nigeria	5
Tongan	Zambia	1
Turkish	Turkey	13
Twi	Ghana	12
Ukranian	Ukraine	32
Urdu	Pakistan	58
Vietnamese	Vietnam	1,960
Yanping	China	6
Yoruba	Nigeria	1
Yugoslavian	Yugoslavia	5
Zambuangan	Philippines	1
Zulu	Swaziland	1
Unknown		

[a]Middle East
[b]People's Republic of China
[c]South East Asia

Georgian, normally a language spoken in Georgia, a former member of the Union of Soviet Socialist Republics, is reported as a language in Indonesia (found in Georgia, Armenia, Azerbaijan, Kasakstan, Russia, Tasikistan, Iran; see Turkey; Pittman & Grimes, 2000). This resulted from the child, a daughter of a diplomat posted in Djakarta, having been born in Indonesia.

Fukien is a dialect of Mandarin, but it is reported separately because families identified themselves as Fukien speakers. Fukien can also be found in Malaysia (sometimes called Hakka), Singapore, Taiwan, and China. In China, related dialects are Xiamen, Leizhou, Lei Hua, Li Hua, Chaoshan, Hainan, Hainanese, Qiongwen Hua, Wenchang, Longdu, and Zhenan Min (Pittman & Grimes, 2000). Thus, some of the designations appear incorrect or inaccurate, but they are reflections of parental reports of students' backgrounds. Additionally, a great deal of political change has taken place in Eastern Europe and Russia. Czechoslovakia has become the Czech Republic, for instance, so some country designations are now no longer accurate. A number of parents reported that their L1 was Hindustani, the Hindi word for Hindi, so they were coded as Hindi. Memon was mentioned as a language in one interview. However, after searching for the language in various references, it became apparent that it may not exist, nor does a close variant of the word. The closest was Monom (also Bonom, Menam, and Monam), an Austro-Asiatic language in Vietnam (Pittman &

Grimes, 2000). It also turns out that Memon is a relatively rare family name in the Philippines.

The measures were selected to assess students who were in Grades 4 to 12. It was believed that primary-level students would benefit from being immersed in English-only instruction. As noted previously, Catherine Eddy, the supervisor of the center, had observed that the demographics of classrooms were changing rather dramatically in the Vancouver school district. She had observed that immigrant students were often enrolled in classrooms that did not have a majority of native English speakers. She instituted a policy to assess primary-age students. Staff at OROC helped to design the experimental primary-level assessment battery described in chapter 2.

Primary Students

Primary students who entered Canada between 1996 and 2001 were administered the experimental primary assessment. There were 1,319 individuals from the following immigration categories: 947 immigrants (71.90%); 230 Canadians (17.40%); 57 students (4.30%); 51 refugees (3.90%); 23 Work Visa (2.00%) 5 diplomats (0.40%); and 2 entrepreneur (0.20%). There were two missing cases. Table 4.2 shows the top 10 countries of origin.

Students came from 82 countries and spoke 63 different languages. The surprising finding was that 12.90% were originally from Canada. These were children born in Canada who were taken back to their parents' home countries, to return as they became old enough to enroll in school in Canada. The 10 most frequent languages are shown in Table 4.3.

TABLE 4.2
The 10 Most Frequent Countries of Origin

Country	Frequency	Percentage
Hong Kong	261	20.10%
China	197	15.10%
Canada	168	12.90%
Taiwan	154	11.80%
Philippines	93	7.10%
Korea	45	3.50%
United States	44	3.40%
India	29	2.20%
Japan	27	2.10%
Iran	21	1.60%

TABLE 4.3
The 10 Most Frequent Home Languages

Language	Frequency	Percentage
Cantonese	352	28.10%
Mandarin	307	24.50%
Tagalog	69	5.30%
Vietnamese	63	4.80%
Korean	47	3.80%
Spanish	47	3.80%
English	43	3.40%
Japanese	28	2.20%
Punjabi	28	2.20%
Farsi	24	1.90%

There were 669 (50.80%) males and 641 (49.10%) females in the sample with 1 unknown case. Interestingly, 150 (15.50%) reported that their children's births had been difficult. About 12% reported that their children had serious illnesses and about 11% indicated their children had allergies. Only 5.00% indicated that their children were required to take special medicines. However, 35% indicated that they had serious concerns about their children's health. This is considerably higher that the percentage reported for older students in the sample (see later discussion). Only 49.10% indicated that their children's hearing had been tested, whereas 43.10% indicated that their children's vision had been tested. Only 38.90% reported that their children had seen a dentist before immigrating to Canada. Twenty-seven percent reported that their children had serious childhood fears.

Two hundred thirty students were born in Canada, some had left and re-entered when they were ready to begin primary school, whereas others were from other Canadian jurisdictions. A number of families, usually from India, reported that they had come to Canada to have their children, but wished them to have early childhoods in their home countries to return to Canada at school age because of better educational opportunities.

About 12.00% (11.60%) reported that their children had serious illnesses, whereas 11% (10.80) reported that their children had allergies. About half (51.10%) reported that their children had not had their hearing tested, whereas 73% (72.60) reported that their children's vision had been tested. Two-thirds indicated that their children had seen a dentist. Nearly 40% (38.10) indicated that their children had childhood fears.

Seventeen (16.70) percent reported that their children could read their first languages, whereas 17.80% thought their children could write their

L1s. About half (47.20%) noted that their children spoke a second language. Interestingly, 41.10% of those reporting stated that English was their children's second language. It will be interesting for the reader to compare parental viewpoints with the results from some of the literacy measures.

Primary Students—Literacy-Related Results

Parents reported that on the average their children began producing single-word utterances at 18.00 (17.99; $SD = 6.20$) months. Korean parents reported the highest mean (22.20, $SD = 9.20$). Overall, their children began walking at 12.50 months ($SD = 3.30$).

Six questions of a personal nature were asked. They included: What's your name? How old are you? Where do you live? Who lives with you in Canada? What food do you like to eat? What game do you like to play? Overall, they scored 61.60% accurately telling their names and 49.30% accurately reporting their ages in English. Only 33.80% could tell in English where they lived and 34.90% with whom they lived. When asked what food they liked to eat, 35.20% were able to respond and 33.00% indicated the game they liked to play.

Students were given six oral directions: Please give me the eraser; put the ruler under the book; open the book; pick up the paper; put the paper in the book; and please close the book and put it on the table. Overall students responded correctly 35.60%, 23.60%, 38.00%, 34.70%, 34.00%, and 34.10% of the time.

Students were shown eight lower-case and eight upper-case manuscript letters and were asked to name them. Table 4.4 shows the results for lower-case letters.

TABLE 4.4
Frequencies—Lower-Case Letters

Letter	Yes/No	Percentages
p	499/820	37.80/62.20
c	548/771	41.50/58.50
e	478/841	36.20/63.80
i	501/818	38.00/62.00
f	467/852	35.40/64.60
m	500/819	37.90/62.10
u	468/851	35.50/64.50
y	477/842	36.20/63.80

Approximately one-third of the students accurately recognized and named the eight lower-case letters presented to them. Students were asked to name eight upper-case letters. Their scores are show in Table 4.5.

Upper-case recognition scores were higher than lower-case scores. There is a well-established history of research support for the contention that upper-case letters are the first letters learned by students. Kindergarten and first-grade teachers introduced them to their students first because they were viewed as being easier to learn than lower-case letters. Students were shown cards containing six different colors and were asked to name them. Their scores are shown in Table 4.6.

Accuracy for naming the colors was surprisingly high, about half. There is a fairly robust history of research in and interest in colors as categories. This research is discussed in some detail in chapter 8. It is no coincidence,

TABLE 4.5
Frequencies—Upper-Case Letters

Letter	Yes/No	Percentages
A	609/710	46.20/53.80
G	521/798	39.50/60.50
N	514/805	39.00/61.00
B	602/717	45.60/54.40
T	535/784	40.60/59.40
S	533/786	40.40/59.60
Q	534/785	40.50/59.50
I	495/824	37.50/62.50

TABLE 4.6
Frequencies of Correctly Naming Colors

Color	Yes/No	Percentages
Red	665/654	50.40/49.60
Yellow	650/669	49.30/50.70
Blue	644/674	48.80/51.10
Black	598/674	48.80/51.10
Green	625/694	47.40/52.60
White	592/727	44.90/55.10

however, that red is the most accurately recognized color. Results for parts of the human body are shown in Table 4.7.

It is interesting that "leg" caused the most difficulty. The picture may have caused some confusion because some individuals may have focused on the "knee" rather than the overall whole "leg." Common school items were included. Results are shown in Table 4.8.

The most difficult item was crayons. Although crayons are a high-frequency item in North American elementary schools, it seems that they do represent a kind of cultural knowledge. It seems somewhat surprising that about 40 to 50% of these young immigrants were able to recognize letters, words, objects, and colors in English. In this respect the group seems quite extraordinary. The lowest percentage was related to "crayons." It is likely that this is a cultural phenomenon. Indeed, the overall responses to "school" items were lower than to body parts and colors. A more interesting finding, however, results when different groups are formed.

Responses by students from China, Hong Kong, Taiwan, and Spanish-speaking countries were separated and compared. Table 4.9 shows their responses to lower-case letters.

TABLE 4.7
Frequencies—Correct Recognition of Body Parts

Word	Yes/No	Percentages
Nose	663/656	50.30/49.70
Hand	601/718	45.60/54.40
Mouth	607/712	46.00/54.40
Leg	436/883	33.10/66.90
Eyes	643/676	48.70/51.30
Head	566/753	42.90/57.10

TABLE 4.8
Frequencies—Correct Recognition of School Items

Object	Yes/No	Percentages
Pencil	627/692	47.50/52.50
Table	540/779	40.90/59.10
Paper	529/790	40.10/59.90
Chair	573/746	43.30/56.60
Crayons	447/872	33.90/66.10

It is interesting that lower-case vowels appear to be the most difficult. However, overall means hide underlying differences. The young immigrants differed in important ways. Differences were due to a number of factors. One important difference is related to socioeconomic status. A very large percentage of the Spanish-speaking students were from refugee families. The most significant factor, however, that appears to separate these groups is related to previous school experiences. Students from Hong Kong often begin school at age 3 and the school is often an English-medium one (see later discussion). Table 4.10 shows the results of the upper-case letter recognition task.

A long history of research suggests that upper-case letters appear to be learned first in schools in North America. I, G, and Q appear to be the most

TABLE 4.9
Correct Percentages of Responses to Lower-Case Letters by Group

Letter	Spanish-Speaking	China	Taiwan	Hong Kong
p	19.10%	31.10%	37.70%	59.40%
c	23.40%	32.70%	45.50%	62.10%
e	19.10%	28.60%	34.40%	57.10%
i	23.40%	28.10%	38.30%	59.80%
f	21.30%	28.00%	30.50%	55.90%
m	21.30%	29.60%	37.70%	61.70%
u	17.00%	28.60%	33.80%	56.30%
y	19.10%	28.10%	35.70%	57.10%

TABLE 4.10
Correct Percentages of Responses to Upper-Case Letters by Group

Letter	Spanish-Speaking	China	Taiwan	Hong Kong
A	25.50%	42.30%	51.30%	65.50%
G	19.10%	32.70%	40.90%	57.90%
N	21.30%	31.60%	39.60%	57.90%
B	25.50%	40.30%	50.60%	65.10%
T	21.30%	33.20%	42.20%	59.40%
S	23.40%	33.70%	42.20%	58.20%
Q	19.10%	31.60%	42.20%	59.80%
I	19.10%	27.00%	37.70%	58.60%

difficult across the groups. The recognition of colors by students from China resulted in the lowest percentages of correct responses as shown in Table 4.11.

There is a body of literature that addresses the issue of color names and color categories. Findings suggest that there are focal members of color categories that are recognized and named more accurately than nonfocal members. This research is addressed in the last chapter.

Students were shown pictures of body parts and were asked to name them in English. Their response broken down by geolinguistic groups is shown in Table 4.12.

Students from China scored the lowest across the six body parts. The assessment included a series of pictures of common school items students were asked to name. Their scores are shown in Table 4.13.

Only 19.10% were reported to have studied English before they entered Canada. However, when scores were broken down by number of years students had been reported to have studied before immigrating to Canada,

TABLE 4.11
Percentages—Correct Recognition Scores for Colors

Color	Spanish-Speaking	China	Taiwan	Hong Kong
red	48.90%	32.10%	48.10%	69.00%
yellow	48.90%	31.60%	48.10%	66.70%
blue	48.90%	29.60%	47.40%	64.00%
black	42.60%	27.60%	40.90%	62.10%
green	46.80%	28.10%	46.10%	65.10%
white	42.60%	28.10%	42.90%	60.50%

TABLE 4.12
Percentages—Correct Recognition Scores for Body Parts

Part	Spanish-Speaking	China	Taiwan	Hong Kong
Nose	46.80%	33.20%	49.40%	69.00%
Hand	34.00%	28.60%	39.00%	67.40%
Mouth	40.40%	29.60%	43.50%	67.40%
Leg	29.80%	20.40%	23.40%	44.40%
Eyes	42.60%	32.10%	48.70%	68.20%
Head	40.40%	26.00%	37.70%	62.80%

there were no differences. Those who had studied 3 years did no better than those who had studied only 1 year overall. Those who had reentered Canada or who had transferred in from another school jurisdiction scored the following: upper-case A (37.50%); G (30.40%); N (30.40%); B (36.90%); T (33.30%); S (32.70%); Q (32.10%); I (29.80%); lower-case p (20.40%); c (35.70%); e (30.40%); l (29.20%); f (30.40%); m (29.80%); u (27.40%); and y (28.00).

Pearson product-moment correlation coefficients were computed to measure the degree of association among the various variables. The total number of coefficients is huge and is not presented here. However, they are described in general terms. Recognition correlations were substantial, as can be seen in Table 4.14.

These recognition tasks were highly related as can be seen by the pattern of correlation coefficients. Students' ability to correctly use English prepositions was related to their ability to follow the six directions (listed earlier), with coefficients of: Direction 1, .71 (1064); Direction 2, .69 (1064); Direction 3, .72 (1064); Direction 4, .75 (1064); Direction 5, .74 (1064); and Direction 6, .73 (1064). The correlations among scores for body parts are shown in Table 4.15.

TABLE 4.13
Percentages—Correct Recognition Scores for School Items

Item	Spanish-Speaking	China	Taiwan	Hong Kong
Pencil	44.70%	32.10%	46.80%	67.00%
Table	27.70%	26.00%	33.10%	58.20%
Paper	38.30%	23.00%	30.50%	57.10%
Chair	36.20%	27.60%	38.30%	59.80%
Crayons	36.20%	19.40%	24.70%	40.60%

TABLE 4.14
Pearson Product-Moment Correlation Coefficients

	Readnum	Alpha	Colors	BParts	SchItems
Count	.81—1086	.78—1098	.75—1092	.73—1092	.73—1082
Readnum		.78—1083	.74—1077	.73—1077	.73—1068
Alpha			.72—1087	.71—1087	.72—1078
Colors				.88—1094	.87—1085
BParts					.92—1086

Note. Includes sample sizes.

Correlations among the scores for the recognition of colors are shown in Table 4.16. These correlations reveal a very high relationship among the recognition scores.

Recognition scores for school items were also highly related, as can be see in Table 4.17.

Overall the correlations among the recognition of capital and lower-case letters were in the .30 to .40 range. They were the lowest of the relationships. In general, a very large percentage of these students were unable to do any of the recognition tasks.

TABLE 4.15
Correlations—Naming Body Parts

	Hand	Mouth	Leg	Eyes	Head
Nose	.85—1180	.84—1180	.67—1180	.92—1180	.81—1180
Hand		.84—1180	.73—1180	.87—1180	.84—1180
Mouth			.71—1180	.89—1180	.85—1180
Leg				.69—1180	.77—1180
Eyes					.84—1180

Note. Includes sample sizes.

TABLE 4.16
Correlations—Colors

	Yellow	Blue	Black	Green	White
Red	.90—1180	.91—1180	.86—1180	.88—1180	.86—1180
Yellow		.89—1180	.88—1180	.89—1180	.87—1180
Blue			.89—1180	.89—1182	.86—1180
Black				.88—1180	.91—1180
Green					.88—1180

Note. Includes sample sizes.

TABLE 4.17
Correlations—School Items

	Pencil	Table	Paper	Chair
Crayons	.70—1180	.74—1180	.75—1180	.76—1180
Pencil		.78—1180	.88—1180	.83—1180
Table			.81—1180	.85—1180
Paper				.82—1180

Note. Includes sample sizes.

Correlations—Personal Predictors

A fascinating finding was that the relationships among personal variables and the language variables all had coefficients lower than .10. Many were essentially zero. For instance, the relationship between age of first words and the recognition of school items had a correlation of .01 (1090). It was anticipated that there would be stronger relationships between such variables.

Primary Students—Achievement Differences

It is clear that overall a majority of primary students enter Canada without the basic English skills measured by the primary assessment instrument developed by the OROC staff. This has consequences for them and for their primary teachers and the mainstream students whose classes they entered. If, as members of the OROC staff believed, the skills measured by their primary assessment represented a set of "readiness" variables, then a large percentage of immigrant students were not ready for the teaching and learning they would encounter in the primary classes they would be enrolled in.

There were significant differences related to age. Older students scored significantly higher on the assessment measures. However, the effect sizes were not impressive. However, there were significant differences in scores on the primary battery related to where students were from. Differences were related to complex interacting variables. Socioeconomic status was a significant variable. Students from lower socioeconomic categories scored significantly lower than those from higher ones. However, the most significant factor related to achievement for those who had English literacy skills appeared to be an instructional variable. This is readily apparent when students from the People's Republic, Hong Kong, and Taiwan are compared.

Recognition scores for lower-case "p," for instance, were: Spanish-speaking 19.10%, PRC 31.10%, Taiwan 37.70%, and Hong Kong 59.40%. There were statistically significant differences across all of the measures. Instruction, as a factor, appears to be related to these differences. Students from Hong Kong were involved in learning to read from age 3. In most cases, these students were in preschools that were also, most often, English-based religious institutions. They were taught English reading skills from a very early age. Spanish-speaking students were primarily from refugee backgrounds. Their educational experiences included interrupted schooling or no school experiences and psychological and physical trauma. Lower English scores are not unexpected, but differences across groups were.

The measures developed by the OROC test revealed that about one-third of the students entered the country with some English language skills. However, in the one-third of students who had some English language skills, groups differed dramatically.

OLDER STUDENTS

The majority of students in this study were those who ranged in age from 12 to 20. Table 4.18 shows older students' ages upon their entry into the Vancouver school district.

The largest group of students was made up of those 8 to 17 years old. As can be seen in Table 4.18, the largest group entering the country was comprised of 9- to 13-year-old students. These findings have interesting ramifications for the study, particularly as it relates to the acquisition of academic language, if one is convinced by the research finding of individuals such as Collier (1987) that they are the most likely students to be successful in learning a second language.

TABLE 4.18
Frequencies of Age on Entry

Age	Frequency	Percentage
12	2,465	9.9%
11	2,515	10.2%
10	2,440	9.8%
9	2,415	9.7%
13	2,017	8.1%
15	1,864	7.5%
14	1,693	6.8%
16	1,643	6.6%
8	1,419	5.7%
17	1,295	5.2%
7	971	3.9%
5	846	3.4%
6	845	3.4%
18	721	2.9%
4	498	2.0%
3	299	0.2%
2	224	0.9%
1	149	0.6%
20	7	00%
Unknown	567	2.30%
Total	24,890	

There was a gender imbalance, with 13,316 (53.5%) boys and 11,549 girls (46.4%) (missing 0.1%, 25) entering the school district. A difference of 1,767 may seem small; however, this number does represent the populations of about six elementary schools or a large secondary school. Landed immigrants had a 52.40/47.60% ratio, refugees 54.00/46%, students 56.30/43.70%, entrepreneurs 51.50/48.50%, diplomats 52.50/47.50%, and the work visa group 60.00/40.00%. There were larger imbalances across countries.

There were differences related to immigration status. Landed immigrant status represented 64.6% (16,078), refugees were 17.1% (4,257), student status 1.4% (349), entrepreneur status 13.1% (3,261), diplomat 0.4% (100), returning Canadians 3.2% (796), and those with work visas 0.2% (49). Landed immigrants are individuals who have applied to and have been granted a visa to enter Canada as permanent residents who can apply for Canadian citizenship after 3 years. There are two categories of refugees, those who enter Canada and claim refugee status and those who are granted such status by the Minister of Immigration. Student visas are given to individuals who study at postsecondary institutions, so the individuals in the study are children of those adult students. Returning Canadians are children who were born in Canada and then left the country, most often to return to their parents' home country in order to be raised in their first cultures and acquire their parents' first languages. Some students accompanied their parents, who entered Canada on work visas. Work visas allow individuals to work in Canada for a fixed period of time. Refugee status was claimed by individuals from the countries shown in Table 4.19.

TABLE 4.19
Countries of Origin for Those Claiming Refugee Status

Country	Number	Percentage
Afganistan	93	2.10%
Angola	2	00%
Bosnia	4	0.1%
Bulgaria	4	0.1%
Bangladesh	26	0.6%
Cambodia	22	0.5%
Chile	9	0.2%
China	419	9.50%
Croatia	7	0.2%
El Salvador	455	10.3%

(continued)

TABLE 4.19 *(continued)*

Country	Number	Percentage
Ethiopia	62	0.1%
Ghana	13	0.3%
Guatemala	97	2.20%
Honduras	52	1.1%
Hong Kong	101	2.3%
Hungary	17	0.4%
India	18	0.4%
Iran	264	6.00%
Iraq	137	3.20%
Kenya	9	0.2%
Nicaragua	273	6.20%
Moldova	1	00%
Peru	8	0.2%
Philippines	21	0.5%
Pakistan	8	0.2%
Poland	205	4.70%
Romania	48	1.1%
Russia	101	2.3%
Somalia	88	2.0%
Sri Lanka	31	0.7%
South Africa	11	0.3%
Swaziland	1	00%
Thailand	35	0.8%
Tanzania	1	00%
Uganda	6	0.1%
Ukraine	86	2.0%
Venezuela	5	0.1%
Vietnam	1,109	25.20%
Yugoslavia	26	0.6%
Unknown	532	12.00%

Some of the countries of origin seem incorrect. Hong Kong, for instance, does not normally represent a country from which one flees as a refugee. However, in the case of Hong Kong the refugees were mostly Vietnamese "Boat People;" many of their children had been born in Hong Kong in refugee camps.

There were a number of families who entered the country who did so under different circumstances. Indeed, they were categorized as "business" or entrepreneurial immigrants. These individuals gained entrance to Canada on the promise that they would invest at least $250,000 in Canada. These individuals often did not have to wait as long to get their visas and to immigrate as other applicants. Table 4.20 shows the breakdown of entrepreneurial class immigrants.

Entrepreneurs also came from Australia, Indonesia, Russia, Mexico, France, Fiji, Brazil, Iran, Singapore, Venezuela, Brunei, India, Israel, South Africa, Norway, Chile, Germany, Switzerland, New Zealand, Bulgaria, Netherlands, Peru, Poland, Argentina, Cambodia, Guatemala, Honduras, Portugal, Romania, Vietnam, Egypt, Kuwait, Burma, Denmark, Italy, Kenya, Panama, Spain, Sweden, Thailand, Ukraine, United Arab Emirates, and Moldova. Differences related to many variables broken down by country of origin and first languages are interesting and complex.

Personal Development

Parents were asked about the births of their children and whether they had been normal or difficult. About 84% (84.10%) reported normal, uneventful births, whereas about 16% (15.9) reported that they had Caesarian or diffi-

TABLE 4.20
The 10 Most Frequent Countries of Origin—Entrepreneurial Immigrants

Country	Number	Percentage
Hong Kong	1,438	44.10%
Taiwan	897	27.50%
Korea	232	7.10%
Japan	186	5.70%
China	125	3.80%
United States	55	1.70%
Malaysia	36	1.10%
Macau	26	0.80%
England	23	0.70%
Philippines	20	0.60%

cult deliveries. Two-tenths of a percent reported extreme difficulties resulting in problems for the child. About 5% (5.3%) of the cases are unknown
because the mother was not involved in the interview as a result of death,
divorce, or separation (Table 4.21).

There were no significant differences in categories across immigration
status. Refugees, for instance, did not report more or less difficulties. On the
average, parents reported that their children had first begun to walk at
12.90 months (SD = 3.53): immigrants 12.90/3.50; refugees 12.90/3.60; students 13.20/4.90; entrepreneurs 12.80/2.90; diplomats 14.00/5.60; Canadian 12.40/23.00; and those with work visas 12.40/6.70. These are
interesting findings in that they appear to support North American medical norms (J. Kline, 2005, physician, personal communication).

An overwhelming majority reported that their children had no serious
childhood illnesses (86.7%), whereas 13.1% reported serious childhood illnesses, and 0.1% reported the illnesses remained a very serious problem for
the child. Individuals with problems were referred to a public health nurse
for further screening and possible referral. Concerns about their children's
health were reported by 13.90% of parents. Ten percent (9.90%) indicated
that their children had allergies and 0.1% indicated they had continuing serious allergies. Asked whether their children had been prescribed any special medications, 2.4% reported yes and 0.2% reported the condition was
serious and long term.

Overall, 87.50% reported that their children's hearing had not been checked
prior to immigrating to Canada, whereas 7.8% reported that they had, and
0.3% reported their children had significant hearing problems. Nearly 87%
(86.40%) reported that their children had not had visual screening and 11.60%
reported that they had, whereas 5.3% reported there was a serious problem.

Interestingly, in 87.00% of the cases, students had seen a dentist, whereas
12.90% had not. Only four individuals reported that there was a serious
problem. Differences in dental care were noted by many individuals who
indicated, for instance, that in many countries the use of anesthesia to control pain was not a normal procedure for dental repairs or extractions. Later
analyses reveal that whether an immigrant had seen a dentist before immigration to Canada was predictive of English proficiency—an artifact of so-

TABLE 4.21
Child's Birth History

No Problem	19,621	84.1%
Yes—Caesarian	3,910	15.9%
Yes/Problem	50	0.2%
Unknown/NA	1,309	5.3%

cioeconomic conditions. Indeed, students who had not seen a dentist scored significantly lower on all of the language measures than those who had seen a dentist (see complex findings later in this chapter).

It is quite extraordinary that such an overwhelming majority of immigrant students had neither their vision nor their hearing tested. Immigrants, with the exception of refugee claimants, are required to have medical examinations. However, the Canadian federal government focuses on the identification of communicable diseases. Vision and hearing are not communicable diseases and are therefore not considered in immigration. There are serious implications of these findings for teachers, school administrators, and public health authorities. This pattern is different from the one obtained for primary-age students. Overall, a larger percentage of primary students had their hearing, vision, and teeth checked than did older students.

Childhood fears were reported for 30.0%, and the overwhelming fear was of dogs. A majority of refugee children (57.50%) were identified as having childhood fears. The item was considered unreliable by OROC staff because many individuals appeared to invent fears, to seem helpful, and its use as an interview item was discontinued.

Families interviewed at OROC varied in size from 1 child to 29. Table 4.22 displays the frequencies. The most frequent was 2 children, representing 45.50% of the cases.

TABLE 4.22
Number of Children in Family

Children	Families	Percentage
1	1170	4.70%
2	11,300	45.50%
3	7,343	29.50%
4	3,335	13.40%
5	1,045	4.20%
6	348	1.40%
7	149	0.6%
8	49	0.2%
9	98	0.4%
10	24	0.1%
12	1	00
14	2	00
16	1	00
29	1	00

The mean was 2.80 children per family; however, there were differences across countries of origin. The average number of children per family ranged from 5.6 in Iraq to 1.00 in several countries such as Iceland and Moldova.

Parents were asked about the type of school their children had enrolled in before they immigrated to Canada. Most, 64.80%, reported urban school settings: 6.50% rural, 2.30% refugee, 26.10% private, and 0.2% special school. There were 14 students who were reported to have private tutors. The relatively high percentage of private schools is related to Hong Kong and Taiwanese immigrants, who generally attended private elementary schools, usually schools established and run by church groups. In both cases, parents reported that their children had attended religious schools, even though they did not necessarily subscribe to the beliefs of the religion, because the schools were prestigious and instruction was often in English.

There was considerable variation in class size across countries and types of schools, but on the average parents reported 37.10 students (11.20), 5.40 days per week (0.50), and 5.80 hours per day (1.60). Korea established a 9-hour school day for elementary students in 1996. Ranges were: class size 1 to 165, school days 1 to 6, and school hours 1 to 10. Many students attended school for more than 5 days per week. In Hong Kong, for instance, some schools alternate 5- and 6-day school weeks, with the sixth day being a half-day. This is also the pattern in a number of other countries, such as India. Refugee schools were generally not the largest. Schools in Africa and South East Asia reported the largest average class sizes.

Students were asked about their favorite and least favorite classes taken in their home countries. Their responses are shown in Table 4.23.

TABLE 4.23
The 10 Most and Least Favorite School Subjects

Most	Least
Math—31.20%	Math—24.70%
Language—10.90%	Language—10.20%
Science—9.70%	Lang. Arts—9.60%
Lang. Arts—8.60%	Soc. Stds. —9.50%
Art—4.50%	History—8.20%
Soc. Stds.—4.30%	Science—8.00%
History—3.90%	Music—4.00%
ESL—3.40%	Geography—3.60%
Music—2.50%	PE—2.80%
Biology—2.20%	Bible Study—2.30%

Overall, frequencies were affected by several complex factors. Bible study was mentioned as a least favorite subject by students from Hong Kong and Taiwan quite regularly. The fashionable preschools and private schools are often Christian schools, chosen because the medium of instruction is English. There were also differences related to such variables as gender, age, L1, and type of school. Students from Taiwan reported that they were required to take a math skills test every single day of their elementary school careers. As a result, they were most likely to report that math was both their most and least favorite school subject.

Books and magazines were available in the homes of 89.40% of the students, whereas in 10.60% they were not. When asked whether they could help their children with their homework, 40.60% said they could not and 59.40% said they could. Refugee parents were nearly evenly split: 49.70% said they could not help with homework, whereas 50.30% reported they could help. This is a very significant finding that reveals a significant difficulty in English-only systems. Many parents are unable to help their children in such tasks as doing homework. Students are left to rely on the educational support provided by the school district. Their success in school may well rest on how well school-based support accounts for their needs and abilities.

Nearly 100% reported that there was a place for their children to study at home (97.80%). This item was unreliable in that nearly all parents reported positively. It is likely that individuals responded in a way they thought interviewers wanted them to respond. This variable was not used in further analyses.

Learning problems, including difficulties with particular subject classes, were reported for 17.20% of the students. Special talents were reported in 5.60% of the cases. The most frequently identified special skill was a talent for art. Ten percent (10.10%) reported their children had repeated a grade, whereas 2.30% reported they had skipped a grade. Differences were noted relative to such variables as gender, immigration status, type of school, and country of origin.

BACKGROUND VARIABLES
AND LANGUAGE DEVELOPMENT

Parents were asked to report at what age their children had begun to produce words. Overall the average was 12.30/4.70 months: immigrants 12.20/4.70; refugees 12.80/5.50; students 12.00/4.20; entrepreneurs 12.00/3.50; diplomats 13.40/6.60; Canadians 12.00/6.10; and those with work visas 11.00/1.60. Table 4.24 shows the data broken down by first language.

These numbers are fairly close to findings that show North American children begin to produce their first words somewhere between 12 and 20 months (Bates, 1976; Bates, Benigni, Bretherton, Camaioni, & Volterra, 1977; Clark & Clark, 1977). In fact, these results are quite extraordinary be-

TABLE 4.24
Age of First Single-Word Utterances, in Months

Language	Age (years)	Number of Speakers
Acholi	12.00/00	2
Afghani	11.80/.89	5
Afrikaans	11.70/.98	3
Akan	24.00/00	1
Albanian	12.00/00 (n = 2)	3
Algerian	Not known	1
Amharic	11.70/3.70	37
Arabic-Asari	11.00/1.73	94
Armenian	13.50/1.24	3
Assamese	8.00/00	1
Assyrian	12.00/00	2
Bahasa	13.00/4.11	31
Bangla	14.00/00	1
Bemba	Not known	2
Bengali	10.00/1.40	43
Bicolono	8.50/2.90	10
Bisaya	Not known	2
Bosnian-Croatian	11.50/3.50	23
Brong	24.00/00	1
Bulgarian	12.30/5.50	40
Burmese	12.00/2.30	8
Busanga	16.00/5.60 (n = 2)	3
Cambodian	13.70/3.40	30
Cantonese	12.30/4.20 (n = 5,602)	9,106
Cebuano	10.30/2.60	11
Chaldean	14.00/00 (n = 1)	9
Chiarati	16.00/00	1
Chiuchow	11.25/.96	5
Creole	12.00/00 (n = 2)	4
Croatian	9.50/3.50	37
Czech	8.70/2.30	40
Danish	12.50/1.80	10
Dari	12.00/6.70	21
Dutch	Not known	15

Egyptian	Not known	2
English	12.30/5.90	997
Ewe	Not known	1
Farsi	11.70/2.30	129
Fijian	11.70/2.00 ($n = 6$)	8
Filipino	10.70/2.40	7
Finnish	12.30/1.20	18
Foochow	12.00/00 ($n = 1$)	17
Fookien/Fukien	16.20/6.30	52
French	13.30/5.90	126
Georgian	14.00/00	1
German	12.70/4.40	47
Greek	9.00/1.00	29
Gujarati	13.90/3.40	30
Hainanese	12.30/3.20 ($n = 10$)	12
Hakka	11.50/3.10	65
Hausa	8.00/00	1
Harari	12.00/00	2
Hebrew	11.50/5.60	61
Henghun	Not known	1
Hiligaynon	18.00/00	1
Hindi	13.40/6.50	335
Hockchew	14.00/00 ($n = 2$)	3
Hokkien	9.80/2.40	45
Hunan	12.00/00 ($n = 1$)	4
Hungarian	13.30/3.20	9
Icelandic	1.40/2.30	9
Ilocano	12.80/5.30	42
Indonesian (Bahasa)	13.00/4.11	26
Iranian	14.00/00 ($n = 2$)	9
Italian	9.00/00 ($n = 2$)	22
Japanese	12.73/3.90	520
Kajai	8.00/00	1
Kanjobal	Unknown	1
Kheh	11.30/2.30	27
Khmer	14.00/2.80	108

(continued)

TABLE 4.24

Language	Age (years)	Number of Speakers
Kiswahili	13.00/00 ($n = 1$)	6
Korean	13.30/3.70	605
Kurdish	15.10/4.40	123
Lao	Not known	8
Lebanese	Unknown	1
Latvian	Unknown	1
Luganda	12.00/00	1
Lukonzo	14.00/00	1
Malay	15.30/2.30	12
Malayalam	11.00/00	1
Maltese	12.00/00 ($n = 2$)	6
Mandarin	12.30/4.00 ($n = 3,028$)	3,882
Marathi	15.00/4.20	3
Memon	Unknown	1
Mihahasa	Unknown	1
Ndebele	Unknown	1
Nepali	10.00/2.80	2
Nuer	Unknown	1
Norwegian	12.30/2.30	10
Ogandian	Unknown	1
Oromiffa	Unknown	3
Oromo	12.00/00 ($n = 1$)	4
Pampango	10.00/00 ($n = 1$)	4
Pangasian	8.00/00	1
Persian	10.80/3.90	134
Pojulu	Unknown	1
Polish	11.97/4.80	416
Pongwli	12.00/00	2
Portuguese	9.60/2.70	114
Punjabi	13.20/7.60	550
Pushtu	12.60/2.30 ($n = 8$)	14
Romanian	11.70/3.80	139
Rusanga	10.00/00	1
Russian	12.60/4.60	245

Saho	13.00/00 ($n = 1$)	3
Sanish	Unknown	1
Sena	12.00/00 ($n = 2$)	4
Serbian	Unknown	1
Serbo-Croatian	12.50/1.40	249
Sesotho	10.00/00	1
Shanghainese	10.00/2.80	2
Shilluk	12.00/00 ($n = 1$)	3
Shona	Unknown	2
Sinhala	14.50/6.40 ($n = 4$)	17
Slovak	14.50/4.90 ($n = 8$)	27
Somali	14.10/7.90	108
Spanish	9.90/3.30	1,327
Sunwoo	8.00/00	1
Swahili	Unknown	1
Swedish	12.10/2.30 ($n = 12$)	19
Swiss	Unknown	1
Tagalog	11.70/5.50	1,091
Taiwanese	12.10/2.90	105
Tamil	11.50/3.70	93
Taosai	10.00/2.80	2
Teochew	11.60/2.30 ($n = 7$)	23
Thai	11.70/5.50 ($n = 8$)	21
Tigrinia	12.20/3.40	29
Tiv	10.00/00 ($n = 2$)	5
Tongan	12.00/00	1
Turkish	12.30/2.60 ($n = 4$)	13
Twi	18.00/00 ($n = 2$)	12
Ukranian	13.10/4.20 ($n = 8$)	32
Urdu	11.58/3.20 ($n = 46$)	58
Vietnamese	Vietnam 15.70/7.10	1,960
Yanping	12.10/2.30 ($n = 3$)	6
Yoruba	Unknown	1
Yugoslavian	12.00/00 ($n = 3$)	5
Zambuangan	Unknown	1
Zulu	Unknown	1

cause they suggest the possibility of a universal in child development across cultures and languages.

Table 4.25 shows ages of single-word utterances broken down by languages. First simple sentences were on the average produced at 20.30 (7.30) months, according to parental reports. It is easily argued that these data are subject to error because of inaccuracies in parental memories. It is also speculative because the definition of a "simple sentence" is unclear and varies from individual to individual. These data are interesting, however.

Parents were asked to report the age when their children had begun to learn to read their first languages, if they had begun to learn to read. A surprising finding was that parents reported their children had first begun to read their L1 at 49.50 months (18.10), with significantly different ages being reported across immigration groups: immigrants 48.00/19.20; refugees 65.80/17.60; students 48.20/15.80; entrepreneurs 44.00/14.30; diplomats 48.90/14.40; Canadians 49.00/17.30; and those with work visas 48.30/16.40. There were striking differences across L1s, with Chinese parents reporting lower average ages than non-Chinese parents. Chinese parents from Hong Kong reported that their children on the average began reading instruction at age 3. This was a surprise. This finding led to further investigation and confirmation that the statement was valid. Ho and Bryant (1997) note, "Children in Hong Kong start learning to read Chinese at the age of 3, which is earlier than what children do in other countries like the U.S. and Britain" (p. 280). Students in the United States often begin to read logos long before they enter school, and Chinese is a logographic language. It is clear from the present research and follow-up inquiries that preschool children in Hong Kong are included in reading instruction involving the recognition of Chinese characters and basic English words. Indeed, instruction involves rote memorization and group oral responses to characters and words shown on flash cards.

Overall, parents reported that their children had begun to produce their first single-word utterances at 12.20 months ($SD = 4.70$). Reports were marvelously similar. The large sample size resulted in statistically significant differences; however, eta squared was .09. In essence, the effect size was minimal. The result showed that there was a remarkable similarity across language groups. Cantonese had a mean of 12.30 ($SD = 4.20$, $n = 5,602$), Mandarin 12.30 ($SD = 4.00$, $n = 3,028$), Korean 13.30 ($SD = 3.70$, $n = 605$), Romanian 11.20 ($SD = 3.80$, $n = 139$), Tagalog 11.70 ($SD = 5.50$, $n = 1,091$), and English 12.30 ($SD = 5.90$, $n = 997$). The Vietnamese mean is higher than these at 15.70 ($SD = 7.10$, $n = 1,960$), but is still within the range typically reported for English speakers, whereas the mean for Spanish speakers was lower 9.90 ($SD = 3.30$, $n = 345$).

TABLE 4.25
Age of First Simple Sentences, in Months

Language	Age (years)	Number of Speakers
Acholi	20.00/00	2
Afghani	15.00/2.80	5
Afrikaans	11.70/.98	3
Akan	36.00/00	1
Albanian	Not known	3
Algerian	Not known	1
Amharic	20.79/4.80 ($n = 22$)	37
Arabic–Asari	16.80/12.90	94
Armenian	20.00/00 ($n = 1$)	3
Assamese	12.00/00	1
Assyrian	Not known	2
Bahasa	23.40/10.70 ($n = 11$)	31
Bangla	Not known	1
Bemba	Not known	2
Bengali	19.50/6.40 ($n = 36$)	43
Bicolono	19.40/4.00	13
Bisaya	Not known	2
Bosnian–Croatian	16.00/6.90 ($n = 18$)	23
Brong	48.00/Oo	1
Bulgarian	18.40/3.60 ($n = 27$)	40
Burmese	24.00/00 ($n = 2$)	8
Busanga	24.00/8.50 ($n = 2$)	3
Cambodian	30.00/12.40 ($n = 8$)	30
Cantonese	19.50/6.40 ($n = 5{,}606$)	9,106
Cebuano	19.50/3.00 ($n = 4$)	11
Chaldean	18.00/00 ($n = 1$)	9
Chiarati	Unknown	1
Chiuchow	15.00/6.00 ($n = 4$)	5
Creole	Not known	4
Croatian	24.10/6.30 ($n = 33$)	37
Czech	30.00/10.40 ($n = 23$)	40
Danish	29.50/7.80 ($n = 2$)	10
Dari	18.80/6.30 ($n = 5$)	21

(continued)

TABLE 4.25 (continued)

Language	Age (years)	Number of Speakers
Dutch	Not known	15
Egyptian	Not known	2
English	21.10/7.80 ($n = 103$)	997
Ewe	Not known	1
Farsi	22.30/8.00 ($n = 47$)	129
Fijian	24.30/7.80 ($n = 5$)	8
Filipino	Not known	7
Finnish	24.00/00 ($n = 4$)	18
Foochow	18.00/00 ($n = 1$)	17
Fookien/Fukien	24.80/6.30 ($n = 36$)	52
French	22.50/8.90 ($n = 107$)	126
Georgian	30.00/00	1
German	22.50/9.20 ($n = 10$)	47
Greek	15.00/2.80 ($n = 5$)	29
Gujarati	23.40/11.20 ($n = 8$)	30
Hainanese	Not known	12
Hakka	18.90/9.90 ($n = 18$)	65
Hausa	14.00/00	1
Harari	18.00/00	2
Hebrew	16.10/4.70 ($n = 24$)	61
Henghun	Not known	1
Hiligaynon	Not known	1
Hindi	21.50/8.80 ($n = 168$)	335
Hockchew	Not known	3
Hokkien	16.30/4.80 ($n = 24$)	45
Hunan	Not known	4
Hungarian	19.50/3.90	9
Icelandic	28.00/00 ($n = 2$)	9
Ilocano	23.50/5.00 ($n = 30$)	42
Indonesian (Bahasa)	23.40/10.70 ($n = 11$)	26
Iranian	14.00/00 ($n = 1$)	9
Italian	16.00/2.80 ($n = 2$)	22
Japanese	22.40/6.10 ($n = 387$)	520
Kajai	24.00/00	1
Kanjobal	18.70/5.00	3

112

Kheh	Not known	27
Khmer	26.60/11.40 ($n = 70$)	108
Kiswahili	36.00/00 ($n = 2$)	6
Korean	24.30/6.20 ($n = 330$)	605
Kurdish	24.30/6.20 ($n = 33$)	123
Lao	Not known	8
Lebanese	Not known	1
Latvian	Not known	1
Luganda	Not known	1
Lukonzo	Not known	1
Malay	24.00/00 ($n = 2$)	12
Malayalam	18.00/00	1
Maltese	Not known	6
Mandarin	19.20/5.90 ($n = 3,663$)	3,882
Marathi	24.00.00 ($n = 1$)	3
Memon	Not known	1
Mihahasa	Not known	1
Ndebele	Not known	1
Nepali	Not known	2
Nuer	Not known	1
Norwegian	18.00/00 ($n = 1$)	10
Ogandian	Not known	1
Oromiffa	Not known	3
Oromo	Not known	4
Pampango	Not known	4
Pangasian	24.00/00	1
Persian	18.50/6.90 ($n = 130$)	134
Pojulu	Unknown	1
Polish	20.60/6.70 ($n = 108$)	416
Pongwli	12.00/00	2
Portuguese	18.30/4.80 ($n = 96$)	114
Punjabi	19.00/5.80 ($n = 351$)	550
Pushtu	22.50/3.00 ($n = 4$)	14
Romanian	18.50/3.90 ($n = 120$)	139
Rusanga	Not known	1
Russian	19.40/6.30 ($n = 250$)	245

(continued)

113

TABLE 4.25 (continued)

Language	Age (years)	Number of Speakers
Saho	24.00/00 ($n = 1$)	3
Sanish	Not known	1
Sena	Not known	4
Serbian	Not known	1
Serbo-Croatian	16.00/6.90 (103)	249
Sesotho	18.00/00	1
Shanghainese	19.90/6.10	51
Shilluk	Not known	3
Shona	Not known	2
Sinhala	20.80/10.70 ($n = 4$)	17
Slovak	Not known	27
Somali	17.50/9.40 ($n = 91$)	108
Spanish	18.70/6.70 ($n = 1,198$)	1,327
Sunwoo	12.00/00	1
Swahili	Not known	1
Swedish	Not known	19
Swiss	Not known	1
Tagalog	20.90/6.20 ($n = 920$)	1,091
Taiwanese	18.90/4.20 ($n = 71$)	105
Tamil	31.80/14.20 ($n = 80$)	93
Taosai	13.00/1.40	2
Teochew	Not known	23
Thai	18.00/00 ($n = 8$)	21
Tigrinia	Not known	29
Tiv	Not known	5
Tongan	Not known	1
Turkish	Not known	13
Twi	Not known	12
Ukranian	24.00/00 ($n = 4$)	32
Urdu	19.90/5.90 ($n = 51$)	58
Vietnamese	22.30/9.80 ($n = 1,770$)	1,960
Yanping	Not known	6
Yoruba	Not known	1
Yugoslavian	Not known	5
Zambuangan	Not known	1
Zulu	Not known	1

There were statistically significant differences in the age at which students began to produce their first simple sentences 20.30 months (SD = 7.20). Eta squared was .13. Cantonese children had a mean of 19.50 (SD = 6.40, n = 5,606), Mandarin 19.20 (SD = 5.90, n = 3,663), Korean 24.30 (SD = 6.20, n = 605), Romanian 18.50 (SD = 3.90, n = 139), Tagalog 20.90 (SD = 6.20, n = 920), and English 21.10 (SD = 7.80, n = 103). These means were within the range of ages observed in studies of English speakers.

There was a significant difference in the reported age at which students began to learn to read their first languages and eta squared was .41. This is a substantial effect size. The overall mean for students beginning to learn to read in their first languages was 49.40 (SD = 19.30). The mean for Cantonese speakers was 38.20 months (SD = 14.70, n = 5,600), Mandarin 45.20 (SD = 14.20, n = 3,680), Korean 50.20 (SD = 10.20, n = 592), Romanian 70.50 (SD = 8.30, n = 120), Tagalog 51.40 (SD = 17.30, n = 847), and English 50/70 (SD = 16.90, n = 92). Spanish speakers began to learn to read at 72.90 months (SD = 11.50, n = 317) and Vietnamese at 66.20 months (SD = 16.20, n = 181). The number of Vietnamese students who were reported to have begun reading in their L1 was extremely low. This is likely a reflection of their overall refugee status. Means across immigration categories were approximately 48 months, except for refugees who reported a mean of 65.20 months. A majority of parents reported that their children used their L1s at home most of the time (94.20%), whereas 4.90% reported their use half of the time and only 0.9% reported they used them seldom. Nearly 100% (99.4) reported that they could communicate with their children in their first languages, whereas 0.6% reported they could not. A small number, 17.70%, reported that they could communicate with their children in English, whereas 82.30% said they could not. Seventy-nine percent indicated that their children liked to hear stories read aloud and 21% said their children did not. A large majority, 89.8%, indicated that their children liked to read alone. Because the responses for these variables are so close to unanimous, their usefulness in further analyses was determined to be doubtful.

ACHIEVEMENT RESULTS

It is important to remember that assessors at OROC, depending on students' age and ability, chose different measures to administer. So, for instance, CELT was used primarily to assess older students (secondary level). The Woodcock was used to assess elementary students. In addition, of the 24,890 students in the database, 5,487 were assessed as 0-level English, no English at all, and no standardized or informal tests were administered. This leaves 19,043, having some measurable English skills. Of this number, 5,928 were administered the Gap, 4,635 the Woodcock, and 7,026 the CELT, a total of 17,589. Because the examiners felt there was a special need, the remaining students were administered various instruments, such as the TONI, the Bilingual Syntax Measure, the Gapadol, or the Slosson.

The Oral Measures

Students' oral English proficiency was measured through the use of the structured holistic assessment described earlier. Their ability to produce tenses was judged according to three categories: yes, no, and weak. The results in Table 4.26 are based on the 19,043 individuals in the database who had some measurable English skills.

Asked to formulate a question, 42.60% were unable, 29.30% weak, and 28.10% able to do so. Some 65.90% were able to say the days of the week (17.40% not able and 16.70% weak), whereas 78.50% were able to recite the names of the letters of the alphabet (4.7% not able and 16.80% weak). Comparable numbers were able to count in English (62.30% yes, 2.80% no, and 34.90% weak) and read numbers at random (76.00% yes, 3.70% no, and 20.30% weak). Students recognized on the average 8.40 colors (3.40) out of 11: immigrants 8.60 (3.20); refugees 7.00 (4.10); students 8.70 (3.30); entrepreneurs 9.10 (3.30); diplomats 9.10 (3.30); Canadians 10.10 (2.30); and those with work visas 10.00 (3.30).

On the average they recognized and correctly named 9.10 (5.50) body parts out of 19: immigrants 9.50 (5.30); refugees 7.70 (6.20); students 8.60 (5.60); entrepreneurs 8.80 (4.50); Canadians 13.60 (5.30); and those with work visas 11.10 (3.20).

Overall, on the average 4.50 (1.90) school items out of 11 were recognized and named in English: immigrants 4.60 (1.80); refugees 3.70 (2.20); students 4.00 (1.90); entrepreneurs 4.50 (1.70); diplomats 4.80 (1.70); Canadians 5.30 (1.10); and those with work visas 6.00 (2.30).

Students correctly produced on the average 3.30 (3.20) prepositions out of 9: immigrants 3.50 (3.10); refugees 2.40; students 3.10 (3.50); entrepreneurs 2.90 (2.70); diplomats 3.90 (3.90); Canadians 5.50 (3.40); and those with work visas 4.10 (3.30).

Students who wrote compositions in English scored a mean of 2.10 (.95). A score of 2.00 on the holistic scale is equated to "Poor" for grade level and age, whereas 3.00 indicates performance judged to be appropriate for students' ages and grade levels. The group producing the highest overall scores were those who entered with work visas, 3.80 (1.20) with immigrants 2.10 (1.00), refugees 1.70 (.90), students 1.90 (1.10), entrepreneurs 2.10 (.80), diplomats 3.10 (1.40), and Canadians 2.70 (1.00). Figure 4.1 shows an 11th-grade student's English composition. This is a reflection of his views

TABLE 4.26
Percentages of Response—Oral Proficiency

	No	*Weak*	*Yes*
Present	25.40%	32.40%	42.10%
Past	54.20%	23.50%	22.30%
Future	51.50%	23.70%	24.70%

of the English courses he had taken in Hong Kong before he immigrated to Canada. It does have an interesting message.

Students were also asked to write in their first languages if possible. Figure 4.2 shows an example written in Hindi.

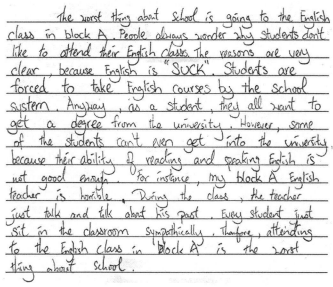

FIG. 4.1.   Immigrant student's English writing sample.

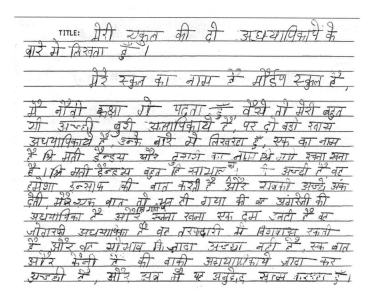

FIG. 4.2.   Immigrant student's Hindi writing sample.

Translation: I am writing about two teachers (ladies) in my school. The name of my school is Modern school. I am in the ninth grade. As such, there are many good and bad teachers, but two are special. That's why I'm writing about them. One is Mrs. X and the other one's name is (?) Y. Mrs. X (not clear) is nice and she always talks about justice and gives good marks to everyone. But I have forgotten one thing and that is she is the English teacher. Mrs. Y. is the complete opposite. She is the geography teacher and holds a specialty in praise. By character she is not very good. One other thing I have to say is the other teachers are more or less good and now I end this writing sample. (Translated by Reginald D'Silva, Department of Language and Literacy Education, University of British Columbia)

Students were asked to write from a selection of topics, including: My Family; My Trip to Canada; A Game I Like to Play; My Home Country; and My School Last Year. Figure 4.2 showed a sample written in Hindi by a ninth-grade student. This writing was judged to be a "2" on the holistic score. Interpreters were convinced that this student was likely enrolled in a Hindi-medium school, and the language he spoke at home was most likely not Hindi. Figure 4.3 shows an example of a composition written in Spanish.

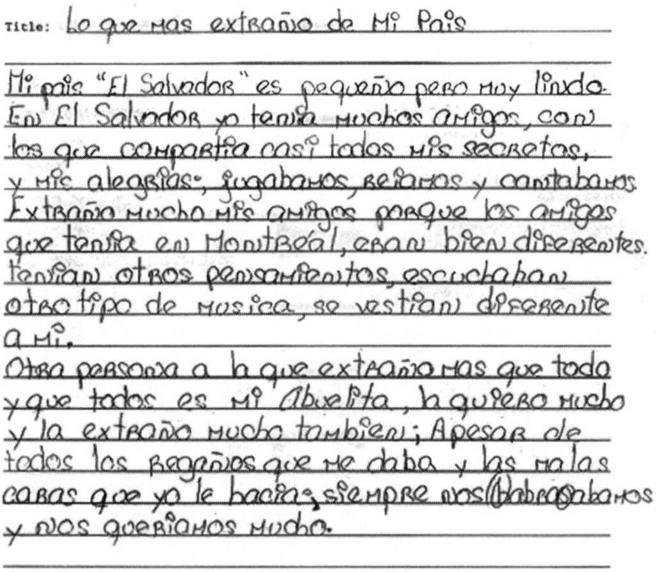
Title: Lo que mas extraño de Mi País

Mi país "El Salvador" es pequeño pero muy lindo.
En El Salvador yo tenía muchos amigos, con
los que compartía casi todos mis secretos,
y mis alegrías; jugabamos, reíamos y cantabamos
Extraño mucho mis amigos porque los amigos
que tenía en Montreál, eran bien diferentes.
tenían otros pensamientos, escuchaban
otro tipo de musica, se vestían diferente
a mi.
Otra persona a la que extraño mas que todo
y que todos es mi abuelita, la quiero mucho
y la extraño mucho tambien; Apesar de
todos los regaños que me daba y las malas
caras que yo le hacía, siempre nos (h)abrazabamos
y nos queríamos mucho.

FIG. 4.3. Immigrant student's Spanish writing sample.

Translation: Title: What I miss the most about my country. My country "El Salvador" is small but very pretty. I had many friends in El Salvador, with whom I shared almost all of my secrets and my joys; we would play, laugh and sing. I miss my friends very much because the friends I had in Montreal were very different. They had different thoughts, listened to different types of music, dressed differently from me.

Another person that I miss more than anything and more than anyone is my grandma. I love her a lot and I miss her a lot also, in spite of all the scoldings I got from her and the long faces I made at her. We always hugged and we loved each other very much. (Translated by Martin Guardado, Department of Language and Literacy Education, University of British Columbia)

This sample of writing reveals a bit about this writer's complex life before she arrived in Vancouver. She and her family first entered Canada in Quebec, where she was enrolled in schools where the language of instruction was French. They then traveled to Vancouver, where, of course, the language of instruction was English.

First-language compositions resulted in a mean of 2.98 (0.91). A score of 3.00 is "Average" for age and grade: immigrants 3.00 (0.90); refugees 2.50 (1.00); students 3.20 (1.00); entrepreneurs 3.10 (0.80); diplomats 3.10 (1.40); Canadians 2.70 (1.00); and those with work visas 3.80 (0.40).

Comparative Findings

Table 4.27 shows the results in the area of oral language production broken down by nine different geographic/linguistic areas. The findings are interesting. It is notable, for instance, that students from Hong Kong, China, and Taiwan had relative difficulties with past and future tenses. There is, in essence, no past or future tense in Chinese. About half of the students from Hong Kong appear to be at a stage where they are able to produce present tense. Present tense is the first verb form learned by second-language learners, for example, I eat, or I am eating. The present progressive "ing" form is the first lexical form that native English speakers seem to develop (Brown, 1973).

Countries in Europe, both Western and Eastern, were considered as a block. However, immigrants from England were not included. They scored 37.10% no, 35.30% weak, and 27.50% yes in present tense, 66.50% no, 16.80% weak, and 16.80% yes in past tense, and 66.50% no, 16.80% weak, and 16.60% yes for future tense.

TABLE 4.27
Percentage Scores—Yes/Weak/No for Present, Past, and Future Tense

Country	Present; Yes/Weak/No	Past; Yes/Weak/No	Future; Yes/Weak/No
Africa	10.4/10.3/65.5	16.7/26.7/56.7	17.2/20.7/62.9
China	18.3/24.2/55.6	8.4/9.7/80.5	9.7/11.7/76.6
Hong Kong	50.8/37.9/11.2	19.7/35.4/44.9	25.5/37.5/37.0
India	22.7/24.0/46.7	17.3/13.3/62.7	17.1/13.2/63.6
Japan	11.3/45.0/41.3	5.1/8.9/83.5	3.9/9.1/85.7
Korea	24.6/17.4/56.5	18.3/2.8/78.9	18.3/8.5/73.2

As noted earlier, 42.60% were unable to formulate a question, 29.30% were weak, and only 28.10% were able to do so. Percentages across area were: Africa 10.20% yes, 3.6% weak, 82.50% no; China 12.4% yes, 16.8% weak, 69.6% no; Hong Kong 32.5% yes, 40.5% weak, 26.90% no; India 19.0% yes, 21.5% weak, 54.4% no; Japan 6.2% yes, 17.3% weak, 75.3% no; Korea 19.7% yes, 16.9% weak, 63.4% no; Philippines 53.9% yes, 26.5% weak, 12.7% no; Spanish 23.3% yes, 24.9% weak, 51.0% no; Taiwan 13.4% yes, 28.7% weak, 56.8% no; and Vietnamese 16.2% yes, 29.3% weak, 54.5% no. Europe resulted in 54.00% no, 25.90% weak, and 20.10% yes.

Some 65.90% were able to say the days of the week (17.40% no and 16.70% weak), whereas 78.50% were able to recite the names of the letters of the alphabet (4.7% no and 16.80% weak). Table 4.28 shows a breakdown of responses across geolinguistic groups.

European immigrants were able in 45.90% of the cases able to produce names of the days of the week, whereas 20.80% were weak, and 33.30% could not. Fifty-one percent were able to produce the letters of the alphabet, whereas 32.60% were weak, and 16.00% could not.

Comparable numbers were able to count in English (62.30% yes, 2.80% no, and 34.90% weak) and read numbers at random (76.0% yes, 3.70% no, and 20.30% weak). Results are broken down by geolinguistic groups in Table 4.29.

European students were able to count (57.10% yes, 34.80% weak, 8.20% no) and to read numbers (63.20% yes, 25.70% weak, and 11.10% no). Students were shown colors and were asked to name them in English as noted earlier. They were also asked to name body parts and school items. Table 4.30 is a breakdown of their scores by geolinguistic groups.

TABLE 4.28
Percentages Correct—Days of the Week and Letters of the Alphabet

Country	Days—Yes/Weak/No	Alphabet
Africa	73.1%/11.5%/15.4%	79.3%/10.0%/3.3%
China	32.1%/40.0%/10.7%	58.8%/22.0%/19.1%
Hong Kong	76.0%/17.5%/6.4%	88.3%/11.0%/.7%
India	71.4%/15.7%/12.9%	83.1%/2.4%/7.2%
Japan	43.6%//20.5%/35.9%	79.0%/16.0%/4.9%
Korea	53.5%/15.5%/31.0%	88.5%/10.3%/1.3%
Philippines	86.7%/8.0%/5.3%	93.2%/2.3%/4.6%
Spanish	45.3%/18.8%/35.9%	46.4%/29.9%/23.7%
Taiwan	55.9%/19.5%/24.6%	79.0%/11.0%/10.0%
Vietnamese	61.0%/15.4%/23.6%	54.1%/35.1%/10.7%

TABLE 4.29
Ability to Count and to Recognize Numbers

Country	Count—Yes/Weak/No	Read Numbers
Africa	12.0%/6.0%/81.9%	13.9%/3.6%/82.5%
China	36.0%/49.4%/12.9%	52.8%/28.7%/18.7%
Hong Kong	68.6%/30.5%/1.0%	84.4%/14.6%/1.0%
India	69.6%/24.1%/6.5%	80.8%/12.80%/6.4%
Japan	54.3%/34.6%/11.1%	63.8%/28.8%/7.5%
Korea	46.8%/48.1%/5.2%	64.5%/31.6%/3.9%
Philippines	79.5%/18.1%/2.4%	93.2%/2.3%/4.6%
Spanish	11.7%/6.6%/82.3%	8.6%/5.5%/81.6%
Taiwan	48.1%/42.4%/9.5%	70.0%/11.0%/10.0%
Vietnamese	11.2%/9.9%/78.0%	11.6%/7.6%/80.8%

TABLE 4.30
Means and Standard Deviations for Colors, Body Parts, and School Items

Country	Colors (1–11)	Body Parts (1–19)	School Items (1–6)
Africa	8.00, 4.10	11.52, 7.1	4.50, 2.10
China	5.50, 4.30	5.50, 5.50	3.20, 2 .10
Hong Kong	9.60, 2.00	10.80, 3.70	5.40, 1.20
India	7.80, 3.60	9.30, 5.90	4.10, 1.80
Japan	8.80, 3.10	6.80, 5.00	3.40, 1.60
Korea	7.50, 3.50	7.60, 5.70	3.30, 2.00
Philippines	10.50, 1.40	14.30, 4.30	5.80, 0.70
Spanish	7.80, 3.60	7.30, 6.60	3.90, 2.20
Taiwan	7.50, 3.50	7.60, 4.50	3.80, 1.80
Vietnamese	6.90, 4.10	7.70, 5.90	3.90, 2.10

European students recognized a mean of 7.00 (4.30) colors, 5.70 (6.00) body parts, and 2.80 school items. It is interesting that those from Europe scored the lowest in school items. There appears to be a significant cultural background knowledge factor in effect in these results. School items, it would seem, are cultural artifacts that vary considerably from country to country. Crayons appear to be purely North American! It also seems that *Sesame Street* has been successful in North America and in other parts of the world such as Hong Kong. Correlations are reported for these measures later in this chapter. A 9-item test of prepositions was administered and students were asked to write compositions in their first languages when possible and in English when possible. Their scores are shown in Table 4.31.

First-language compositions were judged to be appropriate for grade and age for students from China, Hong Kong, Japan, Korea, and Taiwan. English compositions, however, were judged to be poor for students' ages. European immigrants produced good L1 compositions (3.10, 0.98) and poor English compositions (2.00, 1.00). Overall, refugee students had the lowest L1 and L2 compositions.

ENGLISH LITERACY

Assessors at OROC selected what they believed were the age-appropriate tests to administer to students. There was some overlap, however, as can be seen in Table 4.32.

Woodcock Word Identification scores were a mean of 37.10 (25.50), which is equivalent to a grade level of approximately 2.0. The following grade equivalents are based on rounded-off means. The sample size was 4,625 (Table 4.33).

TABLE 4.31
Means and Standard Deviations of Prepositions and L1 and L2 Compositions

Country	Prepositions (1–9)	L1 Compositions (1–5)	L2 Compositions (1–5)
Africa	5.10, 3.60	2.10, 1.20	2.80, 1.10
China	2.10, 3.00	3.00, 1.00	1.70, 1.00
Hong Kong	4.70, 2.60	3.10, 0.80	2.30, 2.60
India	2.30, 3.40	2.30, 0.80	1.80, 1.10
Japan	1.10, 2.10	3.30, 0.80	1.30, 0.80

TABLE 4.32
Number of Students Administered the Woodcock, CELT, and GAP by Age on Arrival (AOA)

AOA	Woodcock	CELT	GAP
8	237	22	16
9	679	28	39
10	803	53	54
11	812	90	89
12	820	170	165

TABLE 4.33
Means and Standard Deviations for Woodcock Word Recognition Test

Status	Mean	SD	Grade Equivalent
Immigrant	38.90	25.70	2.1
Refugee	28.10	20.6	1.7
Student	31.10	27.80	1.8
Business	36.50	26.1	2.0
Diplomat	26.50	23.40	1.7
Canadian	50.20	27.60	2.8
Work Visa	26.00	13.20	1.7

Broken down by geolinguistic groups scores were: Africa 50.40 (32.80); China 26.10 (18.20); Hong Kong 43.20 (21.20); India 36.00 (22.50); Japan 23.30 (26.70); Korea 37.90 (29.80); Philippines 70.60 (34.10); Spanish 29.30 (24.20); Taiwan 27.30 (20.60); and Vietnamese 28.70 (22.40). Mean Woodcock comprehension scores were 16.00 (12.20) or grade level 1.7 ($n = 4,625$). The following are based on rounded means (Table 4.34).

Broken down by geolinguistic areas, scores were: Africa 25.70 (15.60); China 13.30 (12.80); Hong Kong 18.90 (9.60); India 17.00 (15.10); Japan 9.40 (11.00); Korea 16.90 (13.90); Philippines 26.72 (12.40); Spanish 11.50 (12.60); Taiwan 11.80 (10.50); and Vietnamese 11.60 (10.80). The mean of the Gap scores was 22.60 (13.50), which translates into a grade equivalent of 3.3. Overall 5,928 students were administered the Gap. They scored a mean of 21.90 (13.20). Their scores are shown in Table 4.35.

The CELT was administered to 7,026 students, who scored a mean of 34.40 (16.10). These scores are broken down by immigration status in Table 4.36.

CELT percentile scores are based on a number of studies involving secondary foreign students enrolled in high school, nonnative adult university-level speakers, and students enrolled in a community college (Table 4.37). The students in this study scored significantly lower than the CELT norm group (29.30–19.11), who were Grade 10 to 12 students enrolled in a "large suburban high school in the Eastern United States" (Harris & Palmer, 1986, p. 16).

Mean Woodcock scores were computed and broken down by age on arrival (AOA). Scores were converted to grade equivalents. These scores are shown in Table 4.38.

The discrepancy scores are alarming reminders that immigrant students arrive in Canada with potentially significant reading problems. If students require 5 to 7 years to acquire the language necessary to comprehend aca-

TABLE 4.34
Means and Standard Deviations for Woodcock Comprehension Test

Status	Mean	SD	Grade Equivalent
Immigrant	17.80	12.40	1.8
Refugee	12.40	12.60	1.5
Student	16.00	15.50	1.7
Entrepreneur	16.00	10.70	1.7
Diplomat	27.80	15.50	2.6
Canadian	25.00	11.80	2.4
Work Visa	20.90	6.20	2.0

TABLE 4.35
Means and Standard Deviations for GAP Scores

Status	Mean	SD	Grade Equivalent
Immigrant	22.60 (4,765)	13.50	3.5
Refugee	12.70 (255)	11.00	3.4
Student	23.00 (47)	11.80	3.5
Entrepreneur	20.00 (732)	10.10	3.2
Diplomat	28.10 (8)	11.00	3.4
Canadian	26.30 (116)	11.10	3.4
Work Visa	22.00 (5)	9.30	3.1

TABLE 4.36
Means and Standard Deviations—CELT

Status	Mean	SD	Percentile
Immigrant	34.50 (5,554)	15.60	6
Refugee	26.80 (258)	19.70	4
Student	43.90 (50)	19.70	10
Entrepreneur	33.20 (983)	15.30	6
Diplomat	47.30 (12)	20.80	13
Canadian	45.80 (159)	19.20	10
Work Visa	40.20 (10)	20.50	8

TABLE 4.37
Woodcock Comprehension (WoodComp), CELT, and GAP by Geolinguistic
Groups (Means and Standard Deviations)

Group	WoodComp	CELT	GAP
Africa	25.70, 15.60	48.30, 190.90	27.70, 16.20
China	13.40, 12.80	27.10, 17.00	13.30 - 11.00
Hong Kong	18.90, 9.60	35.67, 13.20	23.90, 10.20
India	17.00, 15.00	27.70, 20.80	17.20, 15.40
Japan	9.40, 11.10	23.30, 26.70	14.60, 11.10
Korea	16.90, 13.90	33.70, 17.80	18.20, 12.80
Philippines	26.70, 12.40	37.85, 15.50	27.00, 14.00
Spanish	11.50, 12.60	28.20, 21.50	15.10, 14.50
Taiwan	11.80, 10.50	32.60, 15.60	17.30, 10.20
Vietnamese	11.60, 10.80	25.10, 15.00	12.00, 10.10

TABLE 4.38
Means (and Standard Deviations) of Grade-Level Equivalencies by Age on
Arrival on the Woodcock Word Recognition and Comprehension Measures

Age on Arrival(years)	Word Recognition	Comprehension	Comprehension Discrepancy
8	1.8 (1.6)	2.2 (1.4)	0.2
9	1.8 (1.4)	1.90 (1.5)	−1.1
10	1.8 (1.4)	2.0 (1.4)	−2.0
11	1.9 (1.6)	2.2 (1.8)	−2.8

demic language, then those who arrive at 14 years of age and older face immense challenges to their learning of English reading and academic content. Indeed, Gunderson (2004) concluded, "It seems that, in effect, these students were institutionally disabled because of the serious discrepancy between their English reading abilities and their grade levels" (p. 8).

Gap scores by age on arrival resulted in: AOA 8 years, 25.10, Grade 2.5; 9 years, 21.10, Grade 2.5; 10 years, 27.40, Grade 2.8; 11 years, 23.80, Grade 2.6; 12 years, 25.00, Grade 2.6; 13 years, 17.80, Grade 2.1; 14 years, 19.40, Grade 2.2; 15 years, 20.80, Grade 2.3; 16 years, 23.10, Grade 2.6; 17 years, 23.80, Grade 2.6; and 18 years, 23.30, Grade 2.6.

Students who had not previously studied English before they immigrated had statistically significant higher scores than those who had for the Woodcock, CELT, and Gap. These means are shown in Table 4.39.

TABLE 4.39
Means and Standard Deviations for the Woodcock, CELT, and GAP Broken
Down by the Study of English

Studied English	Woodcock Comprehension	Woodcock Recognition	CELT	GAP
Yes	16.20, 11.70	33.80, 19.10	33.60, 16.80	19.90, 11.10
No	18.00, 12.80	39.30, 29.70	34.90, 15.70	23.70, 14.50

This is an interesting, indeed anomalous, finding in that some students were able to complete the Woodcock, but did not report that they had formal English instruction before immigration. It is extraordinary, however, that students who indicated they had not studied English before immigration scored higher than those who indicated they had. Assessors administered the oral measures to a limited number of individuals who indicated they had not studied English. Mean scores were: Present 2.00 (0.86, $n = 1,307$); Past 1.60 (0.82, $n = 1,261$); Future 1.60 (1.60, $n = 1,259$); Questioning 1.70 (0.83, $n = 1,386$); Days 2.20 (0.88, $n = 1,007$); Counts 2.50 (0.58, $n = 1,348$); Reads Numbers 2.60 (0.61, $n = 1,299$); Alphabet 2.60 (0.61, $n = 1,468$); Colors 7.40 (4.10, $n = 1,133$); Body Parts 7.60 (5.90, $n = 1,049$); School Items 3.70 (2.20, $n = 1,056$); Prepositions 2.30 (3.10, $n = 1,101$); English Composition 1.90 (0.94, $n = 1,130$); and L1 Compositions 2.80 (0.98, $n = 885$). Students who indicated they had studied English scored higher on the oral skills than those who did not. They also produced compositions in both their first- and second-languages that had higher scores than those who had not studied English.

Those who indicated they had studied English did not score very high. To explore further the effects of English language instruction, scores were broken down by number of years students had studied English before immigrating. The number of years was limited to 10 because of the very low numbers of students reported to have studied English for longer periods. This breakdown is shown in Table 4.40.

These results will be discussed in more detail in the next chapter, but it is interesting to note that the word recognition scores appear to be higher than the comprehension scores as predicted by models such as Bernhardt's (1991). However, the total possible raw scores differ dramatically because the recognition test has more items overall. It seems clear that the English instruction these students received in their home countries was not effective in bringing them up to grade level in reading. It is also clear that they did not develop academic language in 5 to 7 years. It is clear that those individuals who studied for 5 to 7 years were not at a reading level that would allow them to read, comprehend, and learn from text. It is also interesting that students appeared to reach a kind of ceiling in scores after about 5 years of English instruction. This may, in fact, be an artifact of instructional techniques or focus of their English programs in their home countries.

BACKGROUND AND LITERACY MEASURES

Language Measures

There were weak correlations between math scores and language scores. The correlation for Gap and CA Math was .22, CELT .04, Woodcock Comprehension .22, Woodcock Recognition .27, L1 Composition .16, and L2 Composition .09. Math scores had similar very low relationships with the oral language measures.

Table 4.41 shows correlations of Gap, CELT, and Woodcock scores with Colors, Body Parts, School Items, and Prepositions. These items varied in values, as described in the preceding chapter.

TABLE 4.40
Woodcock, CELT, and GAP Broken Down by Years of English Study (Means and Standard Deviations)

Number of Years	Woodcock Comprehension	Woodcock Recognition	CELT	GAP
1	9.80, 10.30	24.30, 18.40	20.60, 14.90	12.30, 10.60
2	11.92, 10.00	18.40, 17.10	14.90, 15.80	15.60, 10.70
3	14.70, 10.50	33.20, 17.50	30.00, 16.70	16.90, 10.70
4	16.70, 11.70	39.80, 19.40	32.30, 17.90	17.40, 10.40
5	20.20, 10.80	43.00, 19.20	32.20, 17.60	20.40, 11.50
6	21.60, 11.10	41.10, 20.80	36.00, 16.50	20.70, 10.00
7	20.89, 11.43	37.70, 18.60	33.90, 15.60	20.00, 8.50
8	18.90, 13.30	33.90, 22.50	35.30, 16.50	21.40, 9.80
9	21.20, 11.40	40.50, 12.20	38.00, 14.00	24.20, 10.00
10	23.20, 11.20	41.40, 5.10	36.20, 15.50	22.50, 9.80

TABLE 4.41
Correlations Among GAP, CELT, Woodcock, and Colors, Body Parts, School Items, and Prepositions

	Colors	Body Parts	School Items	Prepositions
GAP	.52, 339	.65, 416	.50, 418	.72, 424
CELT	.41, 259	.48, 328	.44, 328	.58, 332
Woodcock Comprehension	.55, 2120	.76, 2068	.57, 2075	.79, 2116
Woodcock Recognition	.55, 1385	.64, 1391	.55, 1397	.67, 1395

Note. Includes sample sizes.

The significant differences in sample sizes were due to the age of students and the tests selected by assessors at OROC. Table 4.42 shows the correlations among Gap, CELT, and Woodcock scores for variables assessed on a three-level scale (see preceding chapter).

The relationships among the language measures were computed and are shown in Table 4.43.

Pearson product-moment correlations were computed for L1 and L2 compositions, Woodcock Comprehension, CELT, and Gap and are shown in Table 4.44.

TABLE 4.42
Correlations Among GAP, CELT, Woodcock, and Present, Past, Future, Questions, and Days

	Present	*Past*	*Future*	*Questions*	*Days*
GAP	.52, 450	.62, 453	.67, 447	.67, 434	.26, 398
CELT	.49, 328	.50, 327	.55, 322	.60, 316	.20, 310
Woodcock Comprehension	.64, 2234	.68, 2195	.70, 2199	.71, 2283	.48, 2006
Woodcock Recognition	.58, 1330	.57, 1329	.59, 1328	.64, 1329	.52, 1324

Note. Includes sample sizes.

TABLE 4.43
Correlations Among Language Variables

	Present	*Past*	*Future*	*Questions*	*Days*
Colors	.62, 2619	.47, 2594	.50, 2591	.56, 2621	.60, 2560
Body parts	.68, 2634	.65, 2630	.67, 2627	.70, 2624	.58, 2619
School items	.62, 2646	.48, 2641	.52, 2639	.58, 2635	.63, 2631
Prepositions	.65, 2621	.63, 2620	.67, 2619	.71, 2619	.51, 2595

Note. Includes sample sizes.

TABLE 4.44
Correlations—L1 and L2 Compositions, Woodcock, CELT, and GAP

	L2 Composition	*Woodcock Comprehension*	*CELT*	*GAP*
L1 Composition	.34 (n =2778)	.22 (n =1249)	.20 (n =1618)	.20 (n =1701)
L2 Composition		.63 (n =1428)	.55 (n =1908)	.56 (n =2003)

Note. Includes sample sizes.

Interestingly, the correlations between the Woodcock Recognition test and composition scores were .20 for L1 and .60 for English compositions. The measure that best predicted L1 compositions scores was CA Math .443 (1561). The best predictors of English compositions scores for those who indicated that they had studied English previously were: Gap .56 (2003); Woodcock Comprehension .63 (1428); Woodcock Recognition .60 (976); CELT .54 (1908); Present Tense .55 (1635); Past Tense .52 (1632); Future Tense .54 (1630); Questions .57 (1630); and Body Parts .56 (1714).

There were 13,854 who indicated that they had not studied English before entering Canada. However, the number of these students who had some English skills were CELT 4,248, Gap 3,121, Woodcock Comprehension 2,922, Woodcock Recognition 1,189, Present 1,307, Past 1,261, Future 1,259, Questions 1,386, Days 1,007, Count 1,348, Read Numbers 1,299, Alphabet 1,468, Colors, 1,133, Body Parts 1,049, School Items 1,056, Prepositions 1,101, English Composition 1,130, and L1 Composition 885. An exploration of the differences between these two populations is undertaken in chapter 5.

MATH FINDINGS

Two math tests were administered to students at OROC: the Curriculum Associates Math, which is a locally developed math skills test, and a Math Assessment that featured concepts. A total 7,600 students took the Math test for a mean score of 14.30 ($SD = 2.85$) and 5,461 took the CA Math for a mean score of 16.70 ($SD = 6.42$). Math findings are discussed in more detail in chapter 6.

CONCLUSION

Results of two studies have been presented in this chapter. It is important to note that neither of the studies is a rigorously controlled experimental study. Indeed, the two studies represent the planned and unplanned chaos occurring in educational settings that educators understand so well, but others do not. Students in the two studies reported here vary greatly. About 19,000 had some measurable English skills. However, those English skills varied from being able to produce some of the names of the alphabet to producing very good compositions in English. Another set of variables that contributed to the fuzzy nature of the different samples is that from 1989 to 2005 OROC evaluators varied. The criteria used to select test instruments also varied from individual to individual, and that is why there is a fairly large overlap in ages of students who were administered different instruments (see Table 4.32). An attempt has been made to indicate the sample size in all cases.

It is clear that immigrant students arrive with incredibly complex backgrounds. A majority was from groups that spoke Cantonese and Mandarin and were from China, Taiwan, and Hong Kong. The majority were also from socioeconomic backgrounds best described as middle-class or higher. Generally, families from more affluent backgrounds were smaller and had more educational experience.

About one-third of the primary-age students arrived with varying degrees of English ability. The significant difficulty, however, was that English ability varied by geolinguistic grouping. Linguistic markers were visible signifiers of differences in socioeconomic and educational backgrounds. Primary students from Hong Kong had the highest mean scores on the English literacy measures. Students who spoke Vietnamese had the lowest mean scores on these measures. These measures, in effect, were readiness measures developed by the OROC staff. Students from Hong Kong, based on their mean scores, appeared more "ready" to undertake studies in English in their primary classrooms than other groups. Based on their scores it can be concluded that only about one-third of the students appeared ready for their primary classes in English. The picture seems about the same for older immigrant students.

In total, 17,579 elementary and secondary students were administered the Gap (5,928), the Woodcock (4,625), and the CELT (7,026). On all of these measures students were significantly behind their grade levels in reading scores. Indeed, the discrepancy between their grade levels and their reading levels was greater if they were older when they entered the country. In effect, these students were educationally disabled. It seemed apparent that the large majority of them would find it difficult to learn English and to learn academic content in the English-only classrooms they enrolled in. A more detailed discussion of English study in home countries is contained in chapter 5. There were a number of anomalous findings related to scores produced by students who indicated they had not studied English before they arrived in Canada, but who had measurable English skills on the measures administered at the center. Interestingly, a majority of these students were bilingual.

The next chapter explores different models of reading; following that, students' success in schools is explored.

5

Reading Models
and Traditional Analyses

In Hong Kong we memorize, memorize, memorize.
Here we think, think, think. It's easier in Hong Kong.[1]

The purpose of this chapter is to explore whether findings support or refute the model presented in chapter 3. In addition, findings are also evaluated in terms of other models such as Bernhardt's (2000) second-language model and Cummins and Swain's (1986) Common Underlying Proficiency (CUP) model. These analyses are based on the data collected at the time of the immigrants' entry into Canada and their assessment at Oakridge.

ORTHOGRAPHIES—AN ANALYSIS

As mentioned in chapter 2, many authors have suggested that the learning of a second language is affected by a number of factors. In this respect, it has been suggested that there is an advantage for a learner to learn a second language that has an orthography that is similar to that of the second language. It has also been suggested that learning languages that share some linguistic antecedents, such as Italian and Spanish or Norwegian and Swedish, or Japanese and Korean, is aided by the first-language knowledge base. It has also been suggested that the recognition of cognates, for instance, helps one to read and understand in a second language. The English-speaking student who sees the French word "porc" or "chance" in print may recognize they are cognates and understand their meanings. Piper (2001) warns, however, that there are false cognates that she calls false friends that can lead to confusion. It has also been suggested that those who have learned to read a first lan-

---

[1] Female, Cantonese, Hong Kong, 16 years.

guage understand the basic principles of reading such as scanning and decoding that they can apply to the learning of reading in a second language.

Orthographic depth has been discussed as a significant variable (see Aro, 2006). English is written in a "deep" orthography, one in which the phoneme–grapheme correspondences are not always one-to-one. English spelling could be considered as "irregular" because phonemes are not regularly mapped out by graphemes. There are languages, however, that are shallow in that their grapheme–phoneme correspondences are one-to-one. There have been a number of classification procedures to group languages and orthographies such as the one developed by DeFrancis (1989). This system divides orthographies into two broad categories: graphic symbols and alphabetic symbols. These two broad categories are also divided into: syllabic, consonantal, and alphabetic groups. An attempt was made to divide the orthographies in the present study into categories using DeFrancis's scheme. It proved to be too difficult a task.

Efforts were made to categorize the orthographies of the languages represented in the sample in some way that would allow a test to be made of any advantages or disadvantages for students involved in learning English as a second or additional language. This seems like a fairly simple procedure, but it is not. First, a list of the reported home languages was made. It was surprisingly long; however, a fairly low number of different languages represent a majority in the sample. Table 5.1 shows a preliminary breakdown of orthographies for the languages recorded in the study.

It became obvious that categorizing orthographies is extremely difficult, if not impossible. David Diringer's (1968) seminal book was used as a resource, as were a number of online information sites, to help in the process. However, the most useful resource was *The World's Writing Systems,* edited

TABLE 5.1
Orthographies in Study—Preliminary Categorization

Alphabetic	Non-Roman; Alphabetic	Non-Roman; Asian	Syllabary	Semi-Syllabary	Logograph	Mixed
Afrikaans	Arabic	Burmese	Amharic	Assamese	Cantonese	Japanese
Akan	Farsi	Cambodian	Ethiopian	Balinese	Chiuchow	
Armenian	Hebrew	Korean		Bangla	Foochow	
Bahasa	Iranian	Kmer		Bengali	Fukien	
Bisaya	Kurdish	Lao		Chirati	Hainanese	
Bulgarian	Persian	Thai		Dari	Hakka	
Busanga	Somali	Vietnamese		Gujurati	Hengua	
Cebuano				Hindi	Hockchew	
Creole				Malayalam	Hokkien	

Alphabetic	Non-Roman; Alphabetic	Non-Roman; Asian	Syllabary	Semi-Syllabary	Logograph	Mixed
Czechoslova-kian				Marathi	Hopien	
Danish				Nepali	Hunan	
Dutch				Pushtu	Mandarin	
French				Punjabi	Pongwu	
Fijian				Sinhala	Puisze	
Finnish				Tamil	Shanghaiese	
Georgian					Sunwoo	
German					Taisanese	
Greek					Teachow	
Harari					Toishan	
Huasa					Yanping	
Hungarian						
Icelandic						
Ilocano						
Italian						
Latvian						
Malay						
Norwegian						
Oromiffa						
Pampango						
Polish						
Portuguese						
Romanian						
Russian						
Serbian						
Serbo-Croatian						
Slovakian						
Somali						
Spanish						
Swahili						
Swedish						
Tagalog						
Turkish						
Twi						
Ukrainian						
Zambuangan						

by Peter T. Daniels and William Bright (1996). Information was also obtained about various orthographies from www.omniglot.com and a variety of other Internet sources.

It is traditional to divide writing systems into those that represent phonemes (alphabets), syllables (syllabaries), notions (ideographs), and objects (pictographs or logographs). In real life, however, orthographies are seldom so simple. Japanese writing, for instance, uses a syllabary, a logograph, and an alphabet. Korean, according to Diringer, is "the only native alphabet of the Far East" (p. 353). He notes that some have argued that it is one of the most regular alphabets in the world. English, as noted previously, is an alphabetic orthography that has been described as deep because the relationships between graphemes and phonemes are not always one-to-one. Alphabetic languages could have been categorized by depth, although this would have resulted in Korean (Asian alphabet), Spanish (Roman alphabet), and Tamil (Indian semi-syllabary) being included in the same category.

Languages such as Bisaya and Bicolono historically had their own orthographies, but since colonial days these orthographies have disappeared and have been supplanted by Roman-based orthographies. Languages such as Vietnamese have orthographies that have Indian origins for the writing done by hand, but augmented Roman alphabets for that occurring in printed material. French and Spanish were developed from the Roman alphabet, whereas Russian developed from the Greek, so French and Russian are alphabetic "cousins." One could argue that semantically and syntactically English and French are more similar than are English and Russian. English and Russian are also alphabetic cousins.

The purpose for categorizing orthographies is to attempt to measure in some way common underlying proficiencies. The notion is that an alphabetic language that is based on a Roman or augmented Roman alphabet provides a learner an advantage in learning English because there is the possibility that some of the grapheme–phoneme relationships would be the same or similar. However, learning to read English for students who had learned to read an alphabetic language such as Arabic would provide a learner some cues about the process of decoding, but not necessarily a hint about shared grapheme–phoneme correspondences.

Orthographies that were Roman based or Roman augmented were put into the same category. This resulted in some interesting inclusions, in that very dissimilar languages were included, such as Vietnamese and Swahili. Yet they both involve writing systems based on the Roman alphabet. Orthography and history are amazingly and incredibly related. Khmer, for instance, is a semi-syllabary, also called an alphasyllabic system, in which some graphemes represent phonemes and some represent syllables (Schiller, 1996). This orthography is a descendent of an Indic alphabet (the Brahmi script). The difficulty, however, is that modern Khmer is not pronounced the way it was when the Khmer script was adopted. Vietnamese, on the other hand, has adopted an augmented Roman alphabet (Dinh-Hoa, 1996). Africa has about one-third of the languages in the world (Bendor-Samuel, 1996). Colonists brought both their religions and their alphabets to Africa. The Church Missionary Society in 1848 established an approach for writing different African languages using a Roman alphabet (Bendor-Samuel, 1996). In 1928 the International African Institute published "The Practical Orthography of African Languages," which established the "Africa" alphabet (Bendor-Samuel, 1996). Most African languages, mostly Sub-Saharan, are written using either a modified Roman alphabet or the International Phonetic Alphabet. Africa is unique and complex in terms of orthographies (Heine & Nurse, 2000; Prah, 1998).

Table 5.2 represents the orthographies of the students in the Vancouver school system broken down by categories representing the underlying writing principle of their first languages. The purpose for categorizing orthographies is to explore whether there are systematic advantages or disadvantages related to the learning of English as a second language. The classifications represented seem adequate except in the case of students whose first language was Chinese. For them, one feature had to be added, a consideration of instructional strategies in learning to read Chinese. Currently, students in the People's Republic of China are taught to read initially through the use of the international phonetic alphabet (i.p.a.) called Pinyin, as a method to introduce sound–symbol relationships to students. Pinyin was adopted in 1958 (http://en.wikipedia.org/wiki/Zhuyin) to replace the previous system that had been in place, called guóyuzìmu (or bopomofo in Taiwan). In addition, in 1949 the People's Republic of China adopted a simplified orthography (see http://www.omniglot.com/writing/chinese_simplified.htm#simp) so that the first characters students learn are simplified from the classic form. Simplified characters are introduced with Pinyin added so that students are able to "decode" the characters. This system is used until about the third grade, with new characters being introduced with Pinyin, but not thereafter (Hudson-Ross & Dong, 1990).

In Taiwan, students are introduced to a phonetic transcription system that involves non-Roman syllables called zhùyinfúhào or bopomofo. Developed in 1913 by the Ministry of Education in the Republic of China, the system was originally called guóyuzìmu or the National Phonetic Alphabet. In 1986, the Republic of China (Taiwan) adapted the system to assist learners in learning to read and write Mandarin, renaming it zhùyinfúhào (bopomofo). The characters/symbols are based on calligraphic forms and some are derived from Chinese characters (see http://en.wikipedia.org/wiki/Bopomofo). Students in Taiwan learn to read standard, classic Chinese characters that have not been simplified. Finally, in Hong Kong, until recently, learning to read Cantonese was by a system that involved drill and rote memorization of clas-

TABLE 5.2
Languages Represented in Different Categories of Orthographies Among Vancouver Immigrant Students

Categories of Orthographies	Languages of Students
Alphabetic Roman	Afrikaans, Akan[a] Bahasa, Bangla, Bisaya, Bulgarian, Brong, Cebuano, Creole, Croatian, Czechoslovakian, Danish, Dutch, French, Fijian, Finnish, German, Harari, Huasa, Hungarian, Icelandic, Ilocano, Italian, Kanjobol, Kaijai, Latvian, Malay[b], Memon, Norwegian, Pampango, Papiameto, Polish, Portuguese, Serbian, Serbo-Croatian, Slovakian, Somali, Spanish, Swahili[a], Swedish, Tiv, Twi[a], Tagalog, Turkish, Vietnamese, Yugoslavian, Zambuangan
Alphabetic Greek	Armenian, Georgian, Greek, Romanian, Russian, Ukrainian
Non-Roman, Non-Asian; alphabetic	Arabic, Farsi, Hebrew, Iranian, Kashmiri, Kurdish, Lebanese, Pashto[c], Punjabi[c], Persian, Sindhi, Urdu
Non-Roman, Asian; alphabetic	Korean
Syllabary	Amharic, Ethiopian, Oromiffa, Saho, Tigrinia, Twi
Semi-Syllabary	Assamese, Balinese, Bangla, Bengali, Burmese, Busanga, Cambodian, Chiarati, Dari, Gujurati, Hindi, Khmer, Lao, Malayalam, Marathi, Nepali, Pashto, Punjabi, Rusanga, Sanish, Sinhala, Tamil, Thai
Logographic	Cantonese, Chiuchow, Foochow, Fukien, Hainanese, Hakka, Hengua, Hockchew, Hokkien, Hopien, Hunan, Mandarin[a], Pongwu, Puisze, Shanghaiese, Sunwoo, Taisanese, Taiwanese, Teachow, Toishan, Yanping
Mixed	Japanese

[a] i.p.a.
[b] Modern Malay.
[c] Since 1947/1948 writers in Pakistan have used an Arabic orthography.

sic Chinese characters using a "flash card" approach that begins at about age 3 for many students. As noted in the previous chapter, students in Hong Kong often begin formal reading instruction in pre-school at the age of 3. A colleague of this researcher reports that her son was not able to gain admission to a prestigious preschool until he had memorized the required number of Chinese characters (Gloria Tang, personal communication, Vancouver, BC, 2001).

The final orthographic categories to be used in the analyses to explore models treat students who came from Hong Kong, the People's Republic of China, and Taiwan as separate groups.

The Orthographic Categories

Table 5.3 shows immigration status broken down by orthography. There are differences related to immigration status. The percentage of refugees was highest in the group designated as Arabic.

The number of individuals who indicated their first language was English was surprising and was included earlier. Gender was identified as a variable of interest because of the number of studies that report differences in literacy achievement between boys and girls. Table 5.4 shows a breakdown of groups by gender.

Table 5.5 displays means and standard deviations for Woodcock, Gap, and CELT by orthographic category. It also shows sample sizes.

As noted previously, the three different reading assessments were associated in a fuzzy fashion with three different age levels, generally with younger students being assessed with Woodcock, middle students assessed with Gap, and older students using CELT. It is obvious from the table that sample size is a potential problem for analyzing the results of a number of groups. This is especially a problem with the Syllabary group. Other groups, such as the Greek group, will be included in analyses with great caution.

TABLE 5.3
Frequencies of Immigration Status

Orthography	Immigrant	Refugee	Student	Entrepreneurs	Diplomat	Canadian	Worker
Roman alphabetic	3058	864	50	93	22	138	6
Greek alphabetic	181	31	1	11	2	6	1
Arabic	191	146	9	12	0	15	1
Korean	275	0	16	169	6	5	7
Syllabary	22	15	0	0	0	0	0
Indic	830	108	9	17	4	30	0
PRC	698	83	10	82	5	25	1
Cantonese, Hong Kong	4215	50	23	1157	1	139	8
Japanese	109	1	84	143	15	15	2
Taiwan	1565	1	2	684	1	10	0
English	230	30	32	64	3	54	5
Total	11,374	1,329	236	2,432	59	428	31

TABLE 5.4
Frequencies by Gender and Orthography

Orthography	Male	Female	Total
Roman alphabetic	2283	1944	4227
Greek alphabetic	136	117	258
Arabic	200	174	374
Korean	270	207	477
Syllabary	17	17	34
Indic	505	491	996
PRC	469	434	903
Cantonese, Hong Kong	2828	2751	5579
Japanese	180	188	368
Taiwan	1241	1017	2258
English	222	196	418
Total	8,341	7,526	15,867

TABLE 5.5
Means, Standard Deviations, and Samples: Woodcock, GAP, and CELT

Orthography	Woodcock	GAP	CELT
Roman alphabetic	15.60	19.30	32.30
	13.50	14.70	18.40
	990	1010	1235
Greek alphabetic	18.60	22.90	35.40
	13.20	13.60	16.70
	63	53	77
Arabic	17.30	23.80	43.20
	13.80	16.40	20.00
	73	89	95
Korean	16.90	18.20	33.70
	14.00	12.80	17.80
	87	145	207
Syllabary	22.70	14.30	33.00
	11.20	9.30	20.20
	9	9	10
Indic	18.30	18.80	32.10

	13.80	14.00	20.20
	211	240	297
PRC	19.30	20.80	34.80
	13.60	13.70	16.60
	163	336	404
Cantonese, Hong Kong	18.90	24.00	34.80
	10.10	11.70	13.70
	1148	2284	2744
Japanese	9.90	14.90	28.80
	11.80	11.20	15.60
	74	49	54
Taiwan	11.80	17.30	32.60
	10.50	10.20	15.60
	510	756	951
English	32.50	32.40	57.20
	13.40	13.80	15.50
	87	96	116
Total	5,067	3,415	6,190

COMMON UNDERLYING PROFICIENCY (CUP)

To measure CUP would be accomplished best by administering both L1 and L2 literacy tests and comparing the results. As an exploratory study conducted in a given set of circumstances this is not possible. However, there was one measure that was a first-language measure, composition in first language. There were a number of other measures that were predicted to show a relationship with English language and literacy achievement. It was predicted, for instance, that learning to read in a first language would be associated with differences in English reading. Table 5.6 shows the breakdown of reading scores by the number of years students had studied in their first languages in their home countries. As noted previously, English instruction in home countries results in a plateau of scores around 5 to 6 years. Instruction lasting longer than 5 to 6 years appears to have been ineffective in raising students' English reading levels.

Students did not appear to learn cognitive academic language proficiency (CALP) in their English courses in their home countries. Indeed, on the average they appeared to acquire about third grade comprehension skills. This suggests their English courses likely focused on basic interpretive communicative skill (BICS) rather than CALP. Indeed, students' reading scores ap-

TABLE 5.6
Means, Standard Deviations, and Sample Sizes for Woodcock, GAP, and CELT by Years of L1 Study

Years	Parameter	Woodcock	GAP	CELT
3.00	Mean	14.70	16.90	30.00
	n	183	11	10
	SD	10.50	10.70	17.00
4.00	Mean	16.70	17.40	32.30
	n	264	18	13
	SD	11.70	10.40	17.90
5.00	Mean	20.20	20.40	32.20
	n	261	23	19
	SD	10.80	11.50	17.60
6.00	Mean	21.60	20.70	36.00
	n	387	106	85
	SD	11.10	10.00	16.50
7.00	Mean	20.89	20.00	33.90
	n	305	233	220
	SD	11.40	8.50	15.60

peared to hit a plateau at about 5 to 6 years of study. This finding suggests that the acquisition of CALP may be difficult in English as a foreign language (EFL) settings. These findings may also be a condemnation of the English curriculum in non-English-speaking countries (see Table 5.6).

Correlations were computed and revealed .08 (2188) with Woodcock and Years, .24 (2506) for Gap and Years, and .28 (3237) for CELT and Years. There was a .27 (3125) relationship between Years and English Composition scores. This is limited and weak support for CUP. The correlation for the relationship between L1 and L2 composition scores was .34 (2778) for those who had studied in their home countries for more than 2 years.

Correlations were computed for the measures for those students in the categories described above who had studied in their home countries for 3 or more years. Students who had studied the Arabic alphabet showed correlations of .26 (54) between years of study in home country and Gap, .09 (50) with CELT, and .51 (62) with English composition. Students from China had correlations of .42 (131) with Gap, .47 (132) with CELT, .28 (151) with L1 composition, and .20 (121) with English compositions. Those from Hong Kong had correlations of -.05 (66) with Woodcock, .18 (57) with Gap, .15 (72) with CELT, .53 (64) with L1 compositions, and .34 (68) with English compositions. Students from Taiwan had .11 (321) with Woodcock, .24 (472) with Gap, .31 (485) with CELT, .26 (708) with L1 compositions, and .30 (622) with English compositions. Those from a Roman-based orthography resulted in .14 (324) for Woodcock, .21 (255) Gap, .20 (270) CELT, .42 (364) L1 compositions, and .42 (334) English compositions.

The relationship between L1 compositions and the language and literacy variables varied from .10 (1496) for the production of present tense structures in English to .34 (2778) for English compositions. This supports, although not in a strong manner, the notion that there is a common underlying proficiency. Correlation coefficients were calculated for students who had studied for 3 or more years in their home countries between the language and literacy measures and scores on the Woodcock comprehension test broken down by orthographic categories. Cells with fewer than 50 observations are not reported (Table 5.7).

Data were reviewed to assure that the correlation between the Woodcock comprehension and Korean composition was accurate (-.53). The Recognition scores also had a negative correlation of -.40. The correlation with scores for English composition was also reviewed and found to be correct. Table 5.8 contains rankings of the correlations by orthography. The order of presentation of the orthographies has been rearranged on the basis of a hypothesized ordering of informativeness of L1 orthography to English. So,

TABLE 5.7
Correlations Among the Woodcock Comprehension Scores and the Language and Literacy Variables

	All	Arabic	China	Hong Kong	Indic	Japan	Korean	Roman	Taiwan
Pres	.63	.69	.63	.45	.73	.53	.83	.70	.43
Past	.68	.70	.62	.46	.73	.57	.84	.75	.56
Future	.70	.69	.72	.53	.74	.66	.82	.74	.57
Questions	.71	.71	.69	.55	.74	.60	.82	.77	.61
Days	.48	.47	.55	.44	.30	.49	.49	.53	.19
Count	.28	.36	.20	.27	.21	.27	.37	.31	.06
ReadNums	.37	.40	.24	.36	.34	.35	.36	.40	.13
Alpha	.33	.46	.24	.24	.28	.28	.16	.43	.06
Colors	.54	.57	.67	.46	.60	.27	.53	.60	.48
Bparts	.75	.72	.82	.65	.82	.65	.77	.79	.62
Schitems	.58	.54	.67	.39	.62	.63	.59	.60	.48
Preps	.79	.85	.81	.65	.88	.77	.93	.82	.75
L2Comp	.63	.67	.57	.49	.63	.62	.52	.65	.64
L1Comp	.20	IS[a]	.06	.32	.06	.38	−.53	.16	.35

[a] IS; insufficient sample size.

TABLE 5.8
Ranks of Correlations Among Woodcock Comprehension and Language Measures

	Roman	Korean	Arabic	Indic	Japan	China	Taiwan	Hong Kong
Pres	6	3	5.5	5.5	8	7	9	8
Past	4	2	4	5.5	7	8	6	6.5
Future	5	4.5	5.5	3.5	2	3	5	4
Questions	3	4.5	3	3.5	6	4	4	3
Days	10	11	10	11	9	10	11	9
Count	13	12	13	13	14	13	13.5	13
ReadNums	12	13	12	10	11	11.5	12	11
Alpha	11	14	11	12	12.5	11.5	13.5	14
Colors	8.5	8.5	8	9	12.5	5.5	7.5	6.5
Bparts	2	6	2	2	3	1	3	1.5
Schitems	8.5	7	9	8	4	5.5	7.5	10
Preps	1	1	1	1	1	2	1	1.5
L2Comp	7	10	7	7	5	9	2	5
L1Comp	14	8.5	IS[a]	14	10	14	10	12

[a] IS; insufficient sample size.

for instance, Roman is the most similar to English and the orthography of Hong Kong (keeping in mind the instructional differences among China, Hong Kong, and Taiwan) is the least informative of English.

The correlations are similar across orthographies and the language and literacy variables. There are some interesting differences, however. The Korean students' scores resulted in a negative correlation between their Woodcock and Korean compositions scores. This is a mystery that is likely not explainable. The 9-item test of prepositions is a powerful test. Indeed, it is a powerful predictor. The variable appears to be a test of English grammar, although one could also argue that it is a test of English syntax. Cummins's choice of a test of prepositions as a measure of CALP was discussed in chapter 2. It appears there was a high degree of validity in his choice.

The relationships among these variables across orthographies are most interesting and best seen in graphic form. Figure 5.1 shows the highly regular pattern of responses across orthographies. So, for instance, although means differ significantly across orthographies, the trajectory of means is remarkably similar.

These variables represent production. Present, past, future, and questions measured students' abilities to produce correct utterances in English. Days, count, and alphabet measured students' abilities to produce typical reading readiness skills, whereas reading numbers was a recognition skill. The overall pattern of responses suggests a common underlying proficiency. The variables were reordered to represent the range from lowest to highest means. It seems the skill learned first —easiest— was to remember the names of the letters of the English alphabet, whereas the most difficult was producing past-tense verbs (Fig. 5.2). This is an interesting finding in that it suggests an English acquisition order.

It seems apparent that there is a fairly well-established trend across the orthographies in the acquisition of English. The acquisition of English ap-

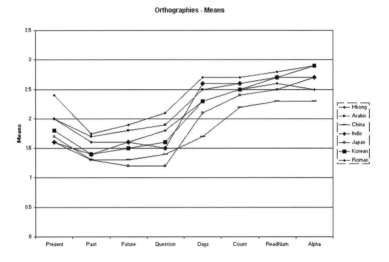

FIG. 5.1.   Mean recognition and production scores for language measures across or-thographic categories.

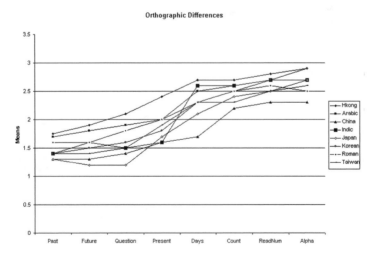

FIG. 5.2.   Language mean scores reordered.

pears to follow an acquisition sequence that is universal. On the other hand, these findings could also represent the teaching sequence followed by English teachers around the world.

Figure 5.3 shows the variables, prepositions, L2 composition, body parts, L2 composition, school items, and colors, computed as proportions across orthographies. There are significant mean differences across orthographies and across the variables. However, the vector of proportions is remarkably similar.

The vector of proportions suggests that there is a common underlying proficiency that is marvelously similar. The variables have been ordered from lowest overall proportion to greatest. Prepositions have been shown to be an extremely difficult syntactic feature to acquire. There appears to be an order of acquisition; colors, school items, body parts, and prepositions in English. Both figures provide evidence that the common underlying factor does not vary according to first language orthography, but is remarkably similar across orthographies. Hong Kong scores are generally higher. The interesting difference is that students from Hong Kong had a higher proportion correct in recognizing and naming school items. Their score for this variable does not fit what seems to be predictable from the general vector of scores. It seems their long experience in schools in Hong Kong made them more aware of school items. Reading scores were turned into proportions and are shown in Figure 5.4.

The Arabic results are somewhat surprising. However, the overall vectors are marvelously similar. It is also interesting to note that the Woodcock comprehension proportion is greater than the recognition proportion. Overall the results shown in the three figures argue for a common underly-

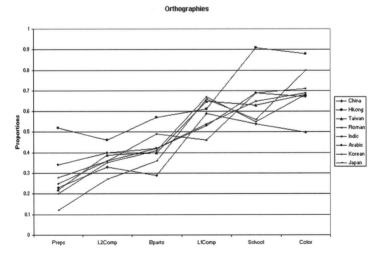

FIG. 5.3. Mean language proportions across orthographic categories.

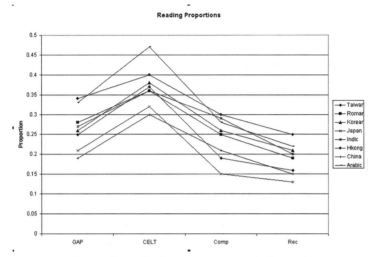

FIG. 5.4. Gap, CELT, and Woodcock proportions across orthographic categories.

ing proficiency. The fascinating feature is that the results across orthographies differ in mean values, but they do not vary relative to the overall pattern of scores. Findings do not appear to support the Differential Base model, but this issue is addressed later. The exception may be Hong Kong, but that has to be explored in a closer fashion.

MULTIPLE FACTOR ANALYSES

Multiple factor analyses were used to explore the pattern of correlations among variables across linguistic and orthographic groups. The exploratory nature of the study supports the approach that "both the theoretical and practical limitations to FA [factor analysis] are relaxed in favor of a frank exploration of the data" (Tabachnick & Fidell, 1996, p. 639). However, FA is sensitive to outliers and to non-normality of distributions of variables. Tabachnick and Fidell (1996) state that "As a general rule of thumb, it is comforting to have at least *300* [emphasis in original] cases for factor analysis" (p. 640). In addition, multiple regression analysis was used to explore the Bernhardt model.

Method

The Zumbo, Sireci, and Hambleton (2003) multigroup exploratory factor analysis approach involving the variables noted earlier, related to letter and word recognition, English reading comprehension, English oral production, and first- and second-language compositions, was used to explore underlying factors. Students' inability to score on particular variables was entered into the analyses. It was hypothesized that there would be a common factor structure across all the orthography groups, including recognition, production, writing, and comprehension measures. However, the pattern of loadings on the four- or five-factor solutions did not match expectations. Instead, all measures seemed to load strongly on one factor.

The first eigenvalue in each of the analyses accounted for 60 to 74% of the variance. The ratio of the first eigenvalue to the second varied from 6.6 to 9.2, meaning one dominant factor could be used as a basis for group comparison (Zumbo et al., 2003). Table 5.9 shows a factor analysis based on one dominant factor across all of the orthography groupings. Table 5.10 shows a ranking of the factor loadings from 1 to 16 for each orthography grouping to reveal which variable has the highest loading (see also Gunderson, 2004).

A principal components analysis (see Table 5.10) of the ranks revealed that all orthographies except that of students from Hong Kong had a great deal of factor structure similarity. The Hong Kong data seem to have shown a second minor factor. Thus, because there was a similar factor across groups with different L1 orthographies, these findings lend support to the notion that there is a common underlying proficiency influencing the second-language reading achievement of these students. The first factor ap-

TABLE 5.9
Factor Loadings

Variable	Arab alphabetic	China	Hong Kong	Indic	Japan	Korean alphabetic	Roman alphabetic	Taiwan
WOODCOMP	.43	.27	.53	.46	.17	.23	.39	.38
WOODREC	.22	.30	.35	.35	.33	.28	.35	.37
PRES	.98	.94	.97	.97	.96	.92	.96	.93
PAST	.97	.92	.95	.97	.88	.95	.95	.94
FUTURE	.98	.94	.96	.97	.96	.95	.95	.95
QUESTIONS	.97	.93	.96	.96	.95	.94	.95	.93
DAYS	.96	.89	.95	.95	.94	.94	.94	.93
COUNT	.89	.80	.96	.94	.92	.89	.90	.89
READNUM	.94	.82	.96	.95	.93	.87	.91	.91
ALPHABET	.89	.78	.95	.93	.89	.84	.91	.88
COLORS	.93	.84	.97	.96	.90	.91	.92	.92
BPARTS	.91	.85	.97	.95	.82	.91	.89	.90
SCHITEMS	.94	.88	.98	.97	.92	.93	.93	.93
PREPS	.80	.73	.90	.81	.52	.70	.75	.70
L2COMP	.39	.41	.35	.43	.27	.36	.40	.28
L1COMP	.35	.38	.36	.33	.45	.41	.34	.39

Note. From "The language, literacy, achievement, and social consequences of English-only programs for immigrant students " (p. 16), by L. Gunderson, 2004. In J. Hoffman and D. Schallert (Eds.), *The NRC Yearbook* (pp. 1–27). Milwaukee, WI: National Reading Conference. Copyright © 2004 by the National Reading Conference. Reprinted with permission.

TABLE 5.10
Ranking of Factor Loadings for the Language Groups

Variable	Arab alphabetic	China	Hong Kong	Indic	Japan	Korean alphabetic	Roman alphabetic	Taiwan
WOODCOMP	4	1	4	4	1	1	3	3
WOODREC	1	2	2	2	3	2	2	2
PRES	16	16	14	14	16	11	16	14
PAST	14	13	6	15	7	15	13	15
FUTURE	15	15	10	13	15	16	15	16
QUESTIONS	13	14	11	12	14	13	14	13
DAYS	12	12	7	9	13	14	12	11
COUNT	6	7	9	7	10	8	7	7
READNUM	10	8	12	8	12	7	9	9
ALPHABET	7	6	8	6	8	6	8	6
COLORS	9	9	15	11	9	9	10	10
BPARTS	8	10	13	10	6	10	6	8
SCHITEMS	11	11	16	16	11	12	11	12
PREPS	5	5	5	5	5	5	5	5
L2COMP	3	4	1	3	2	3	4	1
L1COMP	2	3	3	1	4	4	1	4

Note. From "The language, literacy, achievement, and social consequences of English-only programs for immigrant students " (p. 16), by L. Gunderson, 2004. In J. Hoffman and D. Schallert (Eds.), *The NRC Yearbook* (pp. 1–27). Milwaukee, WI: National Reading Conference. Copyright © 2004 by the National Reading Conference. Reprinted with permission.

TABLE 5.11
Principal Component Analysis: Rotated Component Matrix

Language Groups	Component 1	Component 2
Roman alphabetic	.892	.418
Arab alphabetic	.885	.436
Korean	.881	.343
Taiwan	.874	.451
PRC	.869	.443
Japan	.758	.470
Indic	.714	.634
Hong Kong	.288	.947

Note. From "The language, literacy, achievement, and social consequences of English-only programs for immigrant students" (p. 17), by L. Gunderson, 2004. In J. Hoffman and D. Schallert (Eds.), *The NRC Yearbook* (pp. 1–27). Milwaukee, WI: National Reading Conference. Copyright © 2004 by the National Reading Conference. Reprinted with permission.

pears to be a general English factor, whereas the second factor, the one observed in the Hong Kong group, appears to be a recognition factor. Bolded variables contributed significantly to the factors in the tables.

The striking difference between students from Hong Kong and students from other parts of the world, besides the orthographies they first learned to read, is an instructional one. Most students from Hong Kong were introduced to formal reading instruction at age three. This is about 3 to 4 years earlier than other students from other parts of the world. This instructional variable may have had an effect in these findings. Many students from Hong Kong also were often enrolled in primary schools that were English-based institutions. The difference in response patterns can be seen in Figure 5.3, which shows Hong Kong students' proportion of responses to school items and colors compared to the other groups. Overall, there is support to the notion that there is a common underlying proficiency.

THE BERNHARDT MODEL

Bernhardt (2000) addresses a number of important considerations in developing a second-language reading model. She notes that the selection of tasks is an important variable that "task and the language of response (native or nonnative) exert profound impacts on students' revealed performance" (p. 801). She also notes that in this regard the use of the cloze procedure, although almost extinct from first-language studies, continues to be used in second-language studies. There is evidence that suggests cloze measures "local-level syntactic sensitivity." She also notes that the use of one dependent variable results in an uncertainty about what is being measured. She concludes, "To be succinct, when a measure is taken is it a measure of second language, or first language, or a hybrid of the two?"(p. 802). Finally, Bernhardt argues that "What the research referred to earlier indicates is the constitution of these scores: general literacy ability (about 20% of any given score), grammar (about an additional 30% of any given score, 27% of which is word knowledge and 3% syntax), and 50% of any given score at any particular point in time unexplained" (p. 804).

Assessment at OROC is pragmatic in that assessors choose instruments that are efficiently administered. The three reading measures are all cloze or cloze-like instruments. The other measures were developed to represent a kind of battery of readiness skills for English-only classrooms and to predict what levels of ESL support students would require. The difficulty is to match the variables in this study with the factors Bernhardt notes are important. So, for instance, what measures constitute general literacy ability, grammar, word knowledge, and syntax?

It seems clear that the preposition test is a measure of grammar and that the present tense, past tense, future tense, and questioning measures represent syntactic knowledge, although it could also be argued that they are measures of grammar. Recognizing and naming letters of the alphabet and numbers are also, it seem, kinds of sound—symbol knowledge related to word knowledge. Recognizing body parts and school items seems like a kind of general oral language recognition ability. It is not clear, however, that a measure constituting general literacy ability exists in the present study. First- and second-language composition scores represent literacy in two languages. One could argue that they, in fact, represent general literacy measures.

Measures were entered stepwise. Bernhardt (2004, personal communication, San Antonio, TX) indicated that the method she had employed was stepwise entering of variables. Scores for these measures for all students were entered into a standard multiple regression equation using SPSS Regression with Woodcock comprehension scores as the dependent measure. Eleven variables contributed significantly to the dependent variable. They were Prepositions ($r^2 = .079$, $F(1,4623) = 397.54$); Alphabet ($r^2 = .257$, $F(1,4622) = 1108.43$); Future ($r^2 = .271$, $F(1,4621) = 84.12$); Counting ($r^2 = .290$, $F(1,4620) = 123.085$); Body Parts ($r^2 = .305$, $F(1,4619) = 99.774$); L1 Composition ($r^2 = .317$, $F(1,4618) = 83.99$); Number Recognition ($r^2 = .325$, $F(1,4617) = 52.58$); Days ($r^2 = .329$, $F(1,4616) = 30.85$); English Composition ($r^2 = .333$, $F(1,4615) = 26.05$); Colors ($r^2 = .333$), $F(1,4614) = 7.57$); and School Items ($r^2 = .335$, $F(1,4613) = 9.17$).

Scores for these measures for students from Hong Kong were put into a regression analysis. Six variables contributed significantly to the dependent variable. They were Prepositions ($r^2 = .31$, $F(1,1352) = 42.90$), Alphabet ($r^2 = .207$), Body Parts ($r^2 = .246$), Counting ($r^2 = 256$), Future Tense ($r^2 = 266$), and School Items ($r^2 = 275$). The total amount of variance accounted for by the six variables was .275.

Scores for students from Taiwan were analyzed. Five variables contributed significantly to the dependent variable. They were Prepositions ($r^2 = .136$, $F(1,508) = 79.68$), Alphabet ($r^2 = .282$), L1 Composition ($r^2 = .293$), English Composition ($r^2 = .308$), and Questioning ($r^2 = .314$). The total amount of variance accounted for by the five variables was .314.

Scores for students from languages other than English that use a Roman or augmented Roman alphabet were entered into a standard multiple regression equation. Six variables contributed significantly to the dependent variable. They were Prepositions ($r^2 = .117$, $F(1,988) = 130.30$), Counting ($r^2 = .341$), Body Parts ($r^2 = .361$), Recognizing Numbers ($r^2 = .366$), L1 Composition ($r^2 = .386$), and English Composition ($r^2 = .389$). The total amount of variance accounted for by the six variables was .389.

Tabachnick and Fidell (1996) indicate that "A cases-to-IV ratio of 40 to 1 is reasonable" in the case of the use of stepwise regression (p. 133). The following analyses should be considered exploratory because the number of subjects is less than 560, the recommended cases-to-IV ratio of 40 to 1.

Scores for students who spoke Vietnamese as a first language were entered into a regression equation. Five variables contributed significantly to the dependent variable. They were Prepositions ($r^2 = .130$, $F(1,277) = 41.48$), Counting ($r^2 = .359$), Vietnamese Composition ($r^2 = .400$), Body Parts ($r^2 = .417$), and Alphabet ($r^2 = .440$). The total amount of variance accounted for by the five variables was .440.

Scores for students who spoke Spanish as a first language were entered into a regression equation. Four variables contributed significantly to the dependent variable. They were Prepositions ($r^2 = .324$, $F(1,227) = 109.77$), Counting ($r^2 = .442$), Body Parts ($r^2 = .468$), and Future Tense ($r^2 = .489$). The total amount of variance accounted for by the four variables was .489.

These findings suggest that grammar—knowledge of prepositions—varies in the amount of variance it accounts for in comprehension scores, but it is a significant variable. These findings do not support Bernhardt's model that about 30% of the variance is accounted for by knowledge of grammar. The difficulty with this interpretation, however, is that the measures involved differ from past research and they also involve a measure Bernhardt and others are convinced is not a good measure of reading, the cloze procedure.

Bernhardt mentions the concept of general literacy, but it is not clear what measures could be taken of this concept. There were two interesting tasks in the present study that asked students to write in their first language and in English. It can be argued that composition represents general literacy ability. Students who are able to compose must understand their own first language and the second-language orthography, its grammar and syntax, at least some of its vocabulary, and its writing conventions. First language writing scores have long-term predictive power, however (see chap. 6).

The decision to use the Woodcock data rather than either the Gap or CELT data, even though there were more students involved, was based on a series of preliminary analyses that indicated that they were not as reliably related to the language and literacy variables as the Woodcock data. This was an unfortunate finding.

THE DIFFERENTIAL BASE MODEL

The underlying proposition in the DB model is that because orthographies differ in the way they represent first languages, students who have learned to read in different first language orthographies should differ in their patterns of responses to English. Four hundred and twenty identified themselves as English as a first language with an additional second or third language. English–Hindi (6.50%), English–French (11.00%), English–Cantonese (15.60%), English–Mandarin (7.80%), and English–Tagalog (10.40%) were the largest groups of identified English–Other bilingual speakers. The pattern of responses, including the individuals reporting English as the first language, is shown in Figure 5.5 as proportions.

Those who indicated they were English–Other bilinguals had consistently higher proportions of responses across the measures. On the other hand, 2,959 indicated that they were Other–English bilinguals. It is fascinating to observe that the English–Other bilinguals scored lower on these variables than did the Other–English bilinguals. Tagalog–English bilinguals, for instance, had the following proportional scores: Colors .95; Body Parts .80; School Items .97; Prepositions .62; English compositions .47; and Tagalog compositions .60.

The pattern across the three Chinese orthographic groups is similar (Table 5.12), although the means are significantly different. The one exception to the pattern relates to scores from Hong Kong concerning compositions written in Chinese. The students from Hong Kong had significantly higher

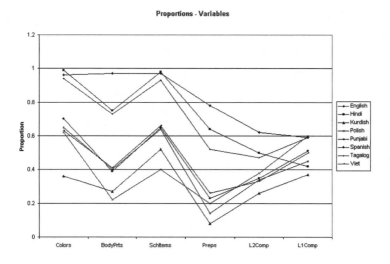

Fig. 5.5. Proportion of Responses.

TABLE 5.12
Proportion Scores for China, Hong Kong, and Taiwan

	Colors	BParts	SchItems	Preps	L2Comp	L1Comp
China	.50	.29	.54	.23	.33	.59
Hong Kong	.87	.57	.91	.52	.45	.61
Taiwan	.68	.40	.63	.22	.39	.65

scores across the variables, except in Chinese compositions. The pattern for students from China and Taiwan are phenomenally similar (Fig. 5.6).

These results do not support the DB model. Figure 5.7 shows these data broken down by languages that represent tokens of the orthographic categories. It is important to note that the sample sizes for the samples shown in this figure are relatively low. They vary from 47 (Greek) to 5,782 (Cantonese). The results appear similar to those noted earlier. The pattern of responses is remarkably similar across orthographies. Greek languages show a bit of a discrepancy in this pattern, but these differences are likely a result of the very small sample size. Variables broken down by selected tokens of orthographic categories are shown in Figure 5.7.

The DB model predicts that there would be different "loadings" on different variables related to their relationship to English and its augmented Roman orthography. In essence, the model predicted that some reading skills related to some orthographies would "transfer" to English, whereas others would "interfere" with it. Bernhardt (1991) noted:

> Transfer and interference data parallel a long-running debate in second-language acquisition research in general. The extent to which first language strategies facilitate acquisition and the extent to which they impede acquisition—in this case, of second-language reading skills—remains unclear. (p. 52)

Mean Woodcock comprehension scores were computed for Cantonese, Mandarin, Indic, and Roman by number of years students had studied English in their home countries. These data were computed to observe whether or not there were differential effects over years of study by individuals from different groups. These data can be seen in Table 5.13.

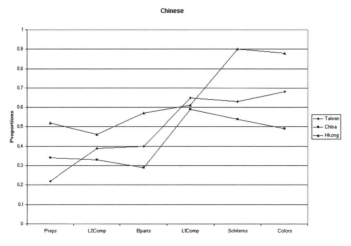

FIG. 5.6. Proportions of scores for students from China, Hong Kong, and Taiwan.

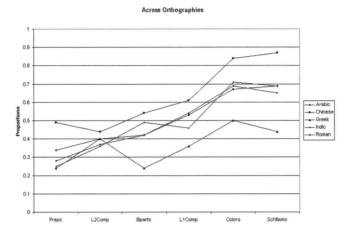

FIG. 5.7.   Proportion scores broken down by orthographic groups.

TABLE 5.13
Woodcock Comprehension Scores by Group by Years of English Study

	1 year	2 years	3 years	4 years	5 years	6 years	7 years
Cantonese	11.80	13.80	14.40	16.30	18.40	20.20	19.70
Mandarin	9.40	12.40	12.60	12.00	24.70	14.60	14.00
Indic	4.70	7.00	13.10	14.30	21.70	18.80	13.60
Roman	10.00	8.90	13.10	14.40	20.50	24.80	21.40

These data suggest that comprehension does increase over the years, but, as noted earlier, there appears to be a plateau effect at 5 to 6 years where scores do not increase. It is not possible, of course, to compute the same calculations for those who indicated they had not studied English before their immigration. It is interesting, however, to plot proportions of scores for those who have and have not reported previous English study. These data are plotted in Figure 5.8.

A careful inspection of the data was undertaken to assure results were not due to some kind of entry error. A number of interesting features that explain these anomalous findings were observed. An astounding half (50.10%) of the students who indicated they had not studied English but were able to score on the reading tests were bilingual, and 70% of them indicated English was their second language. The major countries represented were Hong Kong, Taiwan, the Philippines, and India. Many of these stu-

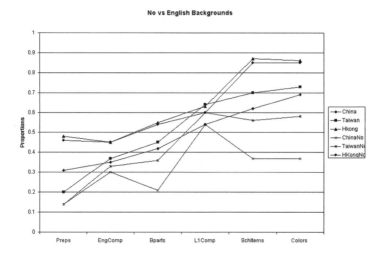

FIG. 5.8.   Proportions by three Chinese groups with and without English instruction.

dents had attended schools where English was the language of instruction. It would seem that their parents' interpretation of the question may have focused on English as a topic, so "Has your child studied English?" was interpreted not to include instruction in English. Or so it would seem. This appears to have been the reason this group scored as well as those who had indicated they had studied English. This remarkable similarity is strong evidence to suggest that there is a common underlying proficiency that provides the foundation for those who are involved in learning English. It seems to be a universal across languages and orthographies.

PRIMARY FINDINGS

Overall findings for primary students (K–3) were described in chapter 4. These findings also suggest that the learning of English construction, words for colors, and lower-case and upper-case letters follows a regular pattern across linguistic and geolinguistic groups. Figure 5.9 shows students' scores broken down by a number of different groups, chosen because they all have substantial sample sizes. Directions were: (a) Please give me the eraser; (b) put the ruler under the book; (c) open the book; (d) pick up the paper; (e) put the paper in the book; and (f) please close the book and put it on the table. The directions involving the words "under" and "in" were then most difficult across the language groups.

The Japanese scores appear to differ somewhat. They appeared to have difficulty with the "command" and also difficulty with the understanding of prepositions. Figure 5.10 shows the percentage of correct responses for upper-case letters for about 1,300 primary students.

Correct Directions

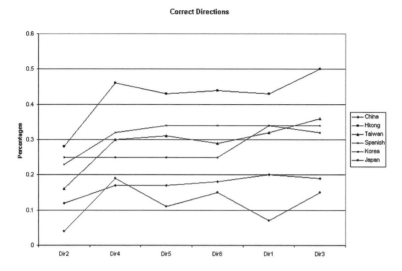

FIG. 5.9.   Percentages correctly following English instructions.

Capital Letters

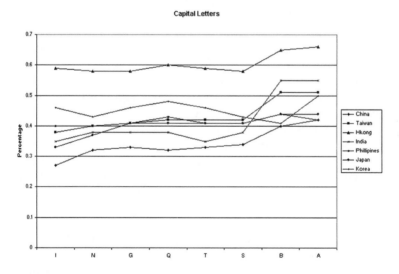

FIG. 5.10.   Percentages of correct responses for capital letters across language groups.

There are significant differences among first languages, but the pattern appears relatively regular. Capital letters A and B resulted in the highest recognition scores, suggesting they were learned first. Figure 5.11 shows the results for four groups.

The pattern is marvelously similar across groups, although there are significant differences in mean scores. There has been a significant and

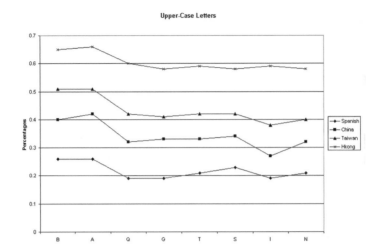

FIG. 5.11.   Proportions of scores for the recognition of upper-case letters.

long-term research interest in the recognition of letters. This literature is discussed in chapter 8. Overall, however, findings suggest that capital letters are recognized more accurately than lower-case letters and they are learned before lower-case letters. Figure 5.12 shows correct scores for the recognition and naming of lower-case letters.

There are differences among the groups, but again the pattern is highly regular from group to group. This can be seen in Figure 5.13, which shows the same four groups referred to earlier.

Colors and letters are interesting categories that may be formed around focal members that are learned first and remembered more accurately than other members of categories. This seems particularly true for colors. Recognition of school items and body parts also shows interesting patterns across groups. Figure 5.14 shows color recognition broken down by the four categories described earlier.

The pattern across the linguistic and geolinguistic groups was essentially the same. This pattern also occurred for the recognition of school items as shown in Figure 5.15.

Finally, students were asked to name pictures of body parts in English. These results are shown in Figure 5.16.

Again, although the means differ from group to group, the pattern remains basically the same across linguistic and geolinguistic groups. Results suggest that the school personnel who developed the two recognition tests of school items and body parts included tokens that were culturally related. These patterns and their implications are discussed in chapter 8. The pattern regularity across groups suggests interesting features of the learning of English.

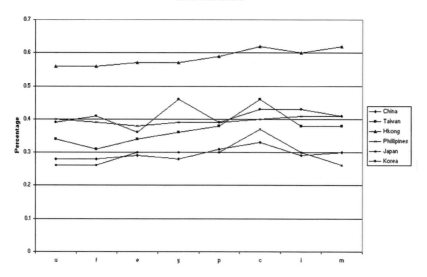

FIG. 5.12.　Percentages of accurate recognition score for lower-case letters.

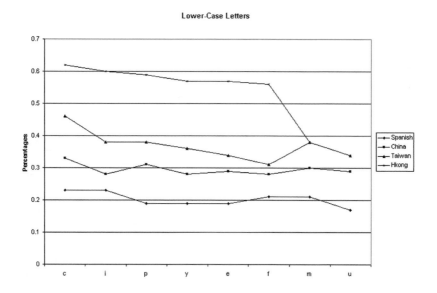

FIG. 5.13.　Percentages of accurate recognition score for lower-case letters, broken down by four language groups.

Colors

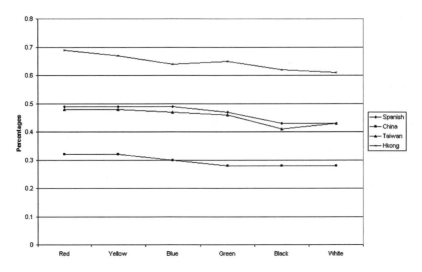

FIG. 5.14.   Percentages of correct recognition of colors.

School Items

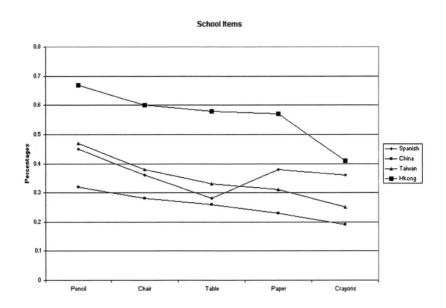

FIG. 5.15.   Percentages of correct recognition for school items.

158

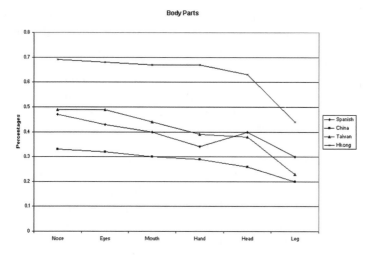

FIG. 5.16.   Percentages of recognition scores for body parts.

CONCLUSION

Mary Ashworth (Gunderson, 1991a) states, "There's nothing more practical than a good theory." The purpose of this chapter has been to explore and
to test models of second-language reading. One of the most widely known
is the Common Underlying Proficiency (CUP) theory developed by
Cummins (1981a) and Cummins and Swain (1986). Most of the proponents
of this theory are researchers and educators in the area of English as a second language, although Cummins and Swain argue the theory holds for
any first- and second-language combination. There was support for CUP in
the findings reported in this chapter. However, discussion is withheld until
chapter 6. It was clear that students who had studied English prior to immigration had not developed CALP in the 5 to 7 years many have observed in
studies in North America.

Bernhardt (1991, 2000) focuses on a theory of second language rather
than an ESL theory. She has rightly noted that the preponderance of ESL
studies have utilized first-language (English) research as models. She also
argues that the measures used in second-language studies are questionable, particularly the use of the cloze procedure to measure reading.

The DB model was developed on the notion that different orthographies
focus their users on different processes and should, therefore, result in different patterns of subskills being transferred to English. Many authors have
suggested that first-language features can either transfer to English features or can interfere with English features.

The measures used in the study were not designed a priori. They were, instead, measures that were available from a school system attempting to cope with thousands of new students whose first languages were not English. They opted to use three different reading tests, all of which are based on the cloze procedure. The other measures were designed to represent home background, schooling, and school language and literacy readiness skills. The system has a lot of noise as a result of assessors having discretion in terms of the measures they used with the individuals they tested. The study has noise. However, it's fairly typical school-based research noise.

There was good evidence to support the notion that there is a common underlying proficiency that transfers from a number of first-languages to English. However, the prediction based on the DB model that the proficiency base would differ from first language to first language was not supported. Instead, the proficiency base appeared to be universal. Although means differed significantly from language to language, the vector of means did not.

The Bernhardt model was not supported by findings of this study. The overall unexplained variance was less than the model predicts. This was likely because of the measures involved.

It was also disappointing to find that the personal developmental variables did not have much predictive power for the language and literacy variables. There were differences in scores related to immigration categories, which are general measures of socioeconomic status.

The next chapter explores the long-term relationships among the variables discussed here and the success in secondary schools of students who take academic classes.

6

Multiple Case Studies, Students' Views, and Secondary Achievement

We waste too much time in school. Too much
time not working. Teachers are too lazy they
don't tell you what to do.[1]

The purpose of this research was to learn about immigrant students' lived lives from different viewpoints. One goal was to come to know how immigrant students were doing in schools where their first language was not the language of instruction or of their socialization into society in general and into the community of secondary students specifically. Another purpose was to explore issues related to identity. To achieve these goals several sources of information were explored: students' grades in secondary school academic courses, teachers' and parents' views, and, of course, the views of the students themselves.

HOW ARE IMMIGRANT STUDENTS DOING?
—THEIR GRADES IN SCHOOL

Students in the Vancouver school district are assigned typical school grades, from failure (F) to outstanding (A). The traditional view is that grades should fall into a normal distribution with the grade of C representing the mean, the median, and the mode, whereas A's and F's represent the bottom and top of the curve. The traditional expectation is, therefore, that average achieving or "normal" students should receive a grade of C.

The use of standardized tests administered at the beginning and end of each school year was abolished in the 1980s in British Columbia at all grade levels,

---

[1] Male, Cantonese, 15 years.

both in elementary and secondary schools. The only required examinations that were retained and continue to be administered are Grade 12 provincial examinations in "examinable" subjects. The student who wishes to attend university in British Columbia must take prescribed courses and pass the appropriate end-of-Grade12 examinations. For purposes of this study, grades were recorded and converted into numerical equivalents as discussed in chapter 3. Grades were recorded for the major examinable subjects: English, Math, Science, and social studies in Grades 8, 9, 10, 11, and 12. In British Columbia, secondary schools enroll students from Grade 8 to Grade 12. The schools in the study varied from populations of 427 to 2,032, with the mean being 1,389.00. In addition, grades and other data were also recorded for English as a second language (ESL) courses the students in the sample had taken. Grades for the examinable subjects were also recorded for students born in Canada for comparison purposes. It should be noted that there were students in this particular sample who were born and remained in Canada, but began speaking home languages other than English. They were, by all definitions, ESL students. For technical reasons it was not possible to identify and eliminate these students from the group categorized as Canadian-born. Eddy (2005) estimates that approximately 5% of the school population consists of students whose first language is not English but who were born and continue to live in Canada. These students are separate from those born in Canada who left for 4 to 6 years to live with relatives in their parents' home country, as described earlier.

Canadian-Born Students

A random sample of 5,000 students born in Canada was selected. Their grades for the examinable courses, English, Math, Science, and social studies, for Grades 8 through 12 were coded and entered into computer files. Figure 6.1 shows these data. Canadian-born students on the average received slightly better than a C average. There was an unusual dip of grade point average in Grade 11. When asked, teachers and administrators thought this was a result of an increase in the difficulty of work in the 11th grade. Students begin to study seriously for university admission during their Grade 11 year. Teachers also confided that they believed Grade 11 teachers graded more rigorously because their students would have to take provincial examinations in Grade 12 and if students have not been properly prepared for them, it would reflect poorly on the teachers. It would appear that Canadian-born students do on the average about as well as, or slightly better than, they should be expected to do so if C does represent the average grade expected of them. The common sense belief that there has been dramatic grade inflation is not supported by these data.

What is not shown in Figure 6.1 is that the number of students enrolled in these courses decreases significantly from Grade 8 to Grade 12. There are a number of reasons for this significant decrease. First, a relatively large

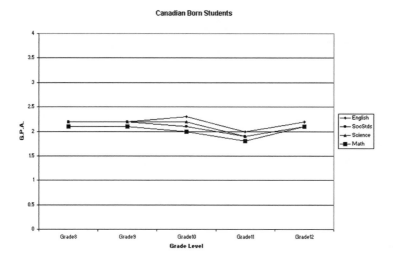

FIG. 6.1.   Grades for Canadian students in Grades 8 to 12.

number of students do not take the examinable courses in Grade 12 because they do not intend to go on to a university. Second, a fairly large number of students leave the school district, for one reason or another, to attend schools in other jurisdictions. Finally, a number of students simply drop out for various reasons. It is not clear what percentage each of these categories represents. However, there were 60% fewer students in Grade 12 taking examinable courses than there were in Grade 8. The interesting feature of the Canadian students' grades in Grade 12 was that they rose from Grade 11. The number of students decreased, from Grade 11 to Grade 12, but the grades for those who remained rose to their pre-Grade 11 levels. Teachers interviewed suggested this rebound occurred because even though teachers were more rigorous in their grading, the students who took Grade 12 examinable courses were better students.

A random sample of 5,000 immigrant students, approximately one-fourth of the number that had been assessed at Oakridge and had been coded into the database, was selected. Of this random sample, only students who had entered Grade 8 on or before 1996 were selected, so that they were old enough to have completed secondary school by the time of the study. The number in the sample was reduced because some had left the district before they had entered secondary school. A total of 2,213 students remained in the sample. A breakdown of this sample by countries of origin is shown in Table 6.1 This reduction in numbers came as a surprise, but it should have been anticipated, considering the sample reduction reported by Collier in 1987.

TABLE 6.1
Students in Random Sample (n = 2313)

Country	Number	Percentage
Hong Kong	909	39.30%
Taiwan	351	15.20%
Vietnam	260	11.20%
China	130	5.60%
El Salvador	72	3.10%
India	67	2.90%
Philippines	53	2.30%
Poland	53	2.30%
Korea	49	2.10%
Japan	37	1.60%
Fiji	28	1.20%
Portugal	26	1.10%
United States[a]	23	.90%
Afghanistan	21	.90%
Iraq	19	.80%
Malaysia	18	.70%
Sri Lanka	18	.70%
Yugoslavia	17	.70%
Ethiopia	15	.60%
Ghana	15	.60%
Honduras	14	.60%
Israel	13	.60%
Laos	12	.50%
Netherlands	11	.50%
Pakistan	10	.40%
Russia	10	.40%
Singapore	9	.40%
Brazil	9	.40%
Bangladesh	8	.30%
Cambodia	7	.30%
Indonesia	6	.30%
Nicaragua	5	.20%

Peru	4	.20%
Romania	4	.20%
Somalia	3	.10%
Egypt	3	.10%
Bosnia	2	.08%
Guam	1	.04%
Georgia	1	

^aSpanish-speaking refugees included in this group.

Their grades for the examinable subjects and for ESL courses were provided by the school district. The examinable course grade averages are shown in Figure 6.2. There is a similar dip in grade point averages in Grade 11, except for math. However, immigrants' grades do not rebound in Grade 12. Their average grade for Grade 12 English, in fact, decreases from the Grade 11 dip. It seems clear that the courses that have been traditionally viewed as requiring advanced language skills, English and social studies, were more difficult for immigrant students.

The overall result, however, is that immigrant students' achievement as measured by grade point average in the same examinable courses is roughly the same as that for Canadian-born students, except for math courses, where their grades are higher. Immigrants' grades in math courses remain extremely stable across the grades and science increases a bit in Grade twelve. On the surface, these data indicate that immigrant students are doing about as well as they would be expected to do if they were Canadian-born students. They also lend some credibility to the notion that C is about an average grade.

Students who entered Canada as members of "regular immigrant" families represented the majority in the population of immigrants. These families applied for immigration to Canada and were required to wait, sometimes as long as 5 years, for their cases to be adjudicated and before they were granted immigrant status. It seems apparent that individuals in these families wanted very much to enter Canada and were patient enough to let the complex Canadian immigration process take place. Their grades in the examinable courses are shown in Figure 6.3. They appear to do extremely well on the average.

However, there are underlying features that put this seemingly good outcome into a less positive context: (a) the disappearance rate, and (b) systematic variations from the immigrants' mean scores. Figure 6.4 shows the disappearance rate for immigrant students who took examinable courses over their secondary school years.

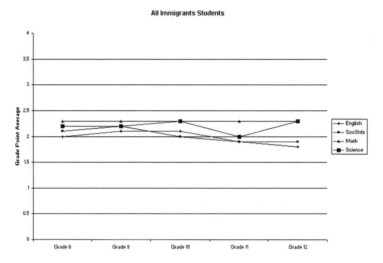

FIG. 6.2.   Grades for all immigrant students.

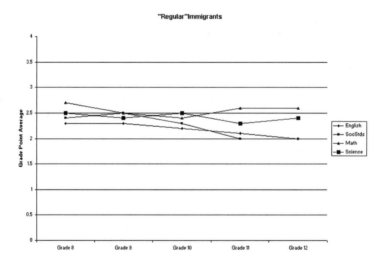

FIG. 6.3.   Grades for students who entered as regular immigrants (not refugees).

Students in the sample who enrolled in English classes decreased from 1,433 in 8th to 651 (45.40%) in 12th grade, in math from 1,576 to 498 (31.60%), in science from 1,482 to 375 (25.30%), and social studies from 1,407 to 326 (23.20%). The decrease was not uniform across immigration categories, however. Indeed, when broken down by immigration status the data reveal a disturbing pattern. The drop in percentage of students in the

Numbers in Random Sample

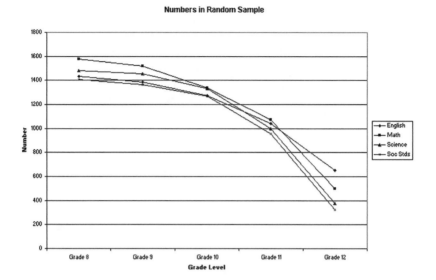

FIG. 6.4.   Decrease in sample sizes from Grade 8 to Grade 12.

sample who were refugees who took examinable subjects is shown in Figure 6.5. Whereas the percentage of students in the "immigrant" category remained relatively stable, although absolute numbers decreased, the percentage of students from entrepreneurial families increased. In science courses, for instance, the variation was from 5.50% in Grade 8, to 4.70% in Grade 9, 7.20% in Grade 10, 8.80% in Grade 11, and 13.10% in Grade 12. The pattern was similar for math (Grade 8, 5.20%; Grade 9, 5.30%; Grade 10, 6.60%; Grade 11, 8.10%; and Grade 12, 10.20%) English (Grade 8, 5.60%; Grade 9, 6.60%; Grade 10, 6.80%; Grade 11, 8.60%; and Grade 12, 9.10%), and social studies (Grade 8, 5.30%; Grade 9, 4.90%; Grade 10, 6.80%; Grade 11, 8.40%; and Grade 12, 7.20%). The overall drop in the number of regular immigrant students who took English 12 was 32% of the number who took English 8. The pattern was the same for math (37%), and science (33%); however, for social studies the number was 6%—94% chose not to take Social Studies 12. This is an extraordinary drop in the number of students who took social studies in Grade 12. It seems apparent that Grade 12 social studies is not very appealing to immigrants. As can be seen in Figure 6.5, Grade 12 social studies also represents the largest drop in number of refugees who took the course. Social studies educators should likely reassess their curricula to discover what features appear to make them generally irrelevant to immigrant students.

The overall averages are shocking and surprising because they suggest that immigrant students are doing about what they should be expected to

Refugee Percentage

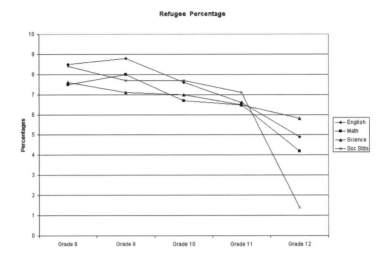

FIG. 6.5.   Percentage enrollment of refugees from Grade 8 to Grade 12.

do and were on par with students born in Canada. As shown earlier, overall means hide some disturbing evidence concerning refugee students' participation in the examinable courses. Students from entrepreneurial families were less likely to disappear from the sample, which suggests they were more established. Refugees had the highest disappearance rate. Another interesting underlying pattern is that there are significant differences between the performance of girls and that of boys (Table 6.2).

Girls outperformed boys in all subjects in Grades 8, 9, 10, and 11. In Grade 12 they continued to outperform boys, although their grade point average did decline. In math and science at Grade 12 boys and girls achieved about the same, whereas in Grade 12 social studies, immigrant boys have a slight advantage. The pattern is similar for Canadian-born students (Table 6.3).

Canadian-born girls outperformed boys across the grades in all academic subjects, except Grade 12 math, where their grade point averages are the same. When they entered Canada, however, there were no significant differences in their literacy and language scores. These results were reported to the school district and were supported by a subsequent province-wide study that created a frenzy in the local press.

Immigrant students were in ESL classes on the average for 3.60 years (*SD* = 2.80). The maximum, of course, was 5 years during their secondary school experiences. There was an inverse relationship between the number of years an immigrant student was in ESL classes and grade point average. Those who were in ESL classes the longest scored lowest on all of the examinable courses and also had the highest disappearance rate.

TABLE 6.2
Immigrant Students: Means and Standard Deviations—Grade Point Averages

Gender	Subject	Grade 8	Grade 9	Grade 10	Grade 11	Grade 12
Male	English	1.80 (1.0)	2.0 (1.1)	2.0 (1.0)	1.75 (1.0)	1.70 (1.0)
Female	English	2.4 (1.1)	2.4 (1.1)	2.2 (1.1)	2.1 (1.0)	1.90 (.90)
Male	Math	2.20 (1.3)	2.2 (1.3)	2.2 (1.2)	2.1 (1.3)	2.2 (1.4)
Female	Math	2.5 (1.2)	2.4 (1.3)	2.4 (1.2)	2.5 (1.2)	2.2 (1.4)
Male	Science	2.1(1.2)	2.1 (1.2)	2.3 (1.1)	2.0 (1.3)	2.3 (1.3)
Female	Science	2.4 (1.2)	2.4 (1.1)	2.4 (1.2)	2.1 (1.2)	2.3 (1.2)
Male	Soc Stds	1.9 (1.2)	2.1 (1.2)	2.0 (1.1)	1.7 (1.2)	1.9 (1.2)
Female	Soc Stds	2.4 (1.1)	2.4 (1.1)	2.3 (1.2)	2.0 (1.2)	1.8 (1.2)

TABLE 6.3
Canadian Born Students: Means and Standard Deviations—Grade Point Averages

Gender	Subject	Grade 8	Grade 9	Grade 10	Grade 11	Grade 12
Male	English	2.0 (1.1)	2.1 (1.1)	2.2 (1.0)	1.9 (1.1)	2.0 (1.1)
Female	English	2.5 (1.1)	2.5 (1.1)	2.5 (1.2)	2.3 (1.1)	2.3 (1.1)
Male	Math	2.0 (1.2)	2.0 (1.2)	2.0 (1.2)	1.7 (1.1)	2.1 (1.2)
Female	Math	2.2 (1.2)	2.1 (1.2)	2.1 (1.2)	1.9 (1.2)	2.1 (1.2)
Male	Science	2.1(1.3)	2.1 (1.1)	2.1 (1.1)	1.8 (1.2)	2.1 (1.3)
Female	Science	2.3 (1.2)	2.3 (1.2)	2.3 (1.1)	2.1 (1.2)	2.2 (1.2)
Male	Soc Stds	2.1 (1.1)	2.1 (1.1)	2.0 (1.1)	1.7 (1.1)	2.1 (1.2)
Female	Soc Stds	2.3 (1.2)	2.3 (1.2)	2.3 (1.2)	2.1 (1.1)	2.2 (1.2)

These results are revealing. However, they focus on groups of students, and overall averages mask significant smaller group differences. Figure 6.6 shows grade point average broken down by one of the larger immigrant groups, Mandarin speakers.

These results are astounding. Mandarin speakers scored significantly higher than Canadian-born students. Their math averages are phenomenally high. However, English and social studies grades decrease over their high school career. English and social studies grades decrease significantly for complex reasons that are discussed later in this chapter. Cantonese speakers represented the largest group of immigrant students in the school district during the period in which data were collected. Figure 6.7 shows their grades.

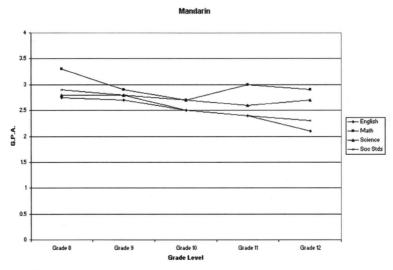

FIG. 6.6.   Grades for Mandarin speakers in Grades 8 to 12.

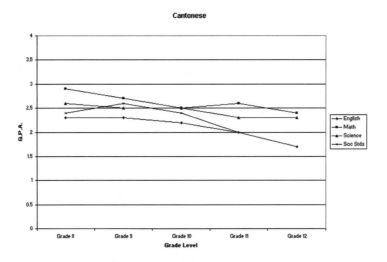

FIG. 6.7.   Grades for Cantonese speakers in Grades 8 to 12.

Cantonese speakers' grades in social studies and English were higher than those of the Canadian-born students until Grade 11, after which they were lower. However, they were lower than the Mandarin speakers' grades. Again, there was a decrease in grade point average, most significantly in English, social studies, and math. Their overall mean grade point averages in English and social studies in Grade 12 were both 1.7. This average lies between a D+ (1.5) and a C– (1.75).

Figure 6.8 shows grade point averages for students whose first language was Spanish. It is important to point out that these students came from a variety of countries and were also more likely to be from refugee families than students from other immigrant groups. One consequence of this phenomenon was that the schools they were enrolled in had different cultural mixes than the schools enrolling Mandarin and Cantonese speakers.

There are a number of distressing elements in the results obtained for Spanish-speaking immigrants. Their overall grade point averages are extremely low. The fluctuation in their grade point averages, to a great extent, is a result of the instability of the number of students at each grade level. The most distressing finding is that in the random sample selected for this study, only one Spanish-speaking student had taken any of the examinable subjects in Grade 12. One individual enrolled in Grade 12 English and completed it with the grade of D. The implications of these findings are both significant and serious. As a group, the Spanish speakers in this sample were at risk educationally.

Results for Vietnamese-speaking students were also subject to significant fluctuations resulting from variable numbers of students in the sample. Vietnamese students also tended to be in particular schools in the school district (Fig. 6.9).

These findings appear, at first, to be encouraging because they are rising. The difficulty is that the number of students decreases dramatically and that the scores in science and math are due to five students in Grade 12 math and four in Grade 12 science. In one case a Vietnamese female, one whose

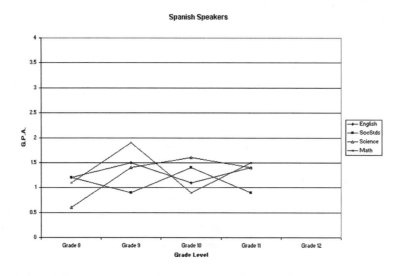

FIG. 6.8.   Grades for Spanish speakers in Grades 8 to 12.

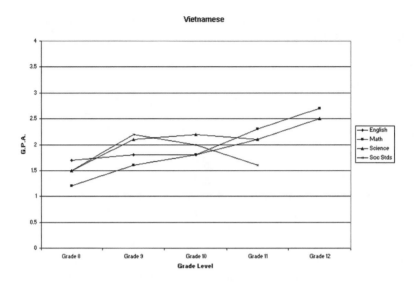

FIG. 6.9.   Grades for Vietnamese speakers in Grades 8 to 12.

family had entered as regular immigrants, had received nearly a perfect 4.00 average across the five grade levels. In all respects, she was an example of a resilient student, one who succeeds against great odds. None of the students in the sample took Grade 12 social studies. Again, these results suggest that as a group the Vietnamese speakers were educationally at risk in this English-only school system because so many of them disappeared between Grade 8 and Grade 12. Results for both the Vietnamese and Spanish speakers suggest strongly that the social studies curriculum should be reviewed because immigrant students appear to avoid taking such courses.

Immigrants from India spoke a number of different languages, but none large enough to form a reliable group across the grade levels. Figure 6.10, therefore, presents data categorized by country, India. Although the numbers enrolled across the grades are relatively stable compared to other groups, their grades do decline significantly. It is interesting to note that the largest decrease is in math grades. There appeared to be some differences in grade point average associated with language within this group of students, but the numbers were too small to be reliable.

These data show that students from India do less well in the examinable academic courses as they progress through secondary school. As fewer are enrolled in ESL classes, their grades decrease. They did progressively worse as they exited from ESL courses. In many respects, these findings are surprising because for many students in India the language of instruction in schools is English beginning at about Grade 4. However, the majority of the population of Indians that immigrate to British Columbia comes from

India

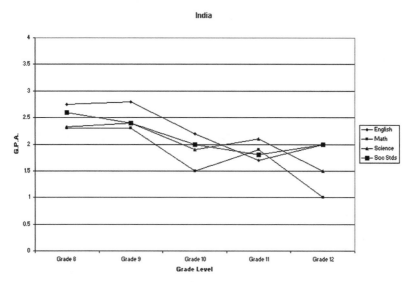

FIG. 6.10. Grades for students from India in Grades 8 to 12.

the Punjab. The Punjab is the "bread basket" of India. It is a major producer of wheat. Although Punjab residents represent only 10 to 15% of India's population, they comprise approximately 85% of Indian immigrants to British Columbia. In addition, although many indicate that Hindi is their first language, actually it was the language of instruction they encountered in primary school. Since the official language of India is Hindi, many from the Punjab preferred to call it their first language, although it was not. Because most of the immigrants from the Punjab come from a farming background, their views about teaching and learning and about school and schooling did not include it being as centrally important to their children's futures as other concerns. Gunderson (2001) observed that Punjabi farmers' views of teaching and learning were considerably different from the views of Canadian teachers. It seems clear that the English-only system failed to account for the needs, abilities, and backgrounds of these students. It is clear that as English support disappeared, students in this group did less well.

Students from the Philippines were another fairly large group. Like those from India, however, no one first language group was large enough to represent a stable group across the grades, so their scores were broken down by country and are shown in Figure 6.11. It is also important to note that the sample size for students from the Philippines decreased dramatically over the five grade levels. The significant dip in Grade 12 grades is associated with a significant decrease in the number of students who were enrolled in the examinable classes. The available data, unfortunately, do not allow one to ascertain whether they stayed in school but opted out of

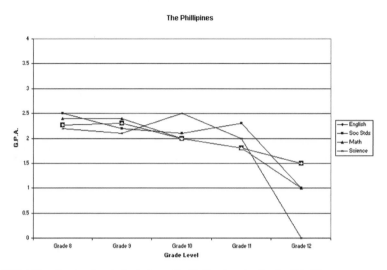

FIG. 6.11. Grades for students from the Philippines in Grades 8 to 12.

taking examinable classes or whether they dropped out or left school. Many of the teachers who were interviewed thought students from the Philippines were, in many respects, model students. They worked hard, they attended class, they attempted to do their homework, and they appeared to be "happy." It was not until the results of this study were revealed to teachers and administrators in the school district that teachers begin to remember that fewer and fewer students from the Philippines actually took examinable courses. This was particularly surprising to everyone because the language of instruction in the Philippines is usually English, except in isolated locations where English-speaking teachers are not available. The English-only school system was not meeting the needs of these students. It is clear that their academic, language, and social needs were not being met. Indeed, as the ESL net disappeared, so did students.

There is a similar pattern in the grade point averages for Korean-speaking students in the sample. Figure 6.12 shows the same extremely significant dip in grades in Grade 12, which were due to one student remaining in the sample. Many of the students from Korea reported that they had studied English before they moved to Canada. This seemed to have helped them succeed in school. It is also important to remember that a fairly high percentage of Korean students were from privileged backgrounds and had entered Canada as entrepreneurs. This status allowed their families to support them educationally. What is not known, however, is why there was such a sharp drop in the number of students in Grade 12. One could speculate that more affluent families found private alternatives. Indeed, the private schools in the city reported extremely long waiting lists, and Korean

Korean Speakers

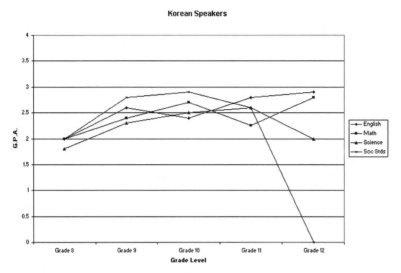

FIG. 6.12.   Grades for Korean speakers in Grades 8 to 12.

families were reported to be among those most interested in having their children attend them.

Figure 6.11 is different from Figure 6.12 in that the student failed to pass Grade 12 social studies rather than science.

SCHOOL ACHIEVEMENT DIFFERENCES

Finding that some groups of immigrant students received higher grade point averages than Canadian-born students was surprising. Some would say this finding is distressing. Finding that differences in achievement were associated with linguistic and national groups was also surprising. However, further analysis reveals that linguistic and national groups differ systematically in other ways. Mandarin speakers did not get better grades than Spanish speakers because of their language. They did not do better than other students because they had greater innate intelligence or aptitude for learning. Their higher level of achievement as measured by grade point averages appeared to be a result of a combination of factors.

The first systematic difference associated with linguistic groupings is socioeconomic. Because of the demographics of immigration to Canada during the 1990s, the Mandarin-speaking group was largely composed of socioeconomically advantaged students from Taiwan. They had the largest percentage of "entrepreneurial" class families (30.20%). Spanish speakers, on the other hand, were largely from refugee families. Cantonese speakers were predominantly from Hong Kong and were economically advantaged (17.30% entrepreneurs), but the distribution of socioeconomic categories was broader than Taiwan's. Beginning in 2000, the largest group of immigrants became those from the People's Republic of China. It will be fascinating to watch how this group, mostly Mandarin speakers, will fair compared to the Taiwanese students since they are from more diverse socioeconomic backgrounds. Figure 6.13 shows grades for refugee students as a group. Again, the difficulty is that not all refugees are from lower socioeconomic statuses. Indeed, there were a number of families with refugee status who were not economically disadvantaged. The overall percentage of advantaged refugees rose from Grade 8 to Grade 12 as the percentage of disadvantaged refugees decreased.

What is interesting is that socioeconomic status alone was not associated with school success. Figure 6.14 shows mean grades associated with students who entered the country as members of entrepreneurial families. They do quite well, but not as well as the Mandarin entrepreneurs shown earlier. Again, Mandarin entrepreneurs do better than the entrepreneur group as a whole for a number of interesting reasons, none of them having to do with intrinsic differences in aptitude. These differences are discussed in some detail later in this chapter when student interview results are described. The causal relationships associated with these amazing differences in achievement are complex. They are associated primarily with socioeconomic status and the alternatives families have to help their children succeed in school.

Differences in socioeconomic status are related to differences in secondary school achievement, but in complex ways. The advantages afforded to immigrants with money are various and they contribute significantly to their school success. Their success in an English-only environment is due to

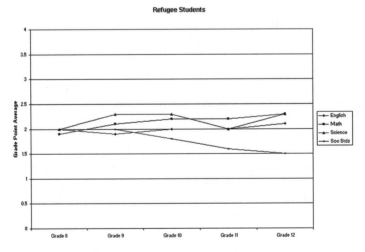

FIG. 6.13.　Grades for refugee students in Grades 8 to 12.

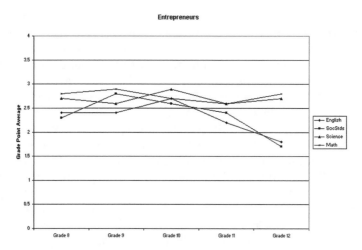

FIG. 6.14.   Grades for children of entrepreneurs in Grades 8 to 12.

a great extent to the many advantages provided by their socioeconomic status, but also to the way in which they use their economic advantages to provide support for their children. These advantages are discussed in detail later in this chapter. However, it is important to note that overall these students, even with considerable support, on the average fall below a C average in English. Indeed, there was a direct inverse relationship between their success in English classes and their participation in ESL classes. However, students and parents from this group were the most vocal in their negative views about ESL classes.

ESL Courses

Two alternative ESL support classes were available to students in the Vancouver School District at the secondary school level: ESL courses in which students spent the majority of the day in classes designed to support their English learning and their academic development, and English language classes designed to provide a period or two of English support per day. Students in ESL courses were integrated into mainstream courses such as physical education when their English proficiency permitted it.

Students in the sample spent, on the average, 3.60 (SD = 2.80) years in ESL classes. There were no significant differences in grade point average between students who spent 1, 2, or 3 years in ESL classes, except that their ESL grades were significantly lower than their academic grades. Indeed, across the board, grades in ESL classes were significantly lower than grades in the examinable classes. There was a small group of students who had been enrolled in ESL classes before they entered secondary school, some for as many as 7 years. Those who had spent 6 or 7 years in ESL classes and were still enrolled in academic classes in Grade 12 received significantly lower grades. Clarke (1997) investigated the performance of a small group of students, a small random sample from the OROC foundational corpus, and found that the students enrolled in ESL classes for more than 6 years appeared to have significant learning problems. Clarke's observations led the school district to develop a special program for students that focuses on their learning strengths. In 2001, based on the findings reported here, personnel from the school district began to develop programs specifically designed to encourage students from some of the identified "at risk" groups to remain in school. Many of the students interviewed were convinced that ESL courses were useless to them, that they got in the way of their preparation for the important academic courses they were required to pass in order to get into university. On the other hand, a number of immigrant students felt ESL courses were designed to help them learn and to survive in school and in society. It is clear, however, that as students exited the ESL program, their grades, particularly in English, fell (Fig. 6.15).

The populations in the courses across the five grade levels decreased in numbers significantly. However, they also varied in composition fairly significantly. Students in Grades 8 and 9 were mostly comprised of immigrants who had been in the country for a fairly short time; a very small minority consisted of students who had been in ESL in elementary school previous to high school and were experiencing difficulty in learning. This picture changed from Grade 8 to Grade 12, however. The number of students with difficulty increased, so that by Grade 12 they represented about 60% of the students in the courses in this database. The dip in grades in these courses that occurs during Grades 11 and 12 is due to the increasing number of stu-

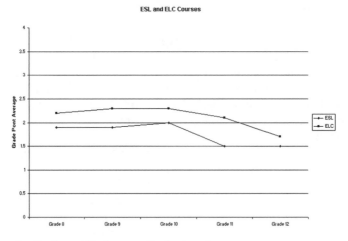

FIG. 6.15.   Grades in ESL classes in Grades 8 to 12.

dents who had difficulty learning English. The largest numbers of students taking ESL and ECL courses were in Grades 8, nine, and ten. The overall numbers begin to decrease in Grade 11 and are lowest in Grade 12.

Grades in ESL8 and ESL9 and ELC8 and ELC9 courses were related positively to students' grades in their academic course. Indeed, the ELC correlations were in the .40 to .50 range, whereas the ESL correlations were in the .30 to .40 range. The better students did in these courses at these two grade levels, the better they performed in their academic classes. This suggests that the ESL support was effective. However, too many students left ESL and ELC courses to be able compute such relationships for Grades 10, 11, and 12 ESL and ELC courses.

The results of these studies show that students from different groups have different achievement levels in the examinable classes. One could argue that the basic responsibility of a school system is to assure that students from different groups have equal opportunity to succeed. This does not appear to be occurring in this English-only system. Students' views of their lived lives, the curriculum, and the schools were recorded and analyzed. Their comments and observations speak eloquently to some of the underlying causes of the achievement discrepancies.

THE STUDENTS SPEAK

A random sample of 1,000 students from the OROC database was selected. Six hundred and eighteen were enrolled in the school district at the time of the study. Of these, 540 were enrolled in secondary schools. School principals were contacted and permission was obtained to contact students' parents and to interview students. Letters of consent written in appropriate languages were distributed. Four hundred and thirty signed letters were returned. In total, 407 interviews were conducted by four independent interviewers (five additional interviews were with native-English-speaking immigrants). Table 6.4 shows the breakdown of this sample by first language.

The reduction in numbers was due to such issues as student illnesses, no shows, and family moves. Interviews were conducted in all 18 senior secondary schools in the school district using the structured protocol described in chapter 2. Interviews were conducted in an open-ended fashion in which interviewers were free to extend discussions and ask questions to encourage students to elaborate on their answers. Interviews took place in empty classrooms, school libraries, conference rooms, and other available areas in the schools.

Living and Learning in Secondary Schools

Life in a western secondary school is patterned within the parameters of the situated culture of the school. As noted in chapter 2, culture is the ideas, cus-

TABLE 6.4
Breakdown of Random Sample of Students Interviewed

Language	Number	Percent	Corpus (%)
Cantonese	158	38.80%	36.60%
Mandarin	62	15.20%	15.60%
Punjabi	24	5.90%	2.20%
Spanish	23	5.70%	5.30%
Vietnamese	19	4.70%	7.90%
Tagalog	15	3.70%	4.40%
Korean	13	3.20%	2.40%
Japanese	12	2.90%	2.00%
Russian	9	2.20%	0.90%
Hindi	8	2.00%	1.30%
Polish	6	1.50%	1.70%
Ukranian	6	1.50%	0.10%
English	5[a]		
Croatian	5	1.20%	0.15%
Farsi	5	1.20%	0.50%
Hokien	3	0.70%	0.18%
Kurdish	3	0.70%	0.50%
Serbo-Croatian	3	0.70%	1.00%
Somali	3	0.70%	0.40%
Urdu	2	0.50%	0.20%
Afghani	2	0.50%	0.02%
Amharic	2	0.50%	0.01%
Cambodian	2	0.50%	0.10%
Bahasa	2	0.50%	0.10%
Bicolono	2	0.50%	0.04%
Fijian	2	0.50%	0.03%
Malay	2	0.50%	0.04%
Portuguese	2	0.50%	0.50%
Romanian	1	0.20%	0.60%
Tamil	1	0.20%	0.04%
Arabic	1	0.20%	0.04%
Bengali	1	0.20%	0.01%

Cebuano	1	0.20%	0.004%
German	1	0.20%	0.20%
Italian	1	0.20%	0.10%
Khmer	1	0.20%	0.04%
Tigrinia	1	0.20%	0.10%
Slovak	1	0.20%	0.10%
Swedish	1	0.20%	0.10%
Thai	1	0.20%	0.10%
Total	407 (412)		

^aEnglish speakers not included in total.

toms, language, arts, skills, and tools that generally characterize a given group of individuals in a given period of time. Secondary school cultures are multiple and complex. They consist, to some degree, of the expected behaviors prescribed by the curriculum guides, and to the multiple cultures within which students have membership. Students do not simply adopt the culture of the school or become bicultural; rather, they acquire and reject some features of the culture, retain and reject some features of their first cultures, adapt some features of first culture to second culture, and become socialized into a system that is uniquely individual, imbued with first- and second-cultural features, that is often, but not always, predictable. In many respects, this could be referred to as an individual "interculture." For immigrant students who are teenagers, learning a new school culture is made more difficult because they do so as human beings whose bodies are filled with the raging hormones of their metamorphosis from children to adults. They are challenged further by the crisis of their developing and changeable multiple identities. In many respects these students belonged to multiple cultures.

School culture constructs the parameters within which students behave, learn, perceive, value, seek friendships, and construct identities. In a very real sense school cultures determine a student's possibilities, how and with whom he or she may interact, for instance. The students in this study were frank and candid about their views of the school. The one feature that was surprising was that, with few exceptions, they were enthusiastic about telling their stories and did so with gusto, often talking well beyond the 40 minutes scheduled for interview sessions. Indeed, in a number of debriefing sessions interviewers likened interactions with students to therapy sessions because the students seemed so anxious to tell their stories and "get them off their minds." Only one student complained about the process. He was angry because it had been scheduled during a review session for one of his important provincial examinations.

One parent refused to allow his son to be involved in the research even after having signed a consent form because he thought it was a waste of time and would take the student away from his "important studies." On the other hand, a number of parents were enthusiastic about the research and spoke animatedly with the researcher about its goals and purposes. One father invited the researcher to his home for dinner to discuss the research and his children's participation. One Chinese-speaking parent volunteered to help the project improve its Chinese writing (the letter describing the research and the permission form). The protocols were reviewed several times, and student responses were recorded and categorized using QSR N5 (NUD*IST). Categories were refined and redeveloped as the protocols were being analyzed.

First and Second Languages

The relationships between first and second language and the effects of knowing different first languages on English were explored in the last chapter using traditional tests and observations. It was clear that there were cross-linguistic differences related to students' achievement as measured by standardized measures. These issues were also explored using different instruments and procedures and are presented here. Students were asked to report about issues related to their first languages. They were asked about how often, with whom, and for what purposes they used their L1 and English. They were asked to evaluate their own English skills: reading, writing, speaking, and listening. They were also asked specifically to comment about how they felt their L1s were useful or not useful in learning English. They were also asked to comment about their use of and ability to use their first languages.

About one-third (34.0%, 138) of the students were convinced that they communicated mostly in their first languages. These students also reported that they mostly used their first languages at home and with friends. About 40% indicated that they used their first and second languages about equally (163), whereas the remainder was convinced they communicated orally most often in English (106, 26.0%). Those who indicated that they had been in Canada the longest also tended to report that they communicated most often in English. Their views were that it took, on the average, about 4 to 6 years before they felt comfortable with their ability to communicate in English. They also reported that their use of language was mostly dictated by their circumstances; L1 was used at home and with friends, whereas English was used at school and in stores. The irony is that students indicated they tried to use English at school, but it was difficult because there were few native English speakers they felt comfortable enough to communicate with. About 45% of the students indicated that they served as translators or interpreters for their parents, usually their mothers, on the telephone or in stores, mostly in stores. A majority (69.0%, 282) reported that their parents thought their oral English ability was better than it actually was. There was an interesting interaction between length of residence (LOR) and students' views of what their parents thought about their English abilities. Overall, those who had been in the country for less than 2 years thought their parents' views of their English were that it was poor (Table 6.5).

Students were asked what language they believed they were strongest in for speaking, reading, and writing. About 75% responded they were strongest speaking their L1s, whereas about 70% indicated they were strongest in reading English and 90% said they were strongest in writing English. Students felt their first-language skills, except for their oral skills, had deteriorated.

Only students who had been in the country less than 2 years felt that their reading and writing in L1 was superior to their reading and writing of English. Indeed, the belief that L1 reading and writing skills had been lost was profound and widespread.

"I forgot how to read Chinese in two years" (male, Cantonese, 17 years).

"Sometimes I read comic books or magazines, nothing more" (female, Japanese, 15 years).

"I write to [my] uncle in China, but I am forgetting how to write Chinese" (female, Mandarin, 17 years).

The degree of loss was related to the time students had been in the country. Ironically, it appeared that only those students who had had a great deal of difficulty learning English and academic content viewed their L1 reading and writing skills as superior to their English skills. Students who had spent more than 5 years in ESL classes all reported that their L1 skills were superior to their English skills. It is unclear, however, whether or not their L1 skills were actually superior.

TABLE 6.5
Length of Residence—Use of L1 and L2

Length of Residence	L1 Mostly	L1–English (½–½)	English Mostly	
6+ Years	11	37	68	116
3–5 Years	29	121	32	182
1–2 Years	98	5	6	109
Total	138	163	106	407

BICS AS CALP

It became clear that students felt their English was less proficient than their parents thought it was. Parents, in fact, seemed to mistake their children's developing ability to communicate orally as an overall estimate of their ability to cope with the English language requirements of the schools. In essence, they assumed that basic interpersonal communicative skill (BICS) was an overall estimate of students' ability to communicate interpersonally and to cope with the language requirements of the school curriculum. It is clear from the data presented in the beginning of this chapter that this is not the case. Indeed, as the number of students enrolled in ESL classes declined from Grade 8 to 12, students' performance in English and social studies, academic subjects many believe require more language proficiency than subjects such as math and science, also declined. Many students and parents had negative views of ESL classes. It is likely that parents' negative views of their children's enrollment in ESL classes were because they thought their communicative ability in English meant they should be able to cope with academic courses.

> "They think my English is okay and I should get good grades, but it is not so good and I have trouble with subjects like socials" (male, Hindi, 15 years).

Writing in English was mentioned as the most difficult school task by nearly 100% of the students in the sample.

> "English is so hard, writing, like when I'm writing essay I have to think what words I know cuz I can only use the words I know. And poems, I don't know how to write poems even in Chinese. I really don't know how to write poems" (female, Cantonese, 17 years).

> "Things like humanities and socials are hard because you have to know a lot of English" (male, Korean, 15).

> "Social studies is so hard because you have to read a lot and do the stuff at the end of the chapter. It's really hard because I read really slow in English" (female, Cantonese, 16 years).

About 40% of the students opined that math and science were difficult, but for interesting language reasons:

> "Math and science are hard because we have to take lots of notes and if we don't then we can't memorize the facts for the test" (male, Mandarin, 15 years).

> "They always make you read these real hard questions, the English is hard, not the math, but you have to know the English before you can know the math question" (female, Cantonese, 18 years).

Students understood that the English required to communicate interpersonally was different from the English required to read and comprehend or to compose essays and assignments. Indeed, when asked, all students in the sample concluded that they preferred multiple-choice tests to tests requiring short essay answers.

> "I am better in multiple choice because if you don't even know the answer you can find out which one is the best answer" (female, Spanish, 17 years).

> "Multiple choice because if you finish a chapter they give you tests chapter by chapter and you can remember" (male, Tagalog, 14 years).

> "Multiple choice tests are the best cuz if you don't know an answer I have 1/5 or ¼ chance of getting it correct. With essays, if you're wrong you're wrong" (male, Cantonese, 16 years).

> "Multiple choice. You got a 50/50 chance of guessing, Should circle answers not use scanner cuz it takes too much time coloring in the bubbles" (male, Cantonese, 15 years).

One student responded thoughtfully to this item:

> "It depends on whether I studied or not, if I did then any kind of test is okay, if I did not, then multiple choice is best" (female, Mandarin, 17 years).

About 40% of the sample concluded that the test that was the least useful to them was the fill-in-the-answer test.

> "The fill in the missing word tests are the worst. They are a waste of time" (female, Cantonese, 17 years).

This response seems like affirmation of the negative view of cloze and cloze-like assessment measures noted by researchers (e.g., Bernhardt, 2000).

Does Knowing How to Read L1 Help to Learn English?

This question was asked explicitly, and students' responses were both thoughtful and insightful and often surprising. However, we asked the question within a series of questions concerning reading habits in L1 and L2 and students' homework practices. It was surprising to learn that students reported that their homework consumed on the average 2.90 hours per evening and as much as 7 hours an evening in one case and as much as 10 to 12 hours during the weekends (Table 6.6). There was some difficulty in coding these data because in some cases the student responded "three to four hours," and we opted to round down, so 3 to 4 hours was coded as 3 hours. The largest group reported they spent 3 (or 3 to 4) hours every day doing homework. What was surprising is that they also reported that they only read, on the average, about 10 minutes per day. This was perplexing at first.

TABLE 6.6
Hours of Homework per Day

Hours	
0	15, 3.70%
1	26, 6.40%
2	83, 20.00%
3	178, 72.40%
4	67, 16.50%
5	35, 8.60%
6	2, 0.50%
7	1, 0.250%

How was it possible to do, on the average, about 3 hours of homework a day and read 10 minutes or less per day? The answer was simple: Reading and studying were not considered to be equivalent terms. Many students considered "reading" to be something done for pleasure, such as reading a novel, a poem, or a comic book. This belief was most obvious in the case of Chinese students. Anderson and Gunderson (2001) found that culturally the difference between the notion of reading for pleasure and "reading" meaning studying is built into some languages. In their article titled "You Don't Read a Science Book, You Study It: An Exploration of Cultural Concepts of Reading," they demonstrated that the words used to represent reading in Chinese and reading to study are distinctly different. Anderson and Gunderson (2001) observed:

> Students were clear in their views of what constituted reading and what did not, and their views were surprising. They indicated that they "studied" about 4 hours a day, but only "read" on average 5 to 10 minutes a day. This was a mystery until the students explained that reading was something they did almost always for pleasure (involving comic books, magazines, or newspapers), and that what they did with schoolbooks was study. For these students, reading a social studies or science text —or any kind of academic book —was not reading, but studying. One tenth-grade student from Hong Kong reported that she "looked at the book and said the words out loud over and over again" until she could remember them. Several students stated that studying a textbook meant scanning the content to isolate items they thought would be on a test. (p. 4)

The relationship between L1 and L2 was explored with the question, "Do you believe that knowing how to read in L1 (your first language) helped you to learn to read in English?" If students answered "no," the follow-up question was, "Why not?" A response of "yes" was followed up with the question, "In what ways?" There were a variety of interesting and culturally based answers, and many were unexpected:

> "It doesn't really matter cuz every time you see a new word you have to memorize it no matter what language it is" (female, 17, Mandarin).

Most believed that knowing how to read a first language to some extent helped them with English (60%), but reasons varied in unexpected ways. It was predicted that students from some languages, languages with augmented Roman or Roman-related alphabets, would benefit. It was also predicted that students from Romance languages would benefit additionally because of the predictability of the sound–symbol relationships, but also from "cognates" they could recognize in print.

> "I never really thought about it, but I guess so. When I first started to read I would translate to Chinese characters so I guess it helped that way" (male, 17, Cantonese).

> "Chinese people have to learn a new alphabet, so when I think about it our alphabets are the same so it was probably easier for me" (male, Spanish, 17 years).

> "I read in Tagalog before coming to Canada. Yeah, some of the words are similar in English. I spoke a little American English in the Philippines, it's different from Canadian, but it helps" (female, Tagalog, 15 years).

> "Yes because most of the letters in Filipino are taken from English. So I had an advantage over the Chinese because it is of no use because they got characters. I've got a bit of an advantage over the Chinese students" (male, Tagalog, 16 years).

> "When I small my auntie, some people come to my home, teach me Vietnamese, but I don't learn much, only some numbers. I cannot read Vietnamese, only a little English" (male, Vietnamese, 14 years).

> "Maybe it help you pronounce words. Some say read a lot and you learn a lot, but I don't think so. You have to learn from direct experience" (male, Vietnamese, 17 years).

> " Yeah, cuz you go to the dictionary and look [up] the word and it tells what it mean in English" (male, Thai, 16 years).

> "No, definitely not cuz they are so different" (female, Cantonese, 15 years).

> "Yes, but I don't know" (male, Vietnamese, 16).

> "I kept up with my Chinese when I came here. Yes. If you read something in English and you don't understand, sometimes if you interpret it into Chinese it can help you understand" (female, Cantonese, 16).

> "Yeah, maybe. Like maybe I don't understand some vocabs and I look in the dictionary and I understand the Chinese" (male, Cantonese, 14 years).

"I think it's the same. No, cuz sometime I think reading in English and reading in Japanese is the same cuz sometimes I don't understand Japanese too" (female, Japanese, 14 years).

"No, not really because English has a different grammar and talking language is difficult. And we don't really know what it is when we have to read so slow in English" (female, Cantonese, 15 years).

"I read Korean first and at the same time there was this person in Korea who knew English so I learned from him" (male, Korean, 14 years).

"No, not much cuz the letters are different and the way you write is different and the way you spell is different and the way you read is different" (male, Kurdish, 15 years).

"No, not at all because Tamil is different. It's no help at all" (female, Tamil, 16 years).

"No help. Arabic go other way. No wrong spelling in Arabic. No words silent letter. English all time have words spell bad" (male, Arabic, 14 years).

Some indicated that they believed they had learned to read English first:

"I kind of learned to read in English before I learned to read in Tagalog. We use the same kind of alphabet. My parents taught me to read in English and then they kind of branched me off into Tagalog. English Immersion school in the Philippines only spoke Tagalog during the Filipino Studies block" (female, 16 years).

A number of individuals complained about the instruction they received and blamed it, to some degree, as the source of their difficulty learning to read English. A Spanish-speaking 15-year-old female noted, for instance:

"No cuz I had to learn the whole language. It was like I was a baby and I had to speak again. "

This was a surprising comment that reveals an interpretation of whole language that should not have been unexpected in older students. There was an undercurrent of dissatisfaction with the educational system that was evident in many of the responses to this item. This negative view was made quite clear in other items and is described and discussed later in this chapter.

About 20% of the responses suggested that the students held what could be called a psycholinguistic view of reading. They suggested in various ways that knowing how to read a L1 trained a reader to make predictions about what is read and this ability helped in learning to read English.

"Yes, I know words in a book make sense and when you know that it helps you because you try to make sense. Sometime it makes you have the wrong answer because you guess wrong" (female, Korean, 18 years).

"Really helps—especially the grammar like knowing past tense. If you know something begins in past tense then everything will be in past tense and this helps you" (female, Spanish, 14 years).

"Kinda, like you can sort of figure books, in Punjabi there is always story in book and English has stories. Stories are like same in English so you can know what will happen" (female, Punjabi, 14 years).

"Yeah, I think so. Cuz you have to know your first language well when you hear English you can compare your language to it or use some grammar or something from your first language" (female, Mandarin, 15 years).

The views of the 60% of the students who believed reading a first language helped in learning to read English broke down into interesting categories related to orthography. Students who had learned to read languages such as Arabic, Kurdish, and Tamil tended to view their L1s as basically unhelpful, whereas those who learned to read alphabetic languages tended to view experiences with their L1s as helpful, mostly because there were "phonics" connections that could be made. Readers of languages such as Chinese, Korean, and Japanese were divided in their beliefs. Many thought that reading L1 was helpful because it allowed them to access English through dictionaries, whereas many others simply rejected the notion that their L1s were of any help at all. Three individuals opined that learning to read a first language had actually interfered with learning to read English.

"Makes it difficult to learn English reading because they are so different. There's some new words I don't know and Chinese doesn't help me to learn them. I don't know. It's hard to say" (male, Cantonese, 14 years).

It is clear that students had opinions about the usefulness of L1 reading to them in learning to read English. It is also clear that they viewed their English proficiency as a factor that made their progress in academic classes very difficult.

Students' responses provided evidence that their difficulties in school were associated with their English proficiency. It is clear also that as the difficulty of their academic classes increased, they did less well, especially for those classes typically viewed as requiring a higher degree of proficiency, English and social studies, but this was also true for the sample of students who were born in Canada. Grades reported previously suggest that even for the immigrant groups that appear to do relatively well, their grades in such courses decreased in Grades 11 and 12. There was a dramatic increase in the number of students who disappeared from the sample in Grades 11 and 12.

If English is the key, then how do students view the ESL classes that were designed specifically to help them to become proficient enough in English to cope with academic courses in which the medium of instruction was English, the complex, difficult, academic language of the schools?

ESL Courses—Do They Help?

Three items explored this issue: Have ESL classes helped you to learn English; have ESL classes helped you with your course work; and what do you think about ESL classes (if negative what suggestions, if positive what would improve them for new students)? Responses to these items were often related to students' backgrounds, particularly their socioeconomic status, in surprising and interesting ways; in other cases they focused on motivation.

> "Well maybe it does. But I don't think learning English is your self problem. If you want to improve your English you can. Even if the ESL program is perfect, if you don't want to improve your English you can't" (female, Mandarin, 15 years).

Responses generally differed among students in ways related to socioeconomic status. Those in lower socioeconomic groups viewed their ESL courses in a generally positive fashion. They were enthusiastic about learning English and about the contributions their ESL courses were making to them. The following was an essay written by one of the students.

> When I knew I was put in the ESL class, I was very disappointed. In the first week, I was totally upset and was in a very low mood because I didn't have many friends, and all things around me were unfamiliar. Besides, I didn't want to be distinct from others. I wanted to be a regular student. However, after the first day of integration, the master of hell told me where heaven was. As I first stepped in the regular classroom, I could easily feel the coldness and bitterness in the air. Everyone was indifferent to me. I was standing in front of the classroom like a fool waiting for the teacher to come. I was so embarrassed that I wanted to cry out and run back to the ESL class. As time went by, I made more friends in the ESL class and we studied together like brothers and sisters. We cared for and helped each other. But I remain an unconcerned visitor in the regular class after six months. I talk to no one. So now I am travelling between heaven and hell, back and forth. (female, Cantonese—Hong Kong, 15 years; also in Gunderson, 2000, p. 687)

About 60% of the students reported that their goal was to go on to college or a university, whereas about 30% wished to find good jobs. About 10% did not know what they wished to do. Generally positive statements included such views as:

ESL forces students to read.

They are fun.

They help student learn to write.

Friends are in the same classes.

Students are all alike.

The teachers are nice.

ESL courses give extra time to focus on English.

They help you learn.

About 95% of the students in high socioeconomic status schools reported that they wished to continue on to college or university. Indeed, many specified their academic goals, such as to become a doctor, an engineer, or a lawyer. Their views of ESL courses were quite negative. Indeed, they viewed them as interfering with their preparation for university education. They noted:

Students speak their own language instead of English.

Student don't learn anything useful in ESL classes.

Students miss classes while attending ESL.

Students don't speak English.

ESL classes repeat stuff students have learned.

ESL classes don't help you to learn to read.

Too many students in each class.

ESL classes take up too much time.

ESL classes segregate students.

ESL classes make students second-class.

They believed ESL classes were for second-class students, those who had little chance to go on to university. They were concerned that ESL classes made students feel inferior, "like those who are crippled or blind." One 16-year-old male Polish student noted, "People make fun of me because I was in ESL." A 14-year-old Mandarin-speaking male suggested that "ESL classes would be better if there were some Chinese teachers" (Gunderson, 2000, p. 699).

"I think it's not that useful for Chinese students because when they go to ESL classes they hang around with kids whose English is not that good. If you were put into a regular class they talk in English and it's better" (male, Cantonese, 14 years).

Students who were positive about ESL classes were especially positive in the cases in which the ESL classes involved academic content.

"I think they were o.k. They were fun. We did a project where English and science were mixed. That was helpful cuz we learned about both. We also learned about computers in that class" (male, Hindi, 17 years).

> "They were the best when they teach you words you need to know in other classes like science" (male, Vietnamese, 16 years).

Those who had negative views often suggested that ESL classes would be better if, in fact, they did include content material.

> "No, they didn't help. You can't understand because it's in English. I think they should have writing every day, write in all subjects. They don't teach you writing except one day a week. They need to teach you paragraphs and how to write stuff about science and socials. It's so hard cuz all our paragraphs are so full of mistakes" (male, Vietnamese, 17 years).

One respondent noted:

> "It was no help at all, but I went to reading circle for a few years at a neighborhood house where they had a program on Thursdays and we read books, lots of books" (male, Mandarin, 14 years).

A number of students thought ESL courses had helped them with English, but not with their course work.

> "A little bit, yeah. They give you grammar and punctuation and all that. And how to spell, but they are no help at all with other course work" (male, Tagalog, 14 years).

One male Korean Grade 12 student, who had been in the country for 2 years, made an interesting series of comments.

> Yes, ESL help a lot. Just to get used to the Canadian school system. But I guess the teachers don't make the students work. The students are ESL so what do they know? They (ESL classes) don't help much with other courses. I spend my grade ten in _____ school, so they taught me grade 8 math. The next years when I transferred to _____ they taught me grade ten math, I just skipped one year, that was really tough. I just felt the students were over confident about their English. They just went out of ESL classes, they want in regular classes. When they didn't do well they just blame the teachers. The teachers don't push them much so they think it's easier, but actually it's not because they have to think independently.

ESL classes appeared to be superior to many students when they included academic content and when they introduced students to content that was academic. Many students were convinced that ESL classes served a valuable social function.

> ESL classes are not so good in teaching English because everyone doesn't speak English and they are at different levels. It's hard for the teacher. The first day I went to regular class I cried all afternoon and I went back to my ESL teacher. I think ESL helped you in a way to adjust. I think if you take a new per-

son and throw them in regular they will fail everything, but I think the ESL program needs to be changed because some students already know English and they didn't learn anything. I don't think they should do away with the whole program, but I think it should be half-half then the kids can talk with more people in English. The ESL program needs to be more regular. Some kids look down on you if you're ESL, so it's hard to make friends. (female, Cantonese, 16 years)

Another interesting point of view concerning the usefulness of ESL classes was, "No, they don't really help in your English but in other courses they make them simpler, easier to understand" (female, Cantonese, 14 years). As shown earlier, students' grades in ESL courses were lower than their grades in academic classes. This is a finding that is contrary to the widely held view that ESL courses are easy.

In ESL classes it's a lot easier. The teachers explain it to you paragraph by paragraph. I think the ESL classes are good for students who come from other countries and just start school here. But sometime some friend of mine are in grade 11/12, but they can't graduate because they are in ESL so they have to go to summer school. ESL takes too much time away from important classes. (male, Punjabi, 16 years)

Students in lower socioeconomic areas suggested that ESL classes were helpful. They complimented the teachers as being concerned and interested in their students' welfare, whereas just halfway across the city students and parents complained bitterly that ESL classes were roadblocks to students' success and they interfered with the learning of examinable courses.

It was, admittedly, difficult to categorize answers because many did not neatly fall into one category and not another. Often, a single response had elements that represented features of responses in different categories. Overall, the decision was made to include a response in a particular category based on the "overall" sentiment of the statement. In general, there was a fair degree of reliability across raters in determining overall sentiment, but only in about 80% of the cases. It is best, therefore, to consider these findings as fuzzy. The statement earlier, for instance, was viewed as a positive statement about ESL classes, although it does include features that are also in the negative ESL category. Some views were impossible to categorize as positive or negative attitudes toward ESL courses because they contained an equal number of strong statements in both perspectives.

English—What Helped?

One underlying, perhaps hidden purpose for conducting research with ESL students is to discover a way or ways to improve their language learning. This was the reason for asking students about what had helped them to learn English and what they would recommend as good strategies for new immigrants. It was surprising that 60% of the students reported that what worked best was television. Nearly 100% of the students indicated that what they would recommend to new immigrants is to communicate with native English speakers. And overwhelmingly they also reported that the difficulty they found was that it was not possible, for various reasons, to speak or interact with native English speakers. The irony is that students in an English-only school system found it difficult to interact with native English speakers. A majority reported that it was impossible to talk to English speakers or to hear English spoken.

> "There are too many Chinese" (male, Cantonese, 15 years).

This student's comment appears racist, but it is not. He complained that all he heard in the hallways and on the schoolyard was Cantonese and that this did not allow him to hear and to practice English. He was concerned that he would never learn "proper English" because he was unable to hear it. He also reported that a number of his Cantonese-speaking friends and their families had moved out of the school district so that they might be "expose to more English." Another commented:

> "There are too many Chinese students in _____. It is hard to practice English. I am happy that I arrived six years ago when there weren't so many Chinese" (male, Cantonese, 18 years).

Students suggested that after-school activities were vital for immigrants, both to learn English and to become acquainted with Canadian students, although a majority also responded that they did not participate in them for various reasons.

> "I can't play P.E. because I can't wear shorts, it's wrong, girls can't stay after school either cuz it's not our beliefs, we have to go home and stay away from boys, Canadian boys specially, and the girls. Girls and boys, teenagers, shouldn't mix, it's bad. Canadian girls have no morals they are bad" (female, Punjabi, 16 years).

Bilingual programs were not viewed as answers to students' learning difficulties. In fact, almost 90% responded that bilingual classes would not help them and that they wished to learn academic material in English because their Grade 12 examinations were in English. About 60% also commented that it would be helpful if they could receive help with their work from someone who knew their first language who could translate a difficult word or explain a difficult concept to them in L1.

> "It would be good if we can ask for explanations in Chinese, especially the difficult things" (female, Mandarin, 17 years).

"You get trouble from teachers if we speak our language. It would be good for people to be able to ask somebody for a word in English in your class. Just one word might help and what's wrong with that? But not whole class in Polish" (male, Polish, 17 years).

Speaking to English speakers was viewed as a good approach and was recommended as appropriate for new students. The biggest problem, however, was that students found it nearly impossible to speak with English speakers. Bilingual programs, on the other hand, were not viewed as being important, although students did feel that some L1 assistance would be helpful.

"It would be good to have teachers who could speak Tagalog cuz they could help you with a real hard word" (female, Tagalog, 17 years).

These findings convinced members of the school district to explore the establishment of a system incorporating what they called "bilingual buddies," who were fellow students who could help translate vocabulary on a limited basis to students having difficulty understanding English.

COMPARING SCHOOLS AND SCHOOL SYSTEMS

Students were asked to compare the schools and the instruction they experienced in their home countries with the experiences they had and were having in Canada. They were also asked what advice they would give new immigrant students. Some of the comments cited here may also be found in Gunderson (2000), who provided a snapshot view of some of the following observations. Students were clear in their views, particularly those who were advantaged economically. Both they and their parents believed that the teaching and learning going on in schools were inferior. It appeared from their comments that most, especially those from countries such as Hong Kong and Taiwan, held a view of teaching and learning that would be best categorized as "bottom-up" (see chap. 2).

"In Hong Kong all we do, memorize, memorize, memorize, day and night, 5 hours homework every day. In Vancouver as we do is think, think, think, nothing more. It's hard to think when the teacher doesn't tell you what to do" (female, Cantonese, 18 years; Gunderson, 2000, p.695).

"In Hong Kong it's harder, they got more stuff and it's harder. You have to know stuff for a test, and they give you the stuff so you don't have to guess" (male, Cantonese, 14 years).

"In China the teacher always gives you homework. School starts at 7 a.m. and you have to get up at 6:00 a.m. You have to memorize and be ready for the exams" (male, Mandarin, 15 years).

"The schools in Canada have no rules. Student can just do what they want and this is not a good thing. The school is too loose. It seems like the students is not studying, they are playing in the classrooms and they do not respect the teachers and they can even swear" (female, Cantonese, 16 years).

"You can't learn nothing if teacher doesn't give it" (male, Russian, 16 years).

"Schools in Canada are too fast. Usually they give you too much homework that they don't talk about. Teachers give many homeworks and the teaching method is just give a formula and then give the homework. They usually can go through one to two chapters at a time and they don't give no help, just tell us to read and learn. That's not right" (female, Cantonese, 14 years).

"Schools in Korea are like more strict. They give you more homework, lots more homework and they go to school on Saturday" (male, Korean, 14 years).

There were very few positive comments about the curriculum. However, there were many observations about difficult conditions in home countries compared to conditions in Canada, with comments such as:

"Schools in Canada are more free. I remember the school in China. We weren't allowed to move at all, just sit all day and listen" (male, Mandarin, 14 years).

"Teachers can hit you in Vietnam and no one care" (male, Vietnamese, 15 years).

"Teachers in Russia don't care, they don't even speak my real language, we have to use school language, Russian, different. They don't know your names and they think we are not so good because we are not real Russian" (male, Russian [Ukrainian], 15 years).

"In Canada school is better than in China. In China it sometimes very dirty and always sick. Here better than in China" (female, Mandarin, 17 years).

"Schools in Canada are better than in the Philippines. They are harder than the schools in the Philippines. Here you get one teacher for one subject. In the Philippines they mostly talk English and sometimes you can't communicate with them cuz you're not good at English" (male, Tagalog, 14 years).

"School is a little bit slower here than over there. They are pretty advanced over there. You have to write. And they don't teach you poetry over there and here they do" (female, Spanish, 15 years).

"Well let's see, I don't know. Well schools here are more fun because well, I don't know, the school in Hong Kong you just sit and listen to the teacher and go home and do your homework. Here they have more projects. You can talk in class. There are more field trips here" (female, Cantonese, 16 years).

"You don't have any freedom in Taiwan. You can't have too long hair, no ear rings, you have to wear uniforms, the same shoes, socks, you have to do lots of homework and you have tests every day" (male, Mandarin, 16 years).

There was strong evidence, however, that differences in achievement, as noted previously, were associated with differences in socioeconomic status.

SOCIOECONOMICS, CLASS, AND IDENTITIES

The most obvious feature of life in a secondary school is groups. Students are nearly always found in groups, standing in groups, eating in groups, talking in groups, and moving in groups. One finds support and affirmation from group membership (Norton, 2000). Indeed, one's sense of identity and self-worth are often related to membership in a particular group. Russian males, for instance, were easily identified in the present study by their greeting rituals involving others in groups. In general, groups were formed on the basis of first language and "ethnicity." Mandarin-speaking students hung out with other Mandarin-speaking students. Group membership seldom included students who were linguistically different. One Korean immigrant in a school with a large Cantonese-speaking population had an interesting viewpoint that supported this observation:

> "I learned English because the only ones who were friendly to me were Canadian students. The Chinese don't talk to me and they don't want to be friends because I am a Korean and I don't speak Chinese and they don't speak English, just Chinese" (male, Korean, 17 years).

Teachers viewed students' proclivity for forming groups on the basis of language and ethnicity as a sign of "standoffishness." They were convinced that immigrant students should "mix" with students from different cultural groups to help them become integrated into Canadian society. Basically, mixing did not occur in anything but an isolated manner. Students' own perceptions of themselves as members of certain groups reinforced their differences. In effect, their group membership was a process of socialization and they reinforced their own views of what was Canadian (not them) and what was not Canadian (them). Students felt that they should integrate, but for many reasons they were unable to do so, except with students who were like them.

It became clear as responses were assessed that there were basic differences in students' views about school, schooling, teaching and learning, and their developing, but often confused, personal and cultural identities that were related to where the students' schools were located, their socioeconomic status, and their first cultures. The schools involved in the study were located in different neighborhoods and they differed from each other socioeconomically. Unlike some jurisdictions, this school district was not involved in a busing program. As a result, school populations reflected the diversity of the neighborhoods in which they were located, not the overall population. An immigrant's socioeconomic status, in many respects, is a determining factor in where his or her family opts to live. In many respects, students' socioeconomic status was mirrored in populations of the schools they attended. Many refugee families were placed in government-supported housing, often low-cost monthly rental hotels. On the other hand, it was not unusual for real estate agents to accompany some economically advantaged new immigrants to OROC in order to identify "desirable" schools and to identify possible homes for them to purchase. Signs asking individuals not to use cellular telephones in OROC had to be posted because individuals from places like Hong Kong and Taiwan used them on a regular basis, so much so that they became a nuisance. There was a fairly persistent rumor that desirable schools were known and had been identified in the press in places such as Hong Kong and Taipei. Parents knew the names of schools that had reputations for being good. One such school was known because it had an International Baccalaureate (IB) program designed for high-achieving students, a French immersion program, and a good view of a nearby island community that allegedly looks like a dragon's eye (a lucky sign) on a map of the region (parental informant, Cantonese, Hong Kong). The IB was a highly desired program. In addition, a number of school sites had "mini schools" that were designed for academically gifted students. Mini schools were part of established secondary schools, but their students were taught in separate, segregated classrooms and the curriculum was designed for gifted students.

Teenagers often experience difficulties with life in general because of the many pressures they face. Such difficulties are often exacerbated by life in a secondary school. It is even more complex and difficult for immigrant students. However, the life of refugees as students may be the most difficult of all.

The Refugees

One could likely classify refugees into about three or four distinctly different groups, and there would be little similarity in members among groups, except for their shared classification as refugees. The difficulty with categories is that they are the inventions of human beings, inventions that are designed to help humans organize and make sense of the world. They turn out to be relative rather than absolute.

Those who were classified as refugees during the 1990s in Vancouver differed in some important ways. There were refugees from wealthy backgrounds who left their home countries for "political" reasons, reasons that varied considerably. A number of refugees from Iran were wealthy refugees. There were refugees who were from advantaged backgrounds in their home countries, but who suffered considerable losses as a result of political changes before they entered Canada as "economically poor, but well-educated refugees." Many of these individuals had been doctors, lawyers, or engineers, but had to leave their home countries for various political reasons. A number of refugees could be best described as "economic refugees" because they traveled to Canada to seek better economic opportunity. British Columbia saw the illegal arrival of several hundred individuals from China who claimed refugee status. It appears, though, that they had entered Canada to seek better economic conditions. Indeed, many indicated that they actually wanted to enter the United States for economic reasons, but it was easier to get into Canada first. Some entered Canada as refugees because they were from war-torn areas of the world where they faced persecution for religious or political reasons. These individuals were often economically disadvantaged in their home countries. There are also a few refugees who did not neatly fit into any of these subcategories. A few entered Canada as tourists, liked the country, decided they wished to stay, and claimed refugee status in order to do so. A number of individuals come to Canada to claim refugee status because of the financial support they will receive from Canada's federal government. Canada is well known in the United States for the individuals who left to avoid the Vietnam War in the 1960s. There are thousands of these who still live in Canada.

It is not possible to identify with any degree of reliability which of these categories students were actually members of, for various, obvious reasons. However, from their parents' comments about their reasons for entering Canada made during their OROC interviews, it appears that about 10% were "advantaged" refugees, about 20% were "well-educated, but economically disadvantaged," and most of the remainder (about 70%) were refugees from strife and war-torn situations. Canadian immigration regulations do not allow individuals to claim refugee status for economic reasons. Because this is so, the number of actual economic refugees is unknown, as to make such a claim would have resulted in denial of the claimants' requests for refugee status.

Overall, students from refugee backgrounds were unhappy, even those who were relieved to be away from the life-threatening war-torn conditions in their home countries. It was difficult to judge whether or not their unhappiness was due to poor conditions for them in their new country, the angst most teenagers everywhere seem to experience, the loss of their friends and acquaintances, their inability to "fit in" to a new community in general (into a new school community specifically), the difficulty learning a second language, the difficulty learning in a second language, the impact of earlier traumas on their lives, or a combination of some or all of these.

The Russians

Russian immigrants interviewed for this study were very verbal about their unhappiness with life and held great disregard for Canada, for the city, for the schools, for the neighborhood in which they lived, and for the way in which they felt they were regarded by teachers, administrators, and others. The graffiti in Figure 6.16 was photographed by the author near the school in which the interviews with Russian refugees were conducted. A portion of the photograph was published in an academic journal (Gunderson, 2000), but the editors chose to edit it so that the left side of the graffiti, perhaps the most interesting part, seen in this figure, was missing. There was a concentration of Russian and Ukrainian refugee families who had been located in a "monthly hotel" in a district of Vancouver that has one of the highest population densities in the country, mostly in high-rise apartments and condominiums. The population includes a large number of retired people and gay men. There are a number of facilities designed for retired individuals, facilities such as government-sponsored retirement apartments and senior centers. There are also a number of gay business establishments and government-sponsored social services for gays and lesbians. Additionally, this is the location of approximately 150 private ESL schools that cater mostly to Korean and Japanese students in their early twenties. They live in the same neighborhood as the Russians. One result of the presence of thousands of young Japanese and Korean students was the proliferation of Japanese and Korean restaurants, grocery stores, and video shops. The high number of retired people (mostly women), gay men, and foreign students (who appeared to be dedicated to hedonism, including skateboarding through traffic, dying hair, piercing multiple body parts, and drinking copious amounts of beer and sake) was all associated to a degree with the way in which Russian students viewed themselves, their lives, and their identities.

One cannot be sure about the identity of the author or authors of these graffiti, but this one in Russian has some interesting clues about the person who wrote it. This Russian graffiti was translated by Daria Semenov of the Language and Literacy Education Department at the University of British

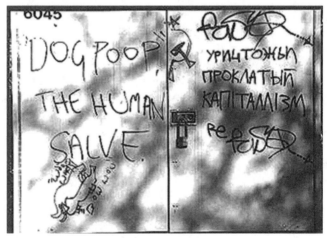

FIG. 6.16.   Russian graffiti near one of the secondary school sites. Photograph by L. Gunderson

Columbia. She indicates that it is an adaptation of an old Soviet slogan reading, "Let's (we will) demolish (destroy) damned (cursed) capitalism." However, Daria, a graduate student from Russia, was convinced that the author was not a native Russian speaker since there are some interesting errors in the graffiti that suggests he or she was a Russian as a second language speaker/writer. First, there are some non-Russian letters, there are some errors in Russian letters, and there is the use of the Roman letter "i". Daria suggested the author may have been from the Ukraine or was possibly a Croatian speaker. Students in the Ukraine in the past most often attended school in which the language of instruction was Russian. The writing on the left-hand side of the photograph may or may not have been written by the same individual. However, they both appeared on the same day and were washed off by a custodian on the same day. The content of the left portion, the one written in English, may be related to the view expressed by one of the students interviewed.

> "They put us in this part where dogs are better than Russian are. We poor house, crowded. All around you see people with dogs, walk dogs. Dogs better than Russians. They put us with old blue ladies, lots of fags, everyone walking around with bags of dog sh—" (male, Russian, 18 years). [2]

These comments reveal a number of statements that need to be contextualized to be understood. The author was the individual who conducted this interview. It seemed clear that the term "blue ladies" referred to women of maturity who dyed their hair. During one of the meetings held between research assistants and the researcher, this interpretation was discussed and was rejected outright by a female research assistant some 20 years younger than the researcher. She explained that hair dyes were no longer as primitive as they had been 20 or so years before the study and that women did not get blue hair as they did at one time (in the 1960s and 1970s) by dying their gray hair. The researcher visited the school and sought out the informant and asked him what he meant by blue ladies. He was told that it referred to the old women in the blue room. The secondary school in question had a public library, an ice-skating rink, a community center, a gym, a district police station, and a center for seniors located in the same building. The blue room was the area in which seniors participated in activities organized for them such as cards. They were, therefore, the blue ladies. There were also blue men, but considerably fewer than blue women.

Because the neighborhood was densely populated and there was a strictly enforced city ordinance to control animal waste, those who walked their dogs, and there were hundreds of them, also carried "Teddy Bags,"

---

[2] A similar version, but with parts removed by an editor, appears in Gunderson, 2000, p. 697.

plastic bags available at free public dispensers, to dispose of their pets'
waste. To be truthful, during early morning and late afternoon hours, it
does appear that a large percentage of the dog walkers are "blue ladies" or
gay men, but this is the researcher's impression that may, in fact, not represent reality. However, the students interviewed in this study were deeply
insulted by having to live with individuals they considered to be inferior
members of society. They viewed their relocation to the neighborhood by
immigration services after their entry into Canada as an indication of the
complete disregard they believed Canadians had for them. These individuals also felt inferior to and resented the affluence of the visiting Korean and
Japanese ESL students. They also expressed a deep resentment for the way
they believed they were perceived.

> "Everybody think we are Russian mafia, they don't talk to us. I live in refugee
> hotel with family. I can not to learning so good the English because we are be-
> ing all Russians in hotel" (male, Russian, 18 years; Gunderson, 2000, p. 696).

The approved interview protocol and procedures for this study did not
include items that explored the political backgrounds of students' families.
No information was available, nor was it permissible to ask students, about
such issues. Interviews with teachers in the school suggested that at least
some of the Russian refugees may have been less than innocent victims.
One teacher, for instance (male, teaching English and physical education),
reported that 3 days after Mother Theresa died, one of the Russian students
had been murdered and was reported in the newspaper to have been a drug
dealer. This teacher reported that a shrine was built in the main entrance of
the school to honor Mother Theresa, including candles, flowers, and cards,
and a similar shrine was built behind the school for the slain student. It also
included candles, flowers, and cards. This teacher thought that the two
shrines and their locations represented an interesting metaphor for the
Russian students' lives in school and in society.

Gunderson (2000), in reference to the student quoted earlier, stated:

> Socioeconomic issues troubled this particular individual. He reported about
> his first visit to a Safeway supermarket in Toronto, his family's port of entry.
> The abundance was overwhelming. Their first stop was the meat display and
> their Canadian-government subsistence check was about to be spent entirely
> on chicken and beef, a shopping-cart full. "But our family's friend asking why
> so much meat and we tell her because next week there will being none." Each
> of us has a view of the world dictated, in part, by our experiences. Children of
> abundance, those who have never had to consider the possibility of empty su-
> permarket shelves, think differently about life than those, like Russian refu-
> gees, who know times of both plenty and scarcity. The transcendence of
> possibility the western child assumes does not exist in the minds of many ref-
> ugee children. They know the good times and the bad, mostly the bad. All of

the refugees spoke of their surprise at the availability of the abundance they associated with the privilege of the rich. (pp. 696–697)

The dropout rate for Russian refugees was extremely high. Indeed, few graduated. It was not clear, from the research conducted for this study, what happened to Russian students after they left school. The number of Russians in the random sample who took examinable courses was very low, only one, and she took none of the Grade 12 courses. Russians did not do well in this English-only school system. However, it is not clear that their difficulties with school and schooling were necessarily and wholly a result of difficulty with learning English or the content of the classes. The student included in the random sample did not flunk any of the courses she attempted. Indeed, her grades ranged from 2.0 (Social Studies 10, English 11) to 3.0 (Science 10), but she did not take any of the Grade 12 examinable courses. It was not apparent whether this was her choice, to not take Grade 12 courses, or whether she left the school system. It does seem that those who were interviewed believed their difficulties were due to their standing in society, at least to the way they believed that others perceived it. It seems that their problems, to a great degree, were beyond the capabilities of teachers and administrators to address. It was also inferred from their comments, their observations, and their attitudes that they had been "advantaged" in some way in their home countries. One indicated, "In Russia we live not poor, we big house, big car, driver" (male, Russian, 18 years). However, there is no good evidence to indicate whether this statement represented reality or fantasy. Russian males were seen in the school, often in dark clothing, speaking to each other (males only) in what appeared to be a kind of ritualized and formal handshake ceremony. Russian students had a great deal of difficulty, and their disappearance from the school system does not auger well for their potential for success in Canadian society. Life was equally difficult for other refugee students.

Spanish-Speaking Students

Spanish-speaking immigrants were from Guatemala, Honduras, El Salvador, Nicaragua, Mexico, Peru, Chile, Venezuela, the United States, Colombia, Costa Rica, Argentina, Panama, Uruguay, and Spain. Forty percent (40.00%) were from refugee families, primarily from Guatemala, Honduras, El Salvador, and Nicaragua. The secondary schools their children attended were generally located in lower socioeconomic areas of the city. As noted previously, only one Spanish-speaking student in the random sample, a male refugee from Honduras, had completed an examinable course. He attempted and completed English 12, but with a grade of D (1.0). The record for this group of students reveals that they were educationally at risk.

"There are bad people from Honduras, they come and sell drugs and steal and make everything hard for you. Everybody think we are all dealers, on the streets. Canadians don't like us, Chinese don't like us, police don't like us, teachers don't like us, no one like us, they think we all bad" (female, Spanish, 16 years).

The difficulty for Spanish-speaking immigrants in general was that the local news media featured a number of articles detailing the cases of a number of well-known Honduran men, mostly in their late twenties and early thirties, who were illegally in the country and were, in fact, involved in the sale of drugs and in prostitution. Indeed, a number of them were known for being deported and for returning repeatedly to reoffend. This promulgated the widely accepted view that Spanish speakers were all involved in crime. Spanish-speaking students in the sample were of the view that ESL courses were not very good because there were too many Chinese speakers and they could not practice English or ask other Spanish speakers for help in English.

"Too much Chinese. ESL class are fill with Chinese. Teachers no good, not stop Chinese talk. No help Spanish. I not passing nothing" (male, Spanish, 14 years).

Unlike entrepreneurial families (see later discussion), Spanish speakers, primarily refugees, did not have the financial base to hire tutors. Overall, their children did not succeed in school. It seems fairly apparent that Spanish-speaking students found the English-only curriculum difficult, and their "identities" were formed, in part, from their failure at school and by being identified with being part of a group considered by many in the community to be criminal.

The author was introduced to a 20-year-old male from El Salvador who had just entered Canada as an independent refugee, while the author was visiting a secondary school to interview other immigrant students. The individual had extremely limited English proficiency and was attempting to enroll in the secondary school to learn English. Twenty-year-olds are not allowed to enroll in classes in secondary school and he was advised to seek programs designed for adults, early evening programs run by the school district itself or programs for adults at the local two-year community college. He had been asked for his passport, and he did not seem to have one, or some other kind of identification, but he did not seem to have any. As the school counselor tried to find out more about the young man, he became more frustrated and finally left in anger; looking back at the small group of individuals trying to "help" him he shouted something, but no one understood what he said.

Spanish-speaking refugees, individuals primarily from Central America, were educationally and socially at risk in the English-only school system and in society in general. It is doubtful that any school system has the resources to deal with the multiple difficulties that confronted this particular group of Spanish-speaking students in this school district. These students' sense of identity was formed by the negative views of teachers, their fellow students, and the media. Ironically, the percentage of students who were refugees rose from Grade 8 to Grade 12, whereas the percentage who were regular immigrants fell dramatically. It seems that the Spanish-speaking families who could afford to do so left the school district. A number of experienced teachers suggested that such families moved to suburban locations where housing was more affordable and which had the added advantage of being away from the difficulties associated with poor areas of a large urban city.

The Vietnamese

Fifty-three percent (53.40%) of the Vietnamese students in the large sample entered Canada as refugees. As noted earlier, members of the refugee category differed quite significantly from one another. This phenomenon appeared especially true for the Vietnamese. Some of the Vietnamese were "boat people" from Hong Kong, where they had been confined to camps and had grown up in circumstances that were harsh. A number of teachers reported that these students were difficult because they appeared to trust no one, had little school experience, and seemed to have developed individual survival skills that were not necessarily "socially acceptable" in Canadian society (female, ESL teacher). Some Vietnamese students were from Malaysia, Indonesia, or the Philippines, where they had landed with their families as "boat people." Many had suffered unbelievable hardships in their journeys to Canada. A number reported traumatic stories about their experiences with pirates, their confinement in refugee camps, and their brushes with violence and death. Other Vietnamese refugees were the sons and daughters of important government officials, professional people, and officers in the armed forces. Their parents' difficulty was that they had the expertise and education to do technical jobs, but not the English skills to pass the required qualifying examinations.

One student argued that the "boat people" were victims of racism, that they were expelled from Vietnam because they were ethnically Chinese, individuals who were hated by those who were ethnically Vietnamese because they tended to be more successful economically. A number of Vietnamese refugees did, in fact, report that they also spoke Chinese (15.00% Cantonese). Twenty-five percent (25.70%) came from Hong Kong and 28.10% reported they had attended refugee schools.

Vietnamese students remained in ESL classes longer on the average than did students from other immigrant groups. Their teachers reported that they appeared to have more difficulty learning English than did students from other immigrant groups. It was evident that Vietnamese students had difficulty in school. It was clear that there were complex sociocultural, socioeconomic, and social-emotional reasons for their difficulty. It also seems that basic differences between English and Vietnamese may have also caused some difficulties for them.

Vietnamese speakers find it difficult to learn English for various reasons (Honey, 1987). Honey (1987) notes,"Because their mother tongue has no inflections, differentiates words by tone, and makes great use of syntax and particles for grammatical purposes, Vietnamese find a language like English, which is so dissimilar to their own, very difficult to learn" (p. 238).

A difficult task for a Vietnamese speaker is related to tone. Vietnamese has six tones. In addition, there is a linguistic feature called voice onset time, which makes the language even more complex. Gunderson (1979) developed a description of Burmese phonemes, a language related to Vietnamese, that has both tonal and voice-onset features. In Burmese the word "ma" has five different meanings, depending on the voice onset of the initial bilabial nasal and the tone of the word. When one produces the bilabial nasal /m/ as in "ma," one normally begins the voicing immediately. However, in Burmese, depending on the intended meaning of the word, the initial portion of the consonant can be voiceless, a short stream of air. Combined with this feature, one can change the meaning by changing the tone. Vietnamese has six tones: high rising, high level, low falling, fall rise, high creaky, and low creaky (cf. Honey, 1987). Creaky voice, by the way, refers to a type of phonation (the production of a speech sound) in which the sound is changed by "mucus" on the vocal chords (Ohala, 1978). Potentially one could produce 12 different words that differed across these features.

Vietnamese has 11 pure vowels and many diphthongs and triphthongs. Vietnamese learners often have difficulty understanding the speech of two different English speakers because they perceive differences in pitch and accent as differences in meaning, even if the two speakers say precisely the same thing. Many of the native English-speaking teachers in this study interpreted Vietnamese speakers' high tones as a feature of age. That is, mature Vietnamese second-language speakers "sounded very young" to their teachers. It seems likely that Vietnamese difficulties in and with school are associated with a number of complex variables, including physical and emotional trauma, that likely also include significant differences between their first language and English. The number of Vietnamese students who appeared to have difficulty in school was on the average higher than for other immigrant groups. The Grade 11 and 12 ESL classes had a disproportionately high percentage of Vietnamese students.

"The white kids are big and loud like gorillas. You have to get out of the way because they so big. They think they own school because they are born here.

> They are so, so loud you can't be a friends with them cuz they don't talk, they scream. They are so rude" (male, Vietnamese, 15 years; Gunderson, 2000, p. 697).

A number of students reported what they viewed as incidents of racism and discrimination. One Grade 9 student reported that he had been kept in after school to talk to his social studies teacher and was asked if he was involved in drugs. His mother was asked to come to school to talk about his problems. On the whole, Vietnamese students appeared to suffer greatly, not only from their lives at school, but from their lives in general in society.

> "ESL students work so hard. Even if you do really well you just get an ordinary job. They have no future, that's why so many drop out. Kids have to work to make enough money for comfortable life, no, not even comfortable life. In school there's gangs, there's drugs, oh, it's horrible thing and school's so small, it's unhealthy. I have a few cousins, they all drop out. There's no future so what's the point? You pay extra to go to better class. Money is so important. Most parents can't afford it" (female, Vietnam, 17 years).

Like the Spanish speakers, Vietnamese students also faced the added difficulty of being members of a group often identified in the media in negative ways. The news media, on a fairly regular basis, reported on criminal activities related to "Vietnamese gangs." Their difficulty with English, their difficulty with examinable courses, their difficulty fitting into secondary schools, all resulted in a very high drop out rate. Indeed, at about Grade 10, the number of Vietnamese students who disappeared from the sample was dramatic. Concerned individuals in the school district, on the basis of the data revealed by this study, established a program to begin in the 2001/2002 school year to try to foster and encourage students to remain in school. The program was developed to focus on interest and motivation, rather than on academics. The difficulties faced by the Vietnamese students in this school district are complex. It is not clear that the school system, by itself, has the resources to adequately address the problems.

Iraq and Iran

Ninety-five percent of the students from Iraq and Iran were refugees. By Grade 12, there were no students from Iraq or Iran in the sample who were taking examinable courses. Students' grades in Grades 8 and 9 were significantly higher than their Grades in 10 and 11. Overall averages for this group varied from .333 (SD = .60) for Grade 10 social studies to 2.80 (SD = .30) for Grade 8 science. Students from Iraq had all suffered emotional and or physical trauma, especially the Kurds, whereas students from Iran were from families that appeared well educated who had left their homeland for political reasons. Students from Iran disappeared from the sample at a faster rate than the Iraqis. Teachers reported that the students from Iran had mostly moved to a suburb where there was an enclave of financially advantaged families from Iran, whereas the Kurds and Iraqis appeared to simply disappear. One of the success stories most talked about in the local press was the refugee from Iran (mentioned in chap. 1) who had sold his extremely successful chain of electronics stories for $400,000,000 (Jamieson & Lazarak, 2001). This successful refugee, however, was an economically advantaged refugee. The Kurds in this study were not from such backgrounds.

> "I'm Kurd, Iraq. No one know (?), no one. Here, many India people, think we being India. Here Chinee people, think India. No one know I not India" (male, Kurdish, 14 years).

This individual suffered from isolation because he felt others thought he was from India and did not choose to become friendly with him. He was also isolated because there were only two other individuals, according to his report, in the whole school who could speak his first language. The difficult irony was that the ESL classes he found himself in were filled with students who mostly spoke a language foreign to him and to Canada, not English.

> "Too much Chinee talk. Too much Chinee people. No English. Bad class, teacher no good, not stop Chinee talk" (male, Kurdish, 14 years).

Secondary students seek out others who share the same language or cultural heritage to help them identify with a group, to help develop their own identities. The difficulty for students like the Kurds is their inability to establish friendships with other students who share similar backgrounds, their inability to establish friendships with other immigrant students, and their inability to establish friendships with native English-speaking Canadians. In essence they are isolated socially, linguistically, and culturally.

> "I spend two years with no friends, no one. I spend two years not talking, anyone. I go school, I go home, I talk only my mother, my brother. Best friend United States. Cry, all time, cry. being sick, all time, sick, stomach hurt, head hurt, heart hurt, all time, bad dream, all time, all time" (female, Kurdish, 16 years).

It seems clear that these students were isolated by their language, by their small numbers, and by their inability to communicate. One concluded that he would be better off if he didn't look Indian.

The Africans and the Europeans

One of the surprising results of the sample selected for purposes of the interviews was that there were few refugees from Europe or Africa. All of the

European refugees had entered Canada as displaced people as a result of difficulties related to armed conflicts, and the pattern was the same for most of those from Africa.

The refugees interviewed for this study were, at best, pessimistic about their life possibilities. Identity and one's feeling of self-worth are constructed through a sense of how one understands his or her relationships within and to the world. Identity, to a great extent, helps to determine or to map out an individual's possibilities within the world. Students from entrepreneurial families also faced significant issues related to their developing sense of identity.

The Entrepreneurs

It seems that children of entrepreneurs, individuals who on the average do fairly well in school, should be happy, but their comments suggested that they were, in fact, far from being totally content. Their reasons for being unhappy were considerably different from those expressed by refugee students. The nine most frequent countries of origin for entrepreneurs (3,261 total) were Hong Kong (44.00%), Taiwan (28.00%), Korea (7.10%), Japan (5.70%), China (3.80%), the United States (1.70%), Malaysia (1.10%), Macau (0.80%), and the Philippines (0.60%).

Because the databases are large, surprises regularly arise. One of the most intriguing was that among the 36 immigrants from Malaysia from entrepreneurial families, none reported that Malay was his or her first language. They reported first languages including Mandarin (38.90%), English (16.70%), Hakka (16.70%), Kheh (11.10%), Cantonese (7.30%), Foochow (2.80%), Fukien (2.80%), and Hokkien (2.80%). It seems likely in this case that Kheh is actually Ke, another name for Hakka spoken in Malaysia (see http://www.ethnologue.com/show_language.asp?code=HAK).

In the large entry database the following, in rank order, were the first languages reported by immigrants from Malaysia: Cantonese (15.40%), Mandarin (15.40%), Hakka (14.00%), English (15.50%), Vietnamese (7.00%), Hokkien (5.90%), Malay (4.30%), Kheh (3.20%), Foochow (2.70%), Tamil (2.70%), Hainanese (1.60%), Hockchew (1.10%), Fukien (0.50%), Henghua (0.50%), Kmer (0.50%), Tagalog (0.50%). It is significant that the majority of immigrants from Malaysia are not Malay speakers. Since Malaysia was a landing place for many "boat people," such languages as Vietnamese were expected. It would seem, however, that the loss of non -Malay-speaking entrepreneurs suggests some underlying discontent on their part. One adult school worker spoke of "bumiputra," the Malaysian version of affirmative action that was designed to increase the percentage of ethnic Malays in professional positions. He suggested this was one reason many ethnic Chinese were leaving Malaysia.

It is significant, in addition, that no students from the People's Republic of China, Russia, or Europe who were entrepreneurs were included in the small interview sample of 407 students. It is significant that no entrepreneurs from these countries were included in the sample of students who took Grade 12 examinable courses. Indeed, overall the number of entrepreneurs who took examinable courses fell from Grade 8 to Grade 12, although, as noted previously, their overall percentage as a group rose in Grade 12.

The Astronauts and the Hong Kong Bungalows

Entrepreneurs too received some less than positive press during the 1990s. There were a number of incidents in which immigrant families created news by demolishing existing old, large "character homes" to build extremely large houses, often huge by Canadian standards. A number of newspaper articles spoke of their multiple kitchens and 20 bedrooms. One family from Hong Kong created controversy by having two 300-year-old cedar trees removed from their property. Newspaper stories often spoke about the astronauts and their families. The term *astronaut* was used as a metaphor to represent the parents who brought their families to Canada, but continued their business affairs in Asia, commuting between work and their Canadian homes, but spending more time out of Canada than in. Children were often left home alone to take care of themselves between their parents' trips. By policy, the Vancouver school district came to insist that parents had to sign documents identifying "legal guardians" for students whose parents did not reside in Canada. There was a series of stories about the difficulties that these teenage immigrant children got into as a result of taking care of themselves, including a number of high-profile automobile accidents.

Students in this group complained a great deal about schools and schooling in Canada. The students from Hong Kong, Taiwan, and Malaysia believed that they were not being given a good education and teachers were not doing their duty. In many respects, they had a skills-based view of teaching and learning, a very bottom-up view of learning. Gunderson (2001), Anderson and Gunderson (1997), and Gunderson and Anderson (2003) concluded that there were serious differences in the views related to teaching and learning between teachers and students and between teachers and parents. Entrepreneurial parents generally viewed learning the way they viewed their business efforts. A teacher, in their view, is responsible for teaching students the many pieces of knowledge, somewhat like products, that they needed to pass a test. The student's responsibility, in this view, is to memorize (acquire) all of the knowledge the teachers deliver. A measure of a student's success and of the teacher's job is the number of items the student gets correct on an examination. Gunderson (2001) developed the material shown in Table 6.7 based on his study of elementary students and their teachers' and parents' views of teaching and learning.

The Chinese secondary school students and their parents in the present study viewed teaching and learning differently than many of their teachers did. The secondary school curriculum for the examinable courses is focused on the creation of thinking, critical learners. As Gunderson (2001) notes, this is a view that is, in effect, a cultural view. Parents of elementary school students were also critical of this view. Indeed, Li (2006) described the difficulties occurring between immigrant parents and their children's teachers because of differences in views of teaching and learning. Secondary school parents were also critical, but they did not appear to take as aggressive a role in the matter as did parents of the elementary students Li studied. They did, however, complain bitterly about the teaching going on in their children's classrooms, as did their children.

> "We waste too much time in school. Too much time not working. Teachers are too lazy they don't tell you what to do" (male, Cantonese, 15 years).

About 90% of the students from Hong Kong and Taiwan felt that the schools were not living up to their expectations and that teachers were not "giving" them the knowledge they needed to succeed in getting into a university. Entrepreneurs were convinced that teachers had the "product" (knowledge), and their task, one they were paid to do, was to make certain the students were given the knowledge. This is a product-oriented view of learning. Indeed, students from Hong Kong and Taiwan, but especially those from entrepreneurial families, were convinced that knowledge was a commodity, one composed of a corpus of facts and operations, that should be transmitted to students. Doing homework was considered evidence that students were actively attempting to master the knowledge given to them by teachers. Finally, a grade was viewed as evidence that students had mastered a set of skills.

In addition to this view, entrepreneurs had some unique comments to make about their lives in school.

> "There aren't enough parking spaces at school" (male, Mandarin, 18 years).

> "The labs are better equipped in Canada, but the teachers don't show us what to do with them" (female, Cantonese, 16 years).

The most interesting interview involved a 16-year-old Cantonese-speaking female from Hong Kong who made her views about Canada (probably her parents' views) quite clear.

> "Canada is really stupid because it builds big beautiful super highways but only let's you go 50 K an hour. That's a waste of money. They waste money on immigrants. They give tax money for immigrants to stay in Canada and all they are doing is taking advantage of Canada. It's not good use of tax. Canada people have to get smart, not waste money on people who don't work."

TABLE 6.7
A Comparison of Teacher and Parental Beliefs About Teaching and Learning
(Gunderson, 2001)

Teachers	Parents
Teaching should be learner-centered	The teacher is the source of knowledge and should not be questioned
Process is more important than product	Correctness of form is important
Meaningful language is intact language	Learning should focus on skills
Active learning is essential so students should contribute to discussions and activities	Students should be told what to learn. It's the teacher who should talk.
Learning should be meaningful	Learning should involve memorizing
Speaking, listening, reading, writing, and watching are integrated, mutually reinforcing language activities	Learning the pieces of language is important A focus on grammar is especially important
The aesthetics of language are fundamental Language is functional	Language is a series of skills to be learned in order
The learning of content and the learning of language are inseparable	Contents represents facts that should be memorized
Learning to read and learning to write involve the learning of process	Learning to read and write means learning phonics, spelling, and how to write.
Error correction does not encourage language acquisition	Errors should be corrected and students should be aware of their mistakes
Invented spelling should be encouraged	Poor spelling represents poor learning
Critical reading and writing are basic	Students should work on material given to them by the teacher
Students should ask questions	The teacher is the source of knowledge and should not be questioned
Students should explore and attempt to solve problems	The teacher should show students how to solve problems
Workbooks are mindless make-work activities	The number of correct items is used to judge students' learning
Skills are learned through interaction with good literature not through explicit teaching	Important skills are learned through explicit teaching and rote memorization
Assessment and evaluation should be holistic	Assessment should focus on how many items a student has learned
Problem solving should be deductive, learning should be exploratory	Problem solving should be taught and students should learn it through induction

Note. From "Different cultural views of whole language," (p. 252), by L. Gunderson, 2001. In S. Boran and B. Comber (Eds.), *Critiquing whole language and classroom inquiry*. Urbana, IL: National Council of Teachers of English. Copyright © 2001 by National Council of Teachers of English. Reprinted with permission.

A majority of students from entrepreneurial families (75%) stated that they were not doing very well in school. However, rather than finding fault in themselves as many of the other students in the study did, they faulted the teachers, the curriculum, and the differences in teaching and learning they found in Canada for their difficulties. An interesting finding was that every entrepreneurial student interviewed had at least one tutor; many had as many as three or four. Tutors were normally university students, most of whom were members of the student body of the author's university. English and math tutors were the most widely hired. Teachers reported that they believed many of the tutors actually did students' homework for them, particularly their writing assignments.

The author was able to speak with a number of tutors, and, interestingly, all of the research assistants involved in the study and the author himself were asked for names and contact information for university students who would be good tutors. Graduate-level students in math, science, and English were the preferred kinds of tutors. One Mandarin-speaking math tutor from Shanghai was a doctoral student in statistics who mainly tutored math and science, but could also tutor English. He indicated that he tutored 15 different Mandarin-speaking secondary students and had done so for about 6 years. He also reported that he had become close enough to several of the families for whom he worked that he had traveled as the children's companion with them, including on an Alaska cruise. For many of his clients he served as tutor over their children's entire secondary school experiences. He interacted with school personnel on behalf of families and students, and for the astronauts he monitored children's activities while their parents were out of the country. He reported that he felt he served as a surrogate father for the students he tutored. Indeed, it was standard practice for him to attend student–teacher conferences on behalf of the parents of the students he tutored. This particular tutor stated that he thought he would make tutoring a career, rather than statistics, because it paid very well and he was able to make significant contributions to the social development of young Mandarin-speaking students. He also admitted quite frankly that he was successful because his students received good grades on their assignment and that he, in fact, did the major amount of work on many of them, especially English assignments.

It is significant that, even with the help of tutors, entrepreneurs found their studies difficult and their grades on the average dropped in Grades 11 and 12. It is also significant that they viewed ESL classes as obstacles to their academic development rather than as assistances and got out of them as quickly as possible. Their parents also viewed ESL classes negatively and thought that they were wastes of time and energy. This group of students held strongly to the view that the only positive outcome of secondary school was their acceptance into a good university, one that would lead them to become a medical doctor, a lawyer, a scientist, or someone with a master of business administration degree. This was the strongly held view of their parents. ESL courses got in the way of their goals because it kept them, they thought, off track in learning what was needed to pass the provincial examinations in the examinable courses. Most were also convinced that because their children were communicatively competent and had studied English in Taiwan and Hong Kong, ESL classes were redundant and useless. They could not conceive of the idea that their children's English was at a level where it was difficult for them to learn their academic subjects. It was convenient to accuse the system of being at fault. The interesting finding is that students who did well in ESL tended to do well in their academic courses. One could conclude that ESL courses actually helped students succeed in academic courses, but the evidence is purely circumstantial.

Their children did succeed. They did so because of their culturally related view of the importance of education, because of the strong support they received from tutors, because of their parents' unrelenting drive to have them succeed in school, and because of their strong work ethic and their willingness to spend long hours working on school-related tasks. They were not more intelligent than other immigrants, but their success was a result of drive, cultural values related to education, hard work, and the financial support to enable them to have the resources to help them in their studies. All of these features "worked" for them. Some entrepreneurs did not succeed as well, in spite of the economic advantages available to them.

The Struggling Entrepreneurs

Not all of the entrepreneurs, of course, were as successful as many of the Mandarin-speaking group and not all of the Mandarin-speaking entrepreneurs were highly successful. In Grade 12 English, for instance, 65.50% of the students received a grade of C or less. In Grade 8 English, the overall means were 1.50 for students from China, 2.00 for Brunei, 2.00 for Japan, 2.30 for Korea, 2.50 for Hong Kong, and 2.80 for Taiwan. It is not easy to succeed in a school system where the language of instruction is different from the home language of a student. Unfortunately, there were no interviews with individuals we could identify as being in this group.

Regular Immigrants

This immigration classification has the widest distribution of backgrounds, languages, and countries in the large database. The one thing they appeared to share in common, however, was that their parents had to have been very patient and determined to enter Canada. The immigration process they endured was long, involved, and often tedious. It is also clear that as a result of Canada's immigration point system they were, to a degree, advantaged in that they tended to be from the trades, or from white-collar or professional occupations. Canada's policy for entry as an immigrant is quite clear. It states:

> Independent immigrants are selected for the knowledge, skills and experience needed in Canada's labour market. Check the information and applications kits available on-line to see if you might qualify. (http://www.cic.gc.ca/english/immigr/guide-ce.html#sheet1)

Potential immigrants are granted points for different background characteristics. It is clear that Canadian policy is to seek individuals—and a premium is given to youth and education—who have the potential to contribute to society, and in particular to the business community. Regular immigrants were, in fact, selected to be "special" in ways determined by Canada's immigration policy. In many respects, Canada's policy appears to seek the most educated individuals within the age categories most likely to be able to contribute over time to Canada. One view of such a policy is that it seeks to attract the "cream of the crop" or to create a "brain drain" of educated individuals.

There were students from 118 different countries in this category, and the 11 most frequent countries were Hong Kong (30.40%), Taiwan (13.60%), the Philippines (8.30%), Vietnam (8.10%), the People's Republic of China (7.60%), India (7.30%), Korea (2.80%), El Salvador (2.20%), Poland (1.50%), Fiji (1.50%), and Malaysia (1.40%). The 10 most frequent languages out of 106 separate languages were Cantonese (40.00%), Mandarin (15.80%), Vietnamese (7.00%), Tagalog (6.90%), Spanish (4.80%), Punjabi (4.10%), Korean (2.60%), English (2.20%), Polish (1.80%), and Hindi (1.70%).

African countries in this group included Ethiopia, Ghana, Egypt, South Africa, Kenya, Zaire, Tanzania, Uganda, Zimbabwe, Nigeria, Morocco, Zambia, Togo, Lesotho, Rwanda, and Mozambique. There were surprisingly few students from Africa in the study observing grade point averages who took examinable courses. In English, grades were English 8, 2.20 (1.00), English 9, 1.90 (1.00), English 10, 2.20 (1.00), English 11, 2.50 (0.50), and English 12, 3.00 (00), where the zero standard deviation resulted from one student remaining in Grade 12 English. Math grades were: Math 8, 1.30 (1.50), Math 9, 2.20 (1.40), Math 10, 1.90 (1.00), Math 11, 1.50 (0.60), and Math 12, none. Science grades were: Science 8, 2.30 (0.35), Science 9, 2.60 (0.90), Science 10, 2.30 (0.50), Science 11, 1.10 (1.00), and none in Grade 12. Social studies grades included: Social Studies 8, 2.0 (0.80), Social Studies 9, 2.10 (0.90), Social Studies 10, 2.60 (0.50), Social Studies 11, 2.00 (0.80), and none in Social Studies 12. Six students from Africa were included in the interview sample of 407. They tended not to answer questions as fully and freely as other students, and they appeared fairly content with school and schooling in Canada.

As a group these students from Africa seemed mostly to miss their friends and relatives and felt alone and isolated. There are few African Canadians in the school district and few immigrants from Africa, so students in this group represented a very small group.

> "It was hard to make new friends. All my good friends are in Somalia. I don't know anyone in _____ school who is from my country" (male, Somali, 16 years).

The students in this group also felt that schools and schooling in Canada were superior to those in their home countries. They also felt that their progress in school was slow. A number thought that school would be better for them if it were conducted in French. These students were also convinced that French actually helped them in learning English.

There were a number of other interesting results, such as the existence of a fairly large group of immigrants from the United Arab Emirates (UAE) who were originally from India. This particular immigration vector was a result of Indian citizens who worked in the United Arab Emirates, and the experience provided them the points they needed to enter Canada. An interesting finding of the study was that there was a fairly well established immigration service run by Canadian lawyers of Indian descent catering to Indians working in the UAE.

The views expressed by these students were extremely varied and seemed related to their neighborhoods (a broad indicator of socioeconomic status), their school backgrounds, and their country of origin. This group of students, although it was the largest, appeared to have fewer complaints about the schools and about Canada in general than did the refugees and the entrepreneurs. On the whole, although they appeared to feel alone and isolated, they did seem somewhat more content and happy with their schools than the entrepreneurs and the refugees. However, they also appeared, in a sense, lost. They seemed to be confused about who they were, about their identities. They seemed to want to become "Canadian teenagers," but felt that for various reasons they were unable to do so and probably never would be able to do so.

ESL STUDENTS, EXAMINABLE COURSES, AND SCHOOL RANKINGS

There is a lamentable inclination across North America to "grade" students and their schools by how they perform on standardized examinations. In British Columbia, schools are graded and ranked by students' performance on the examinable courses by the Fraser Institute (2000; see http://www.fraserinstitute.ca/publications/studies/education/report_card/2000/bc/tables/vancouver.html). Teachers appear to abandon the planned curriculum each year, especially the Grade 12 teachers, to help their students prepare for the Grade 12 examinations. Students' lived lives are focused on the examinations, and all other school activities appear to cease for a time. Schools in British Columbia are ranked by the results of the examination. In 2001 they varied from 1 to 271. What these rankings do not show, however, are some underlying relationships that are meaningful in interpreting what these results mean (Table 6.8).

There is a relatively robust relationship between a school's ranking on the provincial examinations as calculated by the Fraser Institute and the school's overall percentage of ESL students ($r = .74$): the higher the percentage of ESL students, the lower the ranking. The socioeconomic status estimates (high, low, mid) of the schools are based on an interpretation of the Canadian Government's Postal Code assessments of neighborhood incomes (Statistics Canada, 2001; http://www.statcan.ca/english/IPS/Data/13C0015.htm). If one considers the schools in terms of percentage of ESL students, socioeconomic status, disappearance rate, size, and first cultures, students' rankings in the provincial examinations become even more problematic. The difficulty is that statistical comparisons,

TABLE 6.8
Ranking of secondary schools by ESL and Fraser rankings

School	% ESL	BC Rank	Enroll	Grade 12	Percentage	Parents' Education
High A	14%	8	1,521	287	18.90%	16.00
High B	18%	3	427	80	18.70%	17.40
High C	28%	34	989	N/A	N/A	16.00
High D	28%	68	1,112	239	21.50%	17.00
Mid E	30%	104	1,844	313	17.00%	12.70
High F	31%	6	1,308	273	20.90%	16.60
Low G	32%	179	523	N/A	N/A	N/A
High H	37%	8	1,292	282	21.80%	16.10
High I	44%	22	1,999	421	21.10%	14.70
Mid J	50%	45	1,605	383	23.90%	14.90
Mid K	52%	45	2,032	368	18.10%	13.40
Low L	53%	115	970	160	16.50%	12.20
Low M	53%	233	1,414	223	15.80%	12.40
Low N	55%	250	1,220	219	18.00%	13.00
Low O	56%	166	1,196	185	15.50%	12.60
Low P	56%	166	1,861	315	16.90%	12.30
Low Q	75%	241	1,412	204	14.40%	12.40
Low R	85%	239	1,423	233	16.40%	12.80

in this case, cannot be made, because the socioeconomic indicator is school based rather than individually based. Therefore, the variance for individual schools is 0.

The highest in the Fraser Institute rankings in the school district was school B. It is a small school located on the campus of the largest university in British Columbia. Its students are primarily daughters and sons of university professors and graduate students. Parental average in education is 17.40 years, a postgraduate level. This school has the advantage of being small and fairly homogeneous. In addition, students are from families in which education is valued.

School A, known as the "whitest" of the schools in the district, is a large school surrounded by older single-family residences. Its residents are mostly professional people. It has a large French immersion program. Secondary school G was located in a high-density, high-rise neighborhood. It enrolled a large number of First Nations students, and its disappearance rate was the highest of the schools in the study. It had the disadvantages of being small and having a very transient school population. Secondary schools E, L, M, N, O, P, Q, and R enrolled most of the refugee students in the district, whereas schools A, C, D, F, and H had the majority of entrepreneurs. Common sense says that schools are different from one another, but common sense does not provide a clue about how profoundly different they actually are. A student's potential for success is determined, to some degree, by his or her cultural background, his or her family's socioeconomic status, his or her first language and literacy background, and his or her school and its unique character, itself determined in some way by the characteristics of the student's neighborhood. It seems, however, that English-only programs are difficult for second-language students and that as the support of ESL programs is lost, students have even more difficulty succeeding. The most difficult finding for this researcher was that the neighborhood a school was in had fairly high predictive power in identifying who would be admitted to university.

PREDICTING HIGH SCHOOL SUCCESS

These studies were designed to seek out the predictors of success in secondary schools. To a great extent, the studies have been successful. Another goal was to explore the predictive relationships among the assessment measures administered at OROC and students' success in schools as measured by grade point average in the examinable secondary-school subjects: English, math, science, and social studies. The thousands of possible correlations were computed and were generally very low. Another difficulty with these data was that the number of students was lowered very significantly. So, for instance, 7,026 students in the database were administered the CELT. However, by Grade 12 only 162 in the random sample of 5,000 had taken Science 12 courses and had been administered the CELT. This resulted in a correlation of .24. It is important to remember that this is an exploratory study. As such, the following results should be considered as fuzzy or tentative. The following are correlations of interest. It is acknowledged, however, that they are not robust. They may, however, suggest trends that should be explored further.

The overwhelming majority of correlations were essentially zero. For instance, the relationship between first production of single words and grade point average in English 12 was $r = .03$ (137). The relationships among English, math, science, and social studies and factors such as serious illness, allergies, special medicine, concerns about health, hearing tested, vision tested, and previous visit to the dentist were in the range of $r = .09$ to $r = .27$.

There were weak relationships between Woodcock Comprehension scores and grade point averages in English 8 (.32, 144), 9 (.35, 160), 10 (.28, 125), and 11 (.28, 117). There were somewhat more robust relationships among these scores for bilingual students. The number of individuals who had been administered the Woodcock and subsequently took English 12 was only 17, so this correlation is not reported. Correlations between Woodcock and social studies were: .28 (143), .20 (161), .34 (129), and .32 (81). There were less than 50 who had taken Social Studies 12 and the Woodcock. Correlations with Math grades were .20 (226), .22 (212) and, .21 (145). There were less than 50 who had taken Math 12 and the Woodcock. Science correlations were .29 (181), .27 (180), .34 (146), and .09 (80). There were less than 50 in Grade 12. Correlations among Gap scores and grade point averages ranged from .15 to .36. CELT and grade point averages had low correlations varying from .05 to .27. Interestingly, grade point averages across subjects and across grades showed robust relationships ranging from $r = .55$ to $r = .72$. Correlations among the oral language measures and grades were very low, ranging from .05 to .20. In general, these relationships were very weak. The best predictor of grades was first-language composition. They were: English 8, .53; 9, .28; 10, 22; and 11, .37; Social Studies 8, .38; 9, .22; 10, .18; and 11, .37; Math 8, .33; 9, .33; 10, .29; and 11, .44; and Science 8, .47; 9, .16; 10, .16; and 11, .50. Results for Grade 12 subjects are not included because the sample sizes were all less than 50. Indeed, some were empty cells because on entry students had not written a composition in their first language. This is an interesting finding, however, because L1 compositions was not shown to be associated with any significant variance in reading scores in chapter 5. Overall, the disappointing feature of the results was the great reduction in the number of students taking examinable courses.

As noted in chapter 4, students were also administered a math examination. Correlations between math and English grades were: in Grade 8, .12 (220); 9, .12 (158); 10, .01 (141); 11, .20 (131); and 12, .20 (43). There were

low-level correlations between these scores and social studies grades, ranging from .02 to .20; with science, ranging from .18 to .33 (Science 12, $n = 63$);
and with math, ranging from .10 to .33 (Math 12, $n = 95$). Correlations
among grades and the Curriculum Associate Math scores were: English 8,
.25 (129); 9, .32 (162); 10, .25 (132); 11, .24 (67); and 12, .03 (20); Social Studies
8, .21 (131); 9, .32 (157); 10, .39 (121); 11, .25 (86); and 12 (not sufficient numbers); Science 8, .30 (165); 9, .32 (168); 10, .28 (143); 11, .44 (101); and 12, .49
(27); Math 8, .43 (194); 9, .42 (190); 10, .33 (141); 11, .44 (1010); and 12, .49 (35).
The math skills test was a good predictor of science and math grades,
whereas first-language composition was a good predictor of social studies
and English grades.

CONCLUSION

This chapter has contained descriptions of the lived lives of immigrant students in secondary school where they struggled with the learning of English, the learning of academic content, and learning to become part of a
variety of new communities.

The lived lives of the students in this study have not been described to
the degree that they could have been. The databases are large and extensive. The interview data, for instance, are contained in thousands of pages
of responses. The basic approach was to reduce the data to a number of
findings that were somewhat representative across students and groups
using a basic spreadsheet. As noted previously, results reported in this
chapter are fuzzy rather than precise. However, they are both interesting
and provocative.

The most "robust" finding was that students of all ages and grade levels
from all of the immigration categories struggled with their own identities
and were confused about what groups they belonged to. Indeed, the ways
students perceived themselves and their relationships to Canadian society
were determined by a number of featuress such as L1, first culture, socioeconomic status, and immigration status. Gunderson (2000), in a preliminary analysis of the interview data noted:

> Members of the diasporas in this study were lost in the spaces between vari-
> ous identities: the teenager, the immigrant, the first-language speaker, the in-
> dividual from the first culture, the individual socializing into a second
> language and cultures, the individual with neither a dominant first or second
> culture, but one not of either culture. (p. 702)

Gunderson also spoke of the "shadow diasporas," the teachers who
were left with only parts of their first cultures, whose dim first-cultural
memories included foods and festivals, the surface-level façades of cultures lost. These same teachers, it appears, had little empathy or sympathy

for the students who found themselves immersed in a veritable cultural war, one being waged in hallways and classrooms, in the media, and in the "popular" culture along with other individuals who had as much to lose.

Students were convinced that immigrant students would learn English better by integrating with and communicating with native English speakers, but they were unable to do so. Students were concerned that they were not given the opportunity to hear native English speakers. The strange irony is that these students were enrolled in schools where by policy the language of instruction was English, yet they felt they were unable to learn English because they were not exposed to it. They also concluded that a good way to learn English was to watch television.

Bilingual instruction was rejected by students, but limited L1 assistance was thought to be a positive approach. Parents were convinced that their children's English was better than the students themselves thought it was. It seemed clear that students' acquisition of BICS was taken as a sign by parents that they had acquired the English required to learn in school.

Students were divided in their views about whether or not knowing how to read an L1 aided their learning of English. A very small group of students thought it interfered with the learning of English. These students were from languages in which the orthography was different from English (such as Arabic). Speakers of languages such as Chinese and Japanese were convinced knowing how to read their first languages helped them learn to read English because they could use L1 to consult a bilingual dictionary.

Speakers of languages that used augmented Roman and related orthographies were convinced that knowing their L1s helped them to decode words because there were some familiar phonics relationships. Speakers of languages such as Spanish and French were convinced that they were very helpful, because they could decode print, but also because there were cognates in their L1s and English so they could infer meanings.

Students were mixed in their views of the value of ESL classes. Students whose aspirations included university or college careers, particularly those who were from more affluent families, were convinced that ESL classes were roadblocks that made them feel isolated and different. Both they and their parents were very negative in their attitudes concerning their usefulness. Students who did not have aspirations that included university education were more positive about their ESL experiences. However, it was clear from that data that after students left ESL courses, their achievement declined significantly across the board.

It was clear from the data that the disappearance rate for immigrant students varied dramatically relative to the different examinable subjects, with social studies resulting in a 75% disappearance rate. The disappearance rate was highest for refugees. This is a phenomenally high number, but it is reflective of the results of other studies (see, e.g., Roessingh & Field,

2000; Watt & Roessingh, 2000). It was shocking to find that the disappearance rate from the examinable courses was also high for students born in Canada, about 60%. Steffenhagen (2001) reported that Canadian dropout rates were shockingly high, especially for First Nations students. The overall finding of this series of studies is that English-only instruction does not work well, even for the students who had the advantage of multiple tutors and parents who viewed education as being the most important activity their children would undertake.

This series of studies also showed that parental views of teaching and learning often differed from those held by teachers and administrators. This difference resulted in a series of problems for some teachers, some students, and some parents. This is an area that needs to be explored in much more detail. An amazing result is the finding that social studies as a course seemed so irrelevant to students, so much so that many opted not to take it in Grade 12. This should have some significance for teachers, administrators, and curriculum designers.

The central question this research was designed to explore was, "How are immigrant students doing in an English-only school system?" Several sources of data were explored to answer this question from a variety of viewpoints. First, when one uses a standard statistical approach using overall means to compare groups, immigrant students to Canada, most of them fairly well off economically, on the average do as well or better than students born in Canada. They appear to do better in math, but less well in Grade 12 in social studies and English. This is quite an interesting finding, one that can be interpreted by a number of people in a number of ways. The overall means, however, mask provocative differences. When broken down by language or country of origin, there are striking differences in achievement as measured by grade point averages. In essence, scores break down by socioeconomic groups. Students who scored the highest in grade point averages were those from entrepreneurial families, those who could and did hire multiple academic tutors, having deeply rooted beliefs in the benefits of education. Those who scored lowest were from refugee families who had experienced personal trauma and/or interrupted educations. As Yau (1995) found, many refugees come to Canada after having suffered through the perils of war, endured physical torture, and been the subject of intense persecution. In many cases they have had interrupted or no schooling. In addition, they could not afford the scaffolding afforded by tutors observed in this study.

The goal of students in the study appeared to be to pass the Grade 12 examinations. Many students, with an incredible amount of scaffolding from tutors, did succeed in gaining enough knowledge to pass their tests. A number of advantaged students felt a sense of isolation not shared by others because they were members of families in which one or both parents continued to reside and work in their home countries. Other students, those from backgrounds in which the average educational level of their parents was high, also succeeded well. A great number of students, however, simply disappeared.

The life of an individual immigrant is explored in the next chapter. It focuses on his life in a system in which he did not neatly fit.

7

One Immigrant—One Story

I spend two years with no friends, no one. I spend two years not talking, anyone. I go school, I go home, I talk only my mother, my brother. Best friend United States. Cry, all time, cry. Being sick, all time, sick, stomach hurt, head hurt, heart hurt, all time, bad dream, all time, all time[1]

The last chapter was filled with the multiple voices of immigrant students who had entered Canada and had been enrolled in academic courses in high schools. The cumulative picture of their success was not a good one. It was filled with difficulty and disappearing students. This chapter is about one student, Dennis (a pseudonym), who was an immigrant. This chapter also contains discussions about such issues as grade levels and instruction in order to contextualize Dennis's life in and out of school.

EVERYONE AS EXPERTS

It would likely be impossible to find a single human being in all of North America, perhaps the world, who does not have an opinion about teaching and learning, about schools, about what's wrong with today's young people, about how to improve schools, about the right way to teach students to read and write, and about how to get "back to the basics." It seems that the overwhelming majority of North Americans are convinced they know as much, or more, about reading and writing as the thousands of elementary and secondary teachers do who teach their children. There is nothing more frustrating for teachers than to read the constant barrage of negative views promulgated by those who have little or no understanding of the realities of the classroom. The difficulty is that life in the classroom is considerably more demanding and complex than imagined by the armchair critics who

---

[1] Female, Kurdish, 16 years.

believe their simplistic remedies will make it right. Teachers' actions, their personal beliefs, their strategies, their beliefs or theories about teaching and learning, and their ways of viewing the world have subtle but profound effects on their students. Dennis was one such student who believed fervently in the power of reading and writing, mostly because his teachers believed strongly in their power.

DENNIS: ONE IMMIGRANT STUDENT

Dennis arrived with his family from Hong Kong when he was 5 years old. He was a small child with a perpetually runny nose. He spoke no English and his first teacher, Mrs. Van (a pseudonym), nicknamed him "cai doy," her version of Cantonese for naughty boy. Dennis wasn't really so much naughty as he was curious. The vice-principal entered Mrs. Van's classroom one morning to talk to her about some item of school business, probably unimportant in terms of her class. Interruptions are a constant in classrooms; they range from the inane to the important, but the bottom line is that they always arrive at the worst possible moments. Dennis was always interested in everything that happened in his classroom. On this day he came up and put one arm around one of Mrs. Van's legs, sucked his thumb, and watched the conversation going on.

The conversation focused on Mrs. Van's extracurricular glee club and its scheduled winter performance. Her expression changed suddenly during the conversation from patient attention to shocked panic. Dennis had ducked in and was under the tent-like cover of her skirt. She panicked and cried for him to come out, but he didn't. In desperation, she looked at the vice-principal and commented, "He doesn't understand me, he doesn't speak English." Dennis did finally come out. He continued to be a cai doy; he continued to search out things that interested him, most often to the consternation of his teachers, and, for that matter, his fellow students.

Dennis began to learn to speak some English, beginning around the middle of first grade. Before then, he mostly listened, although he was able to swear with alacrity. His favorite was "kick ass." Life in the classroom was difficult for him and for his teachers. He could not learn to read English. He could not learn the names of the letters of the alphabet. He could not recognize written words, even his name, although anything that began with a "D" he called Dennis. Learning handwriting was the most trying task for him, for his teacher, and for his fellow students. He tried and tried, but had difficulty forming letters. His runny nose did not cooperate and his paper turned into a blotchy, runny mess that horrified his teacher and the students that sat near him.

He was referred for testing by one of the district psychologists for what his first-grade teacher thought was a possible learning disability. The psychologist visited the school one afternoon and concluded that Dennis was simply a developmentally delayed child. She concluded that the best course of action was to let him mature a bit. The school psychologist had attempted to administer the WISC (revised), but stopped because Dennis appeared to speak no English and did not appear to understand any of the instructions she gave him. He could not recognize and name any of the letters of the alphabet and did not appear to understand the task of copying letters on the Wide Range Assessment Test (WRAT). He could not recognize any words and was unable to write his name when asked to do so. He was unable to do any kind of math, even when she copied down simple examples for him such as 1 + 2. She concluded that he was zero-level English and that he could neither produce nor understand even simple words or requests. She had the impression that he was immature and she concluded on the basis of her observations of his physical appearance and stature that he was developmentally delayed. Because the psychologist was a monolingual English speaker, she was unable to communicate with Dennis. She asked a Cantonese–English bilingual paraprofessional to help her communicate with Dennis, but the aide concluded that he spoke poor Chinese and could not communicate well. She thought he was "not very smart." However, the aide was not, to say the least, an expert in Chinese language development.

After 4 years in school he continued to be unable to read, except his own name, and often not even that. He could not pay attention, he was hyperactive, he was fidgety, and he could not sit still. He was emotionally labile and as a result everything was distracting to him. He ran to the windows to see what was happening outside or to check out anything and everything his classmates were doing. His parents were convinced he was simply lazy and his father often beat him. His teachers thought he was spoiled, a troublemaker. They all concluded that he would be a good student if only he would pay attention; because he was really very smart and his oral English by the time he entered fourth grade was outstanding.

His fourth-grade teacher was extremely concerned about Dennis and referred him again for testing. The psychologist administered a WISC. This is a standard approach used to identify students with learning disabilities. She determined he had a learning disability. It is important to review what is meant by a learning disability.

LEARNING DISABILITY

The National Joint Committee on Learning Disabilities (2000) published an expanded definition of learning disabilities first developed in 1994:

> Learning disabilities is a generic term that refers to a heterogeneous group of disorders manifested by significant difficulties in the acquisition and use of listening, speaking, reading, writing, reasoning, or mathematical abilities.

These disorders are intrinsic to the individual, presumed to be due to central nervous system dysfunction, and may occur across the life span. Problems in self-regulatory behaviors, social perception, and social interaction may exist with learning disabilities, but do not by themselves constitute a learning disability. Although learning disabilities may occur concomitantly with other handicapping conditions (for example, sensory impairment, mental retardation, serious emotional disturbance), or with extrinsic influences (such as cultural differences, inappropriate or insufficient instruction), they are not the result of those influences or conditions. (NJCLD, 2000, p. 1)

A student may be diagnosed as having a reading disability if there is a large and significant discrepancy between an IQ test score and reading achievement. The U.S. Office of Education (1977) established rules and regulations that operationalized learning disabilities as:

A specific learning disability may be found if (1) the child does not achieve commensurate with his or her age and ability when provided with appropriate educational experiences, and (2) the child has a severe discrepancy between achievement and intellectual ability in one or more areas relating to communication skills and mathematical abilities. (p. 52405)

Gunderson and Siegel (2001), however, argue strongly that the use of an IQ test to identify students with learning disabilities is ill advised and, indeed, invalid with second-language students for various reasons. Students who are likely to be contemplative, for instance, have longer pause times and are graded down because of their slower response times. This is only one of many ways in which culture can affect the outcome of an IQ test.

The school psychologist administered the standard IQ test and concluded that Dennis demonstrated a significant discrepancy between his apparent capacity for language learning and his actual level of functioning. He was placed in a learning disabilities (LD) class for an hour a day. His progress in both his mainstream Grade 4 classroom and his LD classroom was negligible. By fourth grade Dennis had developed a native-like command of oral English. He was completely and often painfully communicative in English. Teachers' impressions were that he was "bright." He simply could not learn to read in English. Unfortunately, he was failing to learn to read English in his mainstream class and he was failing to learn to read in his LD class. In effect, his failure was doubled. At no time was Dennis administered a test in Chinese, even though he appeared to be comfortably bilingual.

One summer day between fourth and fifth grade he ran without looking into a street from behind a parked car and was hit by a delivery van. Dennis lay in the hospital in a coma for 2 months. He had holes drilled into his skull to relieve the pressure on his brain. The neurological trauma he suffered resulted in more problems, more serious learning difficulties, and some added physical disabilities. Dennis eventually returned to school after a lengthy convalescence, one that caused serious problems for his already stressed out family. He was placed in a mainstream fifth-grade class and attended a pull-out learning disabilities class. He continued to fail in school and became a chronic truant. He was slightly more successful in his special class, but not in his mainstream class. His classmates regarded him with loathing, especially when they were asked to choose teammates as part of physical education period. He was uncoordinated and had difficulty running. They believed he made them lose their games.

His parents and teachers could not cope with his inability to pay attention and his inability to learn to read and write. He was constantly in trouble in the classroom. He distracted his fellow students from their studies, he took an inordinate amount of the teacher's time and attention, and he generally interrupted the planned curriculum in a serious way. By all accounts Dennis was learning disabled. His life in school was miserable. His life in general was miserable. Like many disabled students, his potential for success was significantly diminished by his learning disability. When he was at home, he and his father fought, usually ending with his father beating him and kicking him out. Why didn't Dennis find the help he needed in school?

MAINSTREAM CLASSROOMS

It is not unusual to have a learning disabled student enrolled in a mainstream class. Indeed, the notion of inclusive education argues that all students should be enrolled in mainstream classes. The federal "Individuals with Disabilities Education Act" (IDEA) and its 1997 amendments (IDEA, 1997) require schools to educate students with disabilities in mainstream classrooms. Dennis's fourth-grade class had a total of three students classified as learning disabled. Therefore, it was a fairly typical fourth-grade class of 32 students. It was less typical in that it had 20 students for whom English was a second language (ESL). Few were working at grade level, according to the teacher. But what does that mean?

Grade Levels

It seems like nearly everyone has the deeply engrained belief that grade levels actually exist. They do not. They are artifacts of grouping students by age. There is a widespread misconception that "grade level" actually represents in some transcendent fashion the difficulty level of a text or the achievement level of a particular student. This is simply wrong. There are other definitions that refer to specific grade-level designations. Kindergarten to third grade are referred to as primary, fourth to sixth grades, and sometimes seventh, are referred to as middle school and sometimes as junior high school, Grades kindergarten to 7 or 8 are referred to as elementary school, and Grades 8 or 9 to 12 (sometimes to 13) are referred to as high school or secondary school, or senior secondary school. These designations are convenient and they generally differentiate students by age. But what does "fourth grade" really mean?

Many believe that written materials differ by their difficulty level. Some texts are easy, some are more difficult, and some are extremely difficult. It is believed that some material can be read and comprehended by adults but not by children because children have not developed the cognitive abilities to do so. There is the belief that grades differ because older students are better able to comprehend more cognitively demanding material than are younger students. One could say that the primary grades are focused on the development of basic interpersonal communicative skill (BICS) and the higher grades are focused on the use of cognitive academic language proficiency (CALP) in the learning of content or academic material.

It is believed that there is a relationship between age and grade level. It is believed, for instance, that students in the fourth grade can comprehend and learn material that is at the fourth-grade level. Students' cognitive abilities and the difficulty level of the materials are matched. The problem is that life in the classroom is not so simple. First, it is not clear that the difficulty level of material can be judged with any degree of accuracy. Second, human beings differ dramatically in cognitive abilities within age categories. Indeed, Dennis is a good example of difference.

There are two basic methods for determining grade level of written or instructional material: (a) evaluators' (often publishers') estimations and (b) numbers from various readability formulas. The notion of readability is a fuzzy one. An early interest in readability led individuals to try to discover which features made a written text more readable or easy to read. Sherman (1893), for instance, discussed the effects of change in sentence length and the degree of predication in English prose of the 16th century on its readability. The study of readability changed to a focus on formulas for measuring levels (e.g., Chall, 1958; Klare, 1963). Gray and Leary (1935) conducted a study of text features in order to identify elements that affected readability. They surveyed librarians, publishers, and others to ask what features made texts "readable" for adults of low reading ability. Respondents suggested 289 separate features, ,which Gray and Leary categorized into four areas: content features, style features, format features, and organizational features. Gray and Leary rank ordered variables within each category. So, for instance, timely subject matter and theme were ranked highest in the content category. The purpose of the Gray and Leary effort was to identify features that could lead to a measure of readability. They observed that the most easily quantified of the variables were in the style category. The need to quantify features eliminated content features, the most important in the original survey. Eighty-two elements of style were identified, but 18 could not be objectively measured. Their study, which began by investigating 82 readability elements, identified only 21 that were significantly correlated with a comprehension measure. Of these, average sentence length in words, percentage of easy words, and numbers of first-, second-, and third-person pronouns interested readability researchers. Only style variables have been utilized in readability formulas, an unfortunate situation for ESL students because these features do not represent interest or content, and content is the most important variable associated with ESL reading (Gunderson, 1991a).

One standard readability instrument that is widely used is the Fry (1968) readability assessment. Fry involves the counting of syllables and sentence length in 100-word samples. A fourth-grade text, as measured by the Fry procedure, should have approximately 5.8 to 6.5 sentences and approximately 142 to 144 syllables per 100 words. The logic is that a text containing these features should be "readable" by an "average" fourth-grade child who is about 9 years old in September when she or he begins fourth grade and about 9 years and 9 months old in June when she completes fourth grade. An average fourth-grade reading ability is a number usually something like 4.2 (i.e., appropriate for an average student in the third month of Grade 4), estimated by testing students in fourth grade. Testing students' reading ability is also fuzzy. No one can really tell for certain what reading comprehension level a particular student has in general. It's made even more difficult, however, because comprehension levels differ relative to a student's motivation, the difficulty of a particular piece of writing, background knowledge, and so on. Researchers and publishers have expended great energy and creativity in devising methods and approaches to measure reading comprehension.

Dennis's fourth-grade class had students who were all about 9 years of age because age was the sole criterion that determined inclusion in the class. Three were identified as learning disabled, two took prescribed drugs to help them to pay attention, and 20 were identified ESL students. Two of the learning disabled students were also ESL students. The teacher followed a standard fourth-grade curriculum; therefore, materials were selected to be at the "fourth grade" level and lessons were designed to be appropriate for students at the "fourth grade" level.

Dennis never developed the English reading skills necessary to read and comprehend the materials he was required to read and understand in his fourth-grade classroom. Indeed, his English reading skills appeared to be almost nonexistent. This was a serious problem for him because his teacher thought he was really bright because of his oral communication skills; they were superb. His parents were outraged that he could not learn, but the reasons for their outrage were more cultural than academic.

FIRST, SECOND, AND INTERCULTURES

Individuals come to school with rich, complex cultural and linguistic backgrounds they use to understand the world as they attempt to learn both language and academic content. Many of their views of teaching and learning, just as do their teachers' views, differ from each other and from those held by parents, teachers, administrators, and psychologists. Differences in their views and those held by teachers and other school personnel often contribute to the discrepancies that exist between their apparent capacities for learning and their actual levels of achievement.

The majority culture in Dennis's fourth grade class was Chinese and/or Chinese-American. Dennis was from Hong Kong and he and his parents spoke Cantonese. They identified strongly with being Chinese, but even more strongly with being from Hong Kong. The following comments describe cultural features related to those who identify themselves as Chinese (Table 7.1). They have been derived from observations made by expert individuals from the culture and from published material including Helmer and Eddy (1996) and Scarcella (1990). The process began with a focus group of graduate Chinese and Chinese-Canadian students developing a list of categories and contents. In addition, the following information was also derived from additional members of the school community who identify themselves as Chinese. Features have been changed or parts eliminated based on their observations. All of the 18 individuals who reviewed and provided input on the following agreed that it was "generally" and "broadly" representative. Eight of the reviewers were graduate students from Hong Kong, the People's Republic of China, and Taiwan. Two were adults born in Canada but who were self-identified as Chinese.

Individuals of Chinese backgrounds are found in every part of the world. The People's Republic of China has about 1.3 billion inhabitants. It is particularly important, therefore, to keep in mind that the following comments are generalizations that are not necessarily accurate for many of those who are Chinese. Indeed, some Chinese-Canadians and Chinese-Americans interviewed argued that they were "100% Canadian." One Canada-born Chinese-Canadian informant argued that the difficulty with immigration was that new Chinese immigrants were giving Canadian-Chinese bad names by their behavior.

Dennis did not live up to his family's expectations. He was expected to work hard and to do well in school. His inattention at school was considered to be reprehensible. In his parents' view he was a failure and a disgrace. Dennis had become a superb English speaker. His communicative style was very much like his native English classmates. He translated for his parents when they communicated with school personnel. He translated for his teachers when they needed to speak to non-English students. His

TABLE 7.1
Cultural Features of Self-Described Chinese Groups

Geographic origin	China, Hong Kong, Taiwan, Singapore, Thailand, Malaysia, Vietnam, Laos, Cambodia, Fiji, Africa, and the West Indies.
Religious background	Although some people from China may be Roman Catholic or Protestant, most Chinese are traditionally Buddhists. Central notions include: a strong belief that one's past lives influence one's present and future lives (e.g., evil deeds from a past life cause serious illness in the present and threaten the future); man is inseparable from his universe, which is viewed as a vast, indivisible entity. Confucianism also exerts a strong influence in China. Confucius defined the rules that dictate relationships (i.e., between father and son, teacher and student, husband and wife, etc.).
Reasons for immigrating	To live in a modern and agreeable society; to obtain better job opportunities and better educational facilities for their children; to join the relatives who have already settled here; to escape from communist rule, and live in a democratic society.
Naming system	The Chinese name usually consists of a one-word surname followed by a two-word given name. A woman may keep her own surname or use her own and her husband's surnames in hyphenated form. The more traditional Chinese may give a child a second name when schooling commences and a third name when marriage occurs. In Canada the child may have an additional name.
Family dynamics	Structure—A patrilineal extended family system which emphasizes family relationships, duties, discipline, filial piety, obedience, parental authority, and respect for the elderly. The family is often large, extended, living together, headed by the eldest working male, and is a source of pride. It is so important that the Chinese have specific terms for each member. For example, an "uncle" may be called "the second eldest brother of one's mother." The elderly are highly respected and the young are obliged to take care of them. The birth of a male child is considered more desirable than that of a female, because the male carries the family name and is entitled to a larger family inheritance. Roles—Traditionally, the husband interacted with the outside world, and to some extent this still obtains. He works, takes care of finances, usually disciplines the children, and makes the primary family decisions. Women have primary responsibility for the family. Discipline—May appear harsh to the Westerner, and open gestures of affection are seldom displayed. Problem solving—When dealing with conflicts, the Chinese may traditionally be persuaded by others without asserting their own rights. They prefer to listen to what others have to say instead of confronting them directly. And they may nod and smile when they neither understand nor agree with what is being said. They may then reply in an indirect way and try to handle the situation diplomatically.

Cultural values	The Chinese are generally pragmatic people. Hospitality is very important. Work and education are highly valued and are seen as the only means of climbing the social ladder. Harmony is highly valued in all things, a harmonious balance of yin—the negative female energy that produces darkness, coldness and emptiness—and yang—the positive, male energy that produces light, warmth, and fullness. To maintain this balance, one must wholly adjust oneself to the environment.
Common attitudes toward education and society	High priority placed on work and education for children of both sexes. Expending time on jobs and schooling is considered much more important than leisure activities. Difficulties may arise when children do not meet their parents' high expectations of them in school. Parents may feel the rights and privileges accorded children in North America threaten their traditional authority and control. In traditional Chinese families, teachers are highly respected.
Language features	The Chinese people speak more than 80 different languages, not counting the hundreds of dialects and variations of those languages. Chinese language is tonal, noninflectional, and essentially monosyllabic.
Significant social patterns	Time—Time is embedded in a lifestyle marked by formality and politeness. Physical contact—Touching the head or shoulder of another person in casual contact, particularly if he or she is older, is viewed as extremely disrespectful. Eye contact—The avoidance of eye contact is an expression of respect.
Culturally sensitive approaches	Chinese people place great emphasis on work and education, values that influence their education and their use of educational services. Chinese people come from various geographic locations and socioeconomic classes, and vary in culture, religion, beliefs, and experience. It is important to respect each person as a unique individual with a distinct background and values.

parents were convinced he was just a lazy student and they rejected what they thought was his bad attitude toward the value of school and learning. This view was part of a shared set of beliefs. It was based on notions they held that were part of a culturally related set of beliefs. His diagnosed learning disability was viewed as a mental problem, something like "being crazy." Dennis was miserable and unhappy at school and he was miserable and unhappy at home. But was Dennis learning disabled when he entered school? Were his apparent learning problems a result of being a second-language learner?

Learning Disability or Second-Language Problem?

Gunderson and Siegel (2001) note, "Learning disabilities are not always outwardly visible; they must be inferred" (p. 48). The basic definition of a learning disability is something like this: "This individual seems like he/she should be able to learn, but for some reason is unable to learn." In Dennis's case his English communications skills became quite good, but he was unable to learn to read and write. So, as one teacher noted, "He's really smart, but he can't learn to read, I think he's just lazy." This teacher's definition of disability can be described in this fashion: There was a discrepancy between Dennis's apparent language ability (speech) and his actual level of performance (reading).

There are various discrepancy models, mostly involving the use of measures of intelligence. Gunderson and Siegel (2001) argue that notions of intelligence would appear to mean "skills in reasoning, problem solving, critical thinking, and adaptation to the environment" (p. 49). They conclude, based on their analyses of various tests of intelligence, that "They assess only what a person has learned, not what he or she is capable of doing" (p. 49). The use of such tests with immigrant students is questionable because "An IQ test is not culture free, because background is important, nor is it language free, because it requires knowledge of English" (p. 49).

Dennis—Reading and Writing

Dennis wanted very much to learn to read and write in English. The mystery was, however, that he *had* learned to read Chinese. Dennis attended after-school Chinese classes. His Chinese teacher reported that he was able to recognize and read hundreds of Chinese characters (personal communication from Chinese teacher). He had difficulty, however, learning to accurately write the characters. His teacher noted there was a coordination problem with his use of a pen or pencil. She also noted that he was completely inept when asked to use a brush to draw characters. She also reported that his behavior in class was very respectful. He did not appear to have the same degree of distractibility reported by his mainstream classroom teachers. He followed directions well. After his accident, however, he lost his ability to learn more Chinese characters and the ones he had known seemed to have "disappeared." He began to stay away from his Chinese classes because the sessions seemed too difficult for him. His teacher reported that he became more and more frustrated with his inability to remember characters, although his oral Cantonese was intact. There is no real evidence on which to base this conclusion, but one Chinese-English bilingual teacher concluded that Dennis was actually better at communicating orally in English than in Cantonese. Regardless of her view, Dennis was able to translate into Cantonese for his parents and English for his teacher during parent conferences and other school events. Both his parents and teachers and administrators in the school relied on Dennis's bilingual ability, beginning about the end of second grade, to communicate with each other. His parents were surprised and shocked when a bilingual teacher translated the session for them with the school psychologist who sought permission to administer tests to determine whether Dennis had a learning disability.

At 15 years of age he quit attending school altogether. Life at home became so difficult for everyone that he moved out and lived on the street or with friends. After a lengthy series of litigations, Dennis was awarded $19,000 for his injuries, money his parents took on his behalf. He received none of this money and his father told him to never return home. He "crashed" with friends when possible, but his friends and their parents grew tired of him and asked him to stay away. He lived on the streets, sleeping in cardboard boxes at the ends of dark alleys. He was repeatedly mugged and sexually assaulted. He tried to join the armed forces, but they would not take him because he could neither read nor write. He sought work, but always lost his job because he could not pay attention. He was prone to accidents. He occasionally came to the author's school to visit. An arrangement was made with a local Catholic church and Dennis was hired to sweep and clean. One afternoon he jumped from a second-story window and impaled himself on an iron fence. He did not leave a suicide note because he could not write, so no one knows the depth of his despair.

CONCLUSION

The evidence presented in the last chapter shows that immigrant students struggle with school and schooling. Immigrant students suffer because they do not have the English language skills to allow them to understand and to learn the material presented to them in their classes. Dennis was a complex human being who was troubled by the teaching and learning going on in his English-only school. His Grade 4 teacher faithfully taught the curriculum she was asked to teach. It was at fourth-grade level as determined by publishers and other professionals. The curriculum was completely inappropriate for Dennis. He could read and comprehend none of the prescribed textbooks. He could not do fourth-grade math. He could not write. Even though his teachers were dedicated to their jobs, hard working, and sincere in their commitment to teaching and learning, they were ill-equipped to provide the instruction Dennis needed.

Dennis had oral English skills that were superb. Teachers thought he was bright, but was probably having trouble because he was lazy and would not apply himself. Socially he had a difficult time because he could not pay attention to a task for long. Actually, he tended to pay attention to many tasks, but not any one for very long. Teachers worried about Dennis and tried to get help for him. They were concerned. The mystery was that Dennis could speak, read, and write Chinese. He seemed to be able to cope with the stresses of the after-school Chinese classes. He was able to sit still and to learn to read and write. No one in the school actually knew much of this information about Dennis. The school psychologist never tested Dennis's Chinese language skills. Interestingly enough, the policy in the school was that English was the only language that was supposed to be spoken at school. There were signs in many classes, should students forget, reminding them to speak English.

The curriculum in Dennis's fourth-grade class was not appropriate for him. He was not capable of learning to read fourth-grade material in English. He was not able to learn fourth-grade English spelling. He was not able to read and learn the content from his science books, although he was interested in the science taught to him by his learning disabilities teacher. His English-only school did not meet his needs. No one ever really thought about his first language, Cantonese. There was evidence that Dennis did learn to read Chinese and could write it. It is not known, however, whether Dennis was able to read Chinese that was appropriate for his age level. It was not clear whether Dennis could write Cantonese appropriate to his grade level. It was clear, however, that he was considerably more able to learn to read and write in Chinese than he was in English. The sad reality was that the teaching and learning in his elementary school were English-only. He had no chance whatsoever to use his strengths in school. This is, indeed, an unfortunate reality of an English-only school for an individual who has literacy skills in a first language but difficulty learning in English. The school system failed to meet his needs with programs designed to utilize his strengths and to build on them.

The notion of culture developed in this book is that culture is the ideas, customs, language, arts, skills, and tools that generally characterize a given group of individuals in a given period of time, particularly as they relate to its members' learning in North American schools. Students do not simply adopt or adapt a new culture or become bicultural; rather, they acquire and reject some features of the new culture, retain and reject some features of their first culture, adapt some features of the first culture to the second culture, and become socialized into a system that is uniquely individual, imbued with first- and second-cultural features, that is often unpredictable. Dennis sounded very much like a native English speaker by the time he reached Grade 4. He had body language that was very native-like. His oral English was vastly superior to his parents' English. Indeed, his mother spoke almost no English, while his father was able to communicate in a very limited way. The family had moved to North America for economic opportunity and for what they considered superior educational opportunities for their children. They operated very much within the cultural background they brought with them from Hong Kong. Dennis was, at a minimum, bicultural. He learned features of the dominant culture. He was judged by his parents according to their first cultural expectations. He did not succeed in their view because he did not meet their cultural expectations for appropriate behavior in school. Dennis appeared to perform better in classes where the educational context better matched his first-cultural expectations: his after-school Chinese-language classes. The teaching and learning context in his mainstream elementary school focused on his weaknesses—English, reading, getting along with human beings he did not understand—not on his strengths. As a result, he was condemned to failure.

In 2005 a single 18-year-old refugee from Kenya arrived in Canada and was brought to Vancouver. She was from Somalia and was a Midgan-Madiban. This is the lowest caste of human being in Somali society (Samad, 2002). Its members are scorned and reviled in Somalia. Samad (2002) notes:

> To be a Midgan-Madiban, or an outcaste person, in Somali society is to suffer life-long indignities, to be deemed impure, unlucky, sinful, polluting, and thus meriting the disdain, avoidance, and abuse of others. (p. 2)

Samad continues, "Many Midgans have been denied food, medical treatment. And protection just because of their outcaste status by many other Somalis" (p. 2). This student arrived in Canada after a life in a refugee camp in Kenya. She had never been to school and could neither read nor write in any language. She lacked the basic readiness skills measured by the tests used in this study. Her life in English-only schools could only be described as extremely difficult and her potential for success is doubtful. There was no program designed for her, because she was unique. Her needs were unique and her background was unique. In many respects she was like a 2-year-old child. Hers is a dramatic case of someone who lacks background and language capability and a lack of knowledge of what school and schooling mean. However, there are thousands who, like Dennis, do have complex backgrounds that are not utilized in their teaching and learning programs in North America; although their lives do not always end as tragically as Dennis's life, such students fail to learn the skills they need to participate in society. The tragedy is that Dennis had skills and talents that could have been used to help him learn.

Thousands of students like Dennis have talents and abilities that are not recognized in schools. The consequences of continued failure are ominous. Can educators in Canada and the United States and other English-speaking countries afford not to look at alternatives to their prescribed curricula, their approved reading texts, and their programs that do not account for the kind of diversity represented by Dennis and others like him?

Part III

Conclusions and Implications

8

Summary, Conclusions, Speculations, Observations, and Conundrums

ESL program not so good because
you don't learn much. Need more presentations,
more writing. Make communicating with other people
more important. [1]

This chapter contains brief discussions of a number of the most interesting or compelling findings of the studies reported in this book. These discussions are not a comprehensive review of the findings; they are, rather, included because they are noteworthy. The chapter begins with a discussion of the scientific approach as it relates to reading research. The chapter also contains reviews of the methodologies of the present studies within the context of the scientific study of reading.

SCIENCE AND READING RESEARCH

Shapiro (1994) concludes "that educational research should inform our classroom practices is a commonly accepted belief" (p. 434). Educators accept the need for a theory-driven research base to inform those who design instructional programs; however, many find it difficult to identify the research that guides their teaching, referring instead to the generally unspecified authority "they" (Gunderson, 1989). Popkewitz (1984), however, contends that:

---

[1] Male, Mandarin speaker, Grade 10.

> The normative study of the work of research makes it especially potent when applied in schools because schools are designed to impose ideas and work patterns upon children. Much of what occurs in schools is justified and made credible by the activities of the educational research community. Scientific evidence provides the rationale for curriculum development, instructional approaches, and evaluation strategies. (p. 24)

Politicians, researchers, and others have argued strongly that the role of research is important, but that the most important aspect is that the research be scientific. The National Reading Panel (NRP) was established in 1997 in the United States by the Director of the National Institute of Child Health and Human Development (NICHD) as a result of a Congressional request (http://www.nichd.nih.gov/publications/nrp/intro/htm). There were a number of "key themes" developed by the panel. Two of these themes became topics of debate in the reading community: "The need for clear, objective, and scientifically based information on the effectiveness of different types of reading instruction and the need to have such research inform policy and practice; and the importance of applying the highest standards of scientific evidence to the research review process so that conclusions and determinations are based on findings obtained from experimental studies characterized by methodological rigor with demonstrated reliability, validity, replicability, applicability" (p. 3, NICHD, accessed on November 21, 2005). The issue of second-language learning was not included in the Panel because it was to be addressed by a different research review.

An additional National Literacy Panel was established to "conduct a comprehensive, evidence-based review of the research literature on the development of literacy among language minority children and youth" (http://www.cal.org/natl-lit-panel/index.html, p. 1 of 4). The overall purpose of the panel was to produce "a comprehensive report that provides clear, evidence-based conclusions and recommendations for audiences concerned with the education of language minority children and youth." Members of the panel agreed to review studies from various research paradigms, including "quantitative experimental studies, quantitative nonexperimental studies, and qualitative studies" (p. 1 of 4).

In August 2005 The U.S. Department of Education declined to publish the report of the National Literacy Panel, reportedly "because of concerns about its technical adequacy and the degree to which it could help inform policy and practice" (Staff Writer, 2005, p. 1). A number of authors suggested that it was the American government's putative anti-bilingual stance that had caused the document not to be published (see, e.g., Toppo, 2005). Toppo noted, "The government will not publish a report it commissioned on bilingual education—and critics say that's because the Bush administration disagrees with the findings, which cast doubt on the efficacy of teaching immigrant children through English-only lessons" (http://www.nabe.org/press/Clips/clip091605b.htm). Slavin and Cheung (2005), in reference to their article, noted, "The first author was initially a member of the panel but resigned in June 2002 to avoid a 2-year delay in publication of the present article" (p. 253). As noted in chapter 2, Slavin and Cheung reported that there was support, although limited, in favor of bilingual instruction over English-only instruction. The contentious debate between proponents of bilingual versus English-only instruction was reviewed in chapter 2 and is not repeated here. However, the debate is often acrimonious. The context for the debate was made more complex by the passing of the No Child Left Behind (NCLB) act in 2001 in the United States (http://www.ed.gov/nclb/landing.jhtml). NCLB "embodies the four principles of President George W. Bush's education reform plan: stronger accountability for results, expanded flexibility and more local control, expanded options for parents, and an emphasis on teaching methods that have been proven to work" (http://www.ed.gov/print/nclb/overview/intro/factsheet.html, accessed November 21, 2005). NCLB has been the target of criticism from various individuals and from states in the United States who find the issue of funding to be very difficult. The purpose here is not to discuss NCLB, but to mention its focus on scientific research. This appears to be the most important issue in both the NRP and NCLB: the centrality of scientific research. Allington (2005) argues that "There is no scientific research on any of the core programs that have been approved for use, and there is little consistency in the research on the supplemental reading programs" (p. 18). However, the bottom line is that scientific research is considered by some to be the way to answer questions about bilingual versus English-only instruction. The studies reported in this book, therefore, will be scrutinized by some readers to ascertain their adherence to scientific research procedures and if the studies are found lacking, these readers will dismiss the results. This chapter begins with a critique of the methodological approaches followed in the studies reported in this book.

CRITICISMS OF THE STUDIES IN THIS BOOK

The following is the definition of "scientific method" found in the 2000 *American Heritage Dictionary*:

> The principles and empirical processes of discovery and demonstration considered characteristic of or necessary for scientific investigation, generally involving the observation of phenomena, the formulation of a hypothesis concerning the phenomena, experimentation to demonstrate the truth or falseness of the hypothesis, and a conclusion that validates or modifies the hypothesis. (p. 1018)

This is a fairly standard view of the term. The National Reading Panel published the following guidelines for their adjudication of studies[2] (pp. 7–9 of 13):

Design of Study

- Random assignment of participants to treatments (randomized experiment)
  - With vs. without a pretest
- Non-equivalent control group design (quasi-experiment) (Example: existing groups assigned to treatment or control conditions, no random assignment)
  - With vs. without matching or statistical control to address non-equivalence issue
- One-group repeated measure design (i.e., one group receives multiple treatments, considered a quasi-experiment)
  - Treatment components administered in a fixed order vs. order counterbalanced across subgroups of participants
- Multiple baseline (quasi-experiment)
  - Single-subject design
  - Aggregated-subjects design

Independent Variables

a. Treatment Variables
   - Describe all treatments and control conditions; be sure to describe nature and components of reading instruction provided to control group
   - For each treatment, indicate whether instruction was explicitly or implicitly delivered and, if explicit instruction, specify the unit of analysis (sound-symbol; onset/rime; whole word) or specific responses taught. [NOTE: If this category is omitted in the coding of data, justification must be provided.]
   - If text is involved in treatments, indicated difficulty level and nature of texts used
   - Duration of treatments (given to students)

---

[2]National Reading Panel. (2001). Report of the National Reading Panel. Teaching children to read: Addendum, Methodology: Process applied to the selection, review, and analysis if research relevant to reading instruction. Retrieved May 2, 2006, from http://www.nichd.nih.gov/publications/nrp/addendum.htm

- ○ Minutes per session
- ○ Sessions per week
- ○ Number of weeks

- Was trainers' fidelity in delivering treatment checked? (yes/no)
- Properties of Teachers/Trainers

  - ○ Number of trainers who administered treatments
  - ○ Teacher/student ratio: Number of participants to number of trainers
  - ○ Type of trainer (classroom teacher, student teacher, researcher, clinician, special education teacher, parent, peer, other)
  - ○ List any special qualifications of trainers
  - ○ Length of training given to trainers
  - ○ Source of training
  - ○ Assignment of trainers to groups:

    - Random
    - Choice/preference of trainer
    - All trainers taught all conditions
    - Cost factors: List any features of the training such as special materials or staff development or outside consultants that represent potential costs

  b. Moderator Variables: List and describe other non-treatment independent variables included in the analyses of effects (e.g., attributes of participants, properties or types of text)

Dependent (Outcome) Variables

- List processes that were taught during training and measured during and at the end of training
- List names of reading outcomes measured

  - ○ Code each as standardized or investigator-constructed measure
  - ○ Code each as quantitative or qualitative measure
  - ○ For each, is there any reason to suspect low reliability? (yes / no)
  - ○ List time points when dependent measures were assessed

Non-equivalence of groups

- Any reason to believe that treatment/control group might not have been equivalent prior to treatments? yes/no
- Were steps taken in statistical analyses to adjust for any lack of equivalence? yes/no

Result (for each measure)
- Record the name of the measure
- Record whether the difference—treatment mean minus control mean—is positive or negative
- Record the value of the effect size including its sign (+ or −)
- Record the type summary statistics from which the effect size was derived
- Record number of people providing the effect size information

The following set of procedures was used to evaluate studies for inclusion in the review (http://www.nationalreadingpanel.org/Publications/Interim_Report/section5.htm):

> If text is a variable, the coding will indicate what is known about the difficulty level and nature of the texts being used. Any use of special personnel to deliver an intervention, use of special materials, staff development, or other features of the intervention that represent potential cost will be noted. Finally, various threats to reliability and internal or external validity (group assignment, teacher assignment, fidelity of treatment, and confounding variables including equivalency of subjects prior to treatment and differential attrition) will be coded. Each subgroup may code additional items that they deem to be appropriate or valuable to the specific question being studied.

> A study may be excluded at the coding stage only if it is found to have so serious a flaw that its use would be misleading. The reason(s) for exclusion of any such study will be detailed and documented for the record. When quasi-experimental studies are selected, it is essential that each include both pre-treatment and post-treatment evaluations of performance, and that there be a comparison group or condition.

The National Reading Panel was charged with reviewing the research to evaluate which instructional approaches resulted in significantly higher reading achievement in students. The panel was charged to find and review studies that met high standards of scientific rigor, including such features as random assignment of subjects and an assessment of effect sizes. The studies presented in this book would have been excluded from consideration on the basis of a number of methodological issues.

The purpose of the studies presented here was not to test scientifically one instructional strategy against another in a controlled experimental fashion. Results, therefore, do not necessarily provide evidence concerning the efficacy of a particular reading instructional program or strategy over another. The studies presented in this book have a serious and significant subject mortality problem. Students disappeared from the school district in alarming numbers. Their disappearance followed a pattern that demonstrated a significant degree of differential attrition. There is a related serious problem in that students were not equivalent prior to their entrance into schools in the study, for a variety of reasons, mostly socioeconomic. The essential question is whether these results are reliable indicators of immigrant students in schools in other jurisdictions such as the United States. This issue is discussed in some detail later.

Measures used in the study were those utilized by district personnel. The standardized measures were chosen by school personnel because of their relative ease of administration. They could be administered to thousands of students in a fairly efficient manner. The difficulty, of course, is that the standardized reading measures, except for the word recognition test, all involved cloze-like procedures. As a number of researchers have noted, including at least one member of the National Literacy Panel on Language Minority Children and Youth, the validity of cloze as a reading comprehension measure has been questioned. Other assessment instruments were developed by district personnel to measure such variables as the recognition of colors and school items and the writing of L1 and L2 compositions. The data show these assessments have a high degree of reliability across groups. Some readers, however, will question their validity as measures of school "readiness" or of English literacy. The validity of one dependent variable, grades in examinable courses, is questionable. Is success in secondary school measured by whether a student successfully completes the courses that will allow him or her to enter a university? Some will criticize the validity of this as a dependent variable. Random assignment is viewed as important by the NRP. Two groups studied here were randomly selected. The individual student and the thousands of immigrant students were not randomly selected. The individual student was a student in a school in which the author taught and served as a vice-principal. The population of immigrant students was all those who arrived over a particular time period. The following discussion contexualizes results within the limitations noted here.

THE DIVERSITY OF IMMIGRANTS

There is an incredible diversity of backgrounds, languages, school experiences, family experiences, economic circumstances, school histories, and language abilities present in the group of school-age students observed in this book. The largest groups represented in the present studies were from Hong Kong, China, and Taiwan. The distribution of first languages and countries of origin is different from other jurisdictions in Canada (Statistics Canada, 2001) and in the United States (NCES, 2004). Eastern and central Canada have higher percentages of European and Caribbean immigrants than does western Canada, whereas the United States in general has a significantly higher percentage of Hispanic students. The large groups in the population of immigrants in the present study differ from the largest groups in the populations in other parts of Canada and the United States.

However, diversity is a feature of all three. The results of the present study can inform educators in other jurisdictions that have immigrant populations comprised of many small subgroups such as the Kurds, the Hmongs, and the Somalis.

The basic difficulty is that educators and policymakers in various jurisdictions must understand the underlying complexities of their school populations and account for the wide variance in views, cultural attitudes, expectations, skills, and needs of each subgroup, no matter how small, in their educational programs and policies. This is a formidable undertaking.

SCHOOLS AS INSTITUTIONS

Schools are social institutions in which young human beings are involved in instruction designed according to curricula often mandated by administrators, policymakers, or educators in jurisdictions such as provincial Ministries of Education, state Departments of Education, or, so it seems, by federal governments funding certain kinds of instructional programs and not others. They are also institutions where young human beings interact with other young human beings and significant adults. Students spend many hours growing up in schools. Both their minds and their bodies undergo miraculous changes. As social institutions containing micro-societies comprised of students, teachers, administrators, counselors, paraprofessionals, librarians, custodians, secretaries, parent volunteers, occasionally police officers, and others, schools are not the best places to conduct scientific research. The normal state of affairs in a school is one of great flux and change. It is likely impossible to conduct scientific research in a typical school because there are too many confounding variables to control. The present studies took place in schools and in a center operated by a school district.

The instruments used to measure students' family and literacy backgrounds were developed or selected by school personnel to meet their perceived needs. As independent agents, they had the option to select the instruments they administered depending on what they perceived to be the skills, abilities, and needs of each of the thousands of school-age students who entered the school district. In addition, over the years options varied because of changes in the center's budget and changes in the staff. This interesting situation, although typical of a school setting, made control of the background study impossible. The bottom line is that every assessment was not administered to every student in the study. Some students, for instance, were able to write a composition in their first language, but were not able to master any of the English language assessments. They received "0" scores for those measures. The longitudinal study was affected dramatically by disappearing students. Students disappeared from the examinable courses in the schools in the present studies. The disappearance rate can be considered to represent an effect size of great importance. The first notion was to take a random sample of 2,500 immigrant students. A random number generator was used to select students in the database. As their grades were being recorded it became obvious that about half were no longer in the school district. The decision was made to increase the sample size to 5,000.

The size of the resulting sample made it possible to view the achievement of students who were in the school district. However, attrition remained a difficult problem. The number of students who had written compositions in their first language, who were in the random sample, who had taken examinable courses from Grade 8 to Grade 12, and who had also written compositions in their first language and in English was reduced to numbers that hovered around 50 or so. In the best situation, this author would have followed up to find out where the disappearing students were going. This was not possible. With these serious limitations in mind, there were interesting findings.

PURPOSE OF THE STUDIES

The overall purpose of the studies was to describe the lived lives of individuals and groups of immigrant students in various ways. Another purpose was to explore the use of an English assessment battery designed for primary-level students. A third purpose was to describe the life of a single immigrant student within the context of cultural expectations. It was also the goal of the research to provide multiple perspectives on students' lives in secondary schools where they faced the difficult tasks of learning, living, developing identities, and becoming adults, all within the context of new schools, a new country, a new society, and a new language. A central goal was also to explore the interdependence hypothesis (common underlying proficiency, CUP) and, if possible, the threshold principle. The studies were both qualitative and quantitative and therefore necessarily required a variety of analyses.

The relationship between socioeconomic background and success in schools has been investigated in many ways with many populations. In this respect it was predicted that students' achievement, as measured by grade point average, would be related to their socioeconomic backgrounds. It was expected, for instance, that the refugees would have more difficulty in school than those from "entrepreneurial" backgrounds. It turns out that this prediction was substantiated.

It was predicted that students would have identity problems related to their status as immigrant students. It was also predicted that there would be differences in identity problems related to socioeconomic status. Their responses showed that students did, in fact, have great difficulties socializing into their new schools, new society, and new roles as immigrant students.

A student's first language and first-language orthography were predicted to have an affect on the way in which he or she learned English. It was predicted that the relationship between first language and English could be predicted by first-language orthography. There were a number of hypotheses related to classical hypothesis testing involving statistical measures.

It was hypothesized, for instance, that there would be a positive relationship between L2 achievement measured in various ways and students' L1 literacy backgrounds. It was hypothesized that:

1. The number of years of schooling in home country would be positively related to English achievement.
2. There would be a positive relationship between home literacy uses and English achievement.
3. There would be a positive relationship between L1 development and L2 achievement.
4. L2 achievement would be related to age and L1 literacy background.
5. There would be a relationship between socioeconomic status and students' achievement.
6. There would be differences in L2 achievement related to students' first languages.

There were a number of interesting and fascinating findings that should be considered within the limitations noted earlier.

Demographic Findings

The overwhelming majority of immigrants in the developmental study were of "immigrant" status, whereas a number of small groups were from other categories, including a refugee group. Their personal and schooling backgrounds were incredibly diverse, as shown in chapter 4. There were robust findings not affected by attrition. The population was marvelously complex, but it also had some major groups, primarily students from Hong Kong, Taiwan, and the People's Republic of China. It will be interesting to see how these individuals get along with each other as they grow into adulthood and become working members of society because they appear to be separated by fairly strong cultural views, particularly views about their orthographies.

About 19,000 of the students had some English ability as measured by the instruments used at the center. However, this ability varied from being able to recognize some letters of the alphabet in English to being able to produce complex compositions in English and in first language. Generally, the vast majority, about two-thirds, had no or extremely limited English skills. There were no significant differences between the performance of boys and that of girls on these measures upon entry to Canada. Interestingly, however, girls generally outperformed boys in high school. This suggests that the socialization of immigrant students in school has interesting differential effects between girls and boys. It also suggests that differences related to gender may be due to social differences. This is a sobering finding. What feature of instruction or of society results in achievement differentials between boys and girls?

It was surprising to learn that a fairly large number of primary students had been born in Canada, had returned to their countries of origin, and had returned to Canada to go to school. A significant finding was that parents had reported they had come to Canada for better educational opportunities for their children. This is in contrast to the views many expressed in the interview study. Students and their parents rejected many of the features of the education they encountered in their new country. It was reported in the case of three families that they came to Canada because they could not get entrance into the United States. Cultural views of teaching and learning have a significant impact on students' learning. Students who are not able to afford instructional scaffolding (e.g., tutors) appeared to accept ESL and the general curriculum, whereas those who could afford it rejected the teaching and learning occurring in their school (see also Li, 2006).

English Literacy Findings

Many immigrants arrived with some English skills they had learned in their home countries. However, the English programs in their home countries produced students functioning at about third-grade reading comprehension level. A plateau was reached at about 5 to 6 years of English study, however. Students who reported that they studied English for longer periods of time actually had lower English reading comprehension scores. About 4,600 were administered the Woodcock Reading Mastery test. Their scores showed that they entered the school system at reading levels significantly behind their actual grade levels. This has serious implications for instruction. The other reading tests used showed the same patterns. Even those students who indicated they had studied English prior to their immigration did not have the CALP to enable them to succeed in academic classes. Indeed, students who had studied for 5 to 7 years appeared not to have acquired CALP. Students were not prepared to enroll in academic courses in which the language of instruction was English without help. In fact, it appeared that the discrepancies between their ages and the English literacy levels actually defined them as "learning disabled." On the average, they received 3½ years of English support. However, after losing support their grades went down and the disappearance rate rose. There were interesting findings related to their literacy scores, however. These literacy findings were supported by analyses involving good sample sizes.

ESL UNIVERSALS

Over the last few decades it has become unfashionable in the social sciences to speak of universals. Postmodernists argue that knowledge is local, not universal. It was surprising, therefore, to find what seem to be English acquisition universals. Findings strongly suggest that the learning of English as a second language follows a developmental pattern or sequence revealed by the variables assessed at OROC that is similar across language groups. Overall, regardless of first language, the vectors of means showed that students appeared to learn English skills in the following order: names of the letters of the alphabet; reading numbers; counting in English; reciting the days of the week; producing present-tense verbs; producing questions; producing future-tense verbs, and; producing past-tense verbs. There was also a reliable sequencing of skills across language groups on other measures, including recognizing and naming colors; recognizing and naming school items, L1 composition quality; recognizing and naming body parts; English composition quality; and using English prepositions. The vector of scores for these measures was remarkably similar across first-language groups. This is an exciting finding that should be explored further.

There is a substantial research literature and interest related to colors and color categories. The research first gained attention in 1969 when Berlin and Kay suggested that there seemed to be universals related to colors. Human beings live in an environment teeming with a seemingly infinite number of perceivable stimuli that they can differentially discriminate. Human beings are probably unable to cope with infinite diversity, and as a result they divide the world into units so that "nonidentical stimuli can be treated as equivalent" (Rosch, 1977). Rosch argues that the "world does, in a sense, contain 'intrinsically separate things.'" Rosch investigated the categorization of the natural attributes of color. She found that 23 diverse cultural groups selected the same incidence of a color as being the "focal members" of color categories. Thus, the "red" chosen by individuals from various different cultures as being the best example was always the same token. She also found that the names for focal members are shorter than for nonfocal members and are recognized more rapidly than nonfocal members. Rosch argued that names should be more easily learned for focal members than for nonfocal members. She tested this proposal on a group of human beings having a limited color terminology and found her hypothesis to be true. She also argued that the names for focal colors should be learned more eas-

SUMMARY, CONCLUSIONS, SPECULATIONS

ily and were likely to be the names learned first. Interest and debate concerning the universality of these kinds of findings continue today (Regier, Kay, & Cook, in press).

It is interesting that the OROC staff selected white, black, green, yellow, blue, and red as the colors they chose to test. Regier, Kay, and Cook (in press) argue, as did Rosch in the 1970s, that color naming focuses on color prototypes or focal colors. They conclude that across languages these focal colors are related to "six Hering primaries: white, black, red, yellow, green, and blue" (p. 1). It seems that red was the color with the highest mean recognition scores. Similar results were found for the recognition of school items, body parts, and letters.

Letters also represented categories. The category "A," for instance, contains hundreds of tokens varying from lower-case cursive to upper-case Gothic letters. Gunderson (1981) showed that good and poor readers did not vary in their recognition of capital letters but did vary significantly in the ability to recognize lower-case letters. The younger the children, the more difficulty they have in recognizing lower-case letters (Herman, 1959; Smith, 1928). Children who continue to have difficulty with lower-case letters also make progress in learning to read (Gibson et al., 1963; Rystrom, 1969; Super, 1969). Capital letters are more perceptually salient and they are learned first. The immigrant students described in this book appeared to learn capital letters first across linguistic and geolinguistic groups. This is interesting, considering immigrants in this study had learned to read languages represented by different orthographies.

The pattern observed in students' recognition of body parts and school items was similar. There seemed to be a similarity across languages. Interestingly enough, the recognition of "leg" and "crayons" was the lowest. The inclusion of "crayons" as a school item introduced a distinctly first-cultural feature. The inclusion of the leg as an item was unclear because it was not apparent which feature of the picture was actually the focus of the question. It could have been the knee or the ankle, for instance.

Data suggest that there is a universal sequence of English acquisition across the language groups in the studies reported here. These are fairly robust findings since there were substantial sample sizes across a number of language groups. However, this finding may not represent a true universal, simply one associated with the particular variables measured in the study. There was no measure of phonemic awareness, for instance. This is an interesting area to investigate further.

First-Language Universals and the Socially Situated Nature of Reading

Parents across linguistic groups reported that their children begin uttering their first words at about the same time, around 12 to 18 months. They also reported that their children began speaking simple sentences at around the same time, about 18 to 30 months. These reports were not only within the same range from language to language and from country to country; they were very much the same range as the data reported by researchers who have studied the language development of native-English-speaking children.

Parents are good language teachers around the world. However, parents reported significantly different mean times when their children began to learn to read their first languages. The means varied from 36 months to 84 months. Triangulation was accomplished by consulting related curriculum documents and professional educational informants. The findings appeared accurate. It is interesting to note that in the Western world reading historically was an activity limited to priests and noblemen (Mathews, 1965). This also appears to be true in many other parts of the world.

Reading instruction was traditionally placed in the hands of teachers or tutors (Mathews, 1966). Today reading instruction remains primarily in the hands of teachers around the world, although many middle-class parents in North America involve themselves in the language development of their children, including such activities as storybook or bedtime reading, in the hope they will help their children develop into better readers. Most children are taught to read in classrooms with other children. Their reading skills and abilities are fostered in social environments that are imbued with features of their cultural backgrounds. What they value about reading is often a result of the values they learn about reading from their teachers, their parents, their friends, and the characters they read and see in the media. To some, reading is the perfect oral production of speech from the printed form, often the words of God. To others, reading is the source of information. Others view reading as a pleasurable activity that allows them to imagine other worlds and other times, and many view reading as a way to comprehend ideas and notions developed by others. The way we define and value reading is to a great extent determined by the features of the social ways in which we learn to read and our purpose for reading. Classrooms filled with immigrants are also filled with multiple views of reading. When the view of the teacher differs from the views of students, difficulties ensue (Gunderson & Anderson, 2003). This turns out to be one of the instructional conundrums discussed next.

THE LIVED LIVES OF IMMIGRANT STUDENTS

Results reveal that immigrants' lives in secondary schools are, indeed, complex, and often extremely stressful. Immigrant students have various ways of coping with the stress they encounter as they interact with individuals from different cultures, often speaking different languages. First-language students usually congregate to seek the safety of others who are similar to them. Students from very small immigrant groups complain of loneliness and feelings of isolation. Students, teachers, and school administrators believe strongly that immigrants must integrate into the life of the school and participate to be able to learn English and the customs and culture of their new country. As shown in chapter 6, they are wholly unsuccessful for various reasons. The irony is that immigrant students in the studies presented here wanted earnestly to learn to be part of the society in their new country and they wished devoutly to learn English, but they were unable to do so because they did not have easy and socially reasonable access to their English-speaking classmates. It is difficult to believe that students in an English-only environment found it difficult or impossible to interact with native English speakers, except, of course, their teachers.

BICS as CALP

Students reported that they often communicated in English for their parents, almost always their mothers. These English interactions were normally at stores, banks, or on the telephone. Their basic interpersonal communicative skills convinced their parents that they had acquired English and that they should have no trouble in their academic classes. The notion that basic interpersonal communicative skill (BICS) is the same as cognitive academic language proficiency (CALP) caused a great deal of angst for parents who thought that their children's inclusion in ESL courses represented a branding of them as disabled. Most were also convinced that ESL classes were a roadblock to the academic classes their children required for admission to university. It was clear, however, that after students exited ESL classes, their grades decreased and the disappearance rate increased. It was clear that the average of 3½ years of ESL support was not sufficient for the immigrants in the studies. It was also clear that those students who received good grades in ESL classes also received good grades in their academic classes.

Students were asked their views of what would improve ESL classes. A large majority reported that ESL classes would be improved and would be more useful if they involved academic content. This supports the notion held by many in the ESL research community that instruction should include an integrated approach, that content and language should be taught at the same time (see, e.g., Early, 1990).

Socioeconomic Status and Academic Support

Immigrants from more affluent families were more likely to complete secondary school and to gain admission to university than were those from less affluent groups. However, immigrants from higher socioeconomic groups found their studies to be extremely difficult. They reported struggling with English and with their academic classes. They also reported that they were successful, in most cases, because their parents were in the position to afford to employ tutors. Many students reported that they had the assistance of multiple tutors.

Séror, Chen, and Gunderson (2005) conducted a study of resilient students, those who had entered Canada as immigrants and ESL students (in the same school district as those in the present studies) and had subsequently been admitted to university. These authors note, "Analysis of the data suggests that the keys to their resilience were found in individual effort and the existences of strong social networks that provided the support and resources they needed" (p. 62). They also concluded, "This suggests a social rather than an individual definition of resilience, one based on a strong awareness and/or understanding (whether conscious or unconscious) of the strategies that allow one to access, develop, and maintain relationships" (pp. 62–63). Indeed, "All the students in the study displayed a strong developing social capital based on good relationships and strong networks: parents, peers, and teachers or tutors" (p. 63). Students who appeared to lack such support and networking disappeared from the examinable courses. Refugee students received the lowest grades, the lowest literacy scores on entrance into the country, and disappeared from examinable courses at a higher rate than other immigrant groups.

Socioeconomic status was a factor in where students' families were able to live in the school district. Like any large city, there are neighborhoods that differ in that some have expensive housing and others have less expensive housing. Students attended the closest school to their homes in their neighborhoods. The 18 secondary schools in the studies had student bodies that differed in systematic ways related to the socioeconomic status of their families. The location of the secondary school had a relationship to the likelihood that a student successfully completed high school and went on to university. Students in schools in poorer neighborhoods were less likely to go to university than students in schools in more affluent neighborhoods. This is, indeed, a lamentable finding.

THE HIGH SCHOOL CURRICULUM

Students had definite views concerning the value of and their interest in the courses they were taking. As noted earlier, many students and their parents had strong negative feelings about ESL courses. Exceptions to this view can be seen in chapter 6. Indeed, there were a number of students who found the ESL courses to be very important and highly valued. It was obvious that one area of the high school curriculum was viewed with considerable loathing: Students disliked social studies courses. In fact, the disappearance rate was higher for social studies courses than it was for the other examinable courses. This was a difficult finding for the secondary social studies teachers to understand because they believed immigrant students should have had an active interest in learning about their new country, Canada. Two of the required social studies courses involved the history and geography of Canada. Students found them essentially irrelevant. They indicated they would prefer courses that involved current or modern views of Canadian society that would help them to succeed.

READING MODELS AND THE PREDICTION OF SUCCESS

The following integrates discussions of results related to reading models and to the prediction of school achievement because they turned out to be related. It was hypothesized that the number of years of schooling in home country would be positively related to English achievement. Results showed there was a very weak relationship and that there appeared to be a plateau effect of about 5 to 6 years, after which students' reading comprehension scores decreased. The prediction that there would be a positive relationship between home literacy uses and English achievement was not confirmed. The relationships were extremely low. In addition, the prediction that there would be a positive relationship between L1 development and L2 achievement was not confirmed. The prediction that achievement would be related to age and L1 literacy background was partially confirmed. Although the sample size was low, findings showed there was a relationship between students' first-language compositions and Grade 8 English grades. This relationship decreased from Grade 8 to Grade 11. There were too few students in Grade 12 to compute reliably this relationship.

It was predicted that there would be a relationship between socioeconomic status and students' achievement and there would be differences in L2 achievement related to students' first languages. There was a significant and powerful relationship between socioeconomic status and achievement. Less affluent students had a higher disappearance rate from the examinable courses than students from more affluent families. Less affluent students had lower grade point averages in the examinable courses than more affluent students. The hypothesis that differences in achievement would be related to first language difference was made on the premise that those who had learned to read in a language that had an orthography similar to the augmented Roman alphabet used in English would score higher than those who had learned a language with an orthography that was dissimilar to the English orthography. There were significant differences related to first language, but they were not related to first orthography.

Findings of the study—in particular, conclusions drawn from interviews of students and parents—showed that they had a view of reading and reading instruction that was clearly bottom-up. This was a well-entrenched first-cultural view that resulted in many of them, both parents and students, rejecting the teaching and learning going on in the schools.

Linguistic Markers of Socioeconomic Status and Identity

One artifact of the state of affairs in the world that came to light was that linguistic groups and immigration status were related in unfortunate ways. Immigrants who arrived in the school district who spoke Mandarin differed from those who arrived as Spanish speakers in more than just first language. A significant number of Mandarin and Cantonese speakers were entrepreneurs who arrived with substantial amounts of financial resources, while a significant number of Spanish and Vietnamese speakers were refugees who arrived with limited or no financial resources. The social consequences of this artifact continue to be serious for students and for the social system in which they live. One consequence is that the linguistic markers take on features that are negative. "Vietnamese" has to a great extent become the "signifier" for "gang member." This is scandalous. It condemns a whole group, including the hard-working, law-abiding, participating members, in a grossly unfair manner.

There were interesting geolinguistic differences that caused significant turmoil among immigrant groups. A group of Mandarin-speaking parents in one high school volunteered to set up a Chinese New Year's display in the foyer of the building. Rather than being a wonderful addition to the multicultural spirit in the community, however, it caused great anger in another group of Mandarin-speaking parents. A group visited the principal of the school and strongly demanded the display be removed. They argued that the writing was "communist." The first group of Mandarin speakers was from the People's Republic of China. They had used "simplified" Chinese characters (see chap. 5). The second group of Mandarin speakers was from Taiwan. They objected vehemently to the inclusion of the offending communist characters (T. Carrigan, personal communication, 1999). Generally, Cantonese speakers avoided Mandarin speakers while attending school. Mandarin speakers from Taiwan viewed those from the People's Republic of China as "country folk" who were unsophisticated. There were a number of other instances in which individuals speaking the same language as others perceived the others as "different." Students from Mexico indicated they were different from those who came from Central America and/or South America, especially Argentina.

Models

As noted in chapter 2, a model, as a set of theoretical propositions, allows a researcher to analyze logically the possible relationships within a particular system. Further, it permits the design of procedures to isolate and to test empirically the association of variables in the theorized component relationships. Teachers design reading instruction based on their view or model of reading. First-language researchers, primarily from the United States, have formulated a number of reading models for English-speaking learners generally referred to as bottom-up, interactive, top-down, and whole language models. The second-language community has often adopted such models and applied them to situations in which students are learning a second language (Bernhardt, 1991). Most often the second language is English.

Cummins and Swain (1986) proposed a "common underlying proficiency" (CUP) model based on the notion that "literacy-related aspects of a bilingual's proficiency in L1 and L2 are seen as common or interdependent across languages" (p. 82). Literacy experience in either language promotes the underlying interdependent proficiency base. This view suggests that "common cross-lingual proficiencies underlie the obviously different surface manifestations of each language" (p. 82).

There have been a number of studies that suggest that some skills appear to transfer to a second language and some appear to interfere in the learning of a second language. Bernhardt and Kamil (1995) argued that second-language reading is "a function of L1 reading ability and second-language grammatical ability." The present studies cannot be used to inform a general second-language model because they involve the learning of English as the second language. They also employ measures that Bernhardt (2000) argues are invalid.

A model was developed (see chap. 2) that was called the differential base (DB) model to represent the hypothesized variable effects different languages would have on English as a second language. In essence, the model predicted that logographic orthographies would not provide as much information about English reading as would augmented Roman orthographies.

Results did not support Bernhardt's (2000) second-language model. The test of English prepositions, a test of second-language grammar, accounted for large proportions of the variance in reading scores across orthographies. There were no measures of first-language reading in the present study. However, there was a measure of L1 writing. It did not account for any significant amount of the variance in reading scores. English composition scores accounted for a very small amount of the variance in reading scores. L1 writing scores did predict success in secondary school academic subjects.

Results did not support specifically the proposed DB model. Scores varied significantly among orthographic groups. However, the multigroup exploratory factor analysis indicated there was essentially one underlying factor (general English), except for the group from Hong Kong, who seemed to have a second minor factor (recognition). There appeared to be a common underlying proficiency across orthographies. Students from Hong Kong begin reading instruction at 3 years of age. It was suggested that this instructional variable was probably associated with the difference in factor loadings. This is partial support of the DB model. Mean scores were transformed into proportions in order to observe their relative contributions. The vector of proportions was incredibly similar for the measures across orthographic and linguistic groups. Students who learn English as a second language show a remarkable pattern of skills that is the same across orthographies. Regardless of first orthography, the pattern of the acquisition of English skills is remarkably similar. The proportion of scores in the production of English past-tense verbs is the lowest across all of the orthographic and linguistic groups, whereas the proportion of scores for the production of letter of the alphabet is always the highest across orthographic and linguistic groups. This is a unique and exciting finding. Were students, regardless of their first languages, introduced to English skills in a prescribed order? Or do the results suggest some kind of acquisition order related to English? Hong Kong students differed somewhat. The breakdown of their scores compared to others shows they had higher recognition scores for school items than all of the other groups. This clearly suggests an instructional difference.

Caution must be taken in considering these findings because they may be a result of the measures used. This is a difficulty in almost all studies, however. Naming the letters of the alphabet in English resulted in the highest scores across the groups. Is this the first skill they acquire? Or, was there another skill that is acquired first that was not measured? As Leu (1981) notes, "Typically, investigators have constructed models of the reading process based on a set of specific empirical results, often from their particular paradigm, or investigative approach" (p. 96). Common underlying proficiency was also suggested by the finding that first-language compositions scores predicted achievement in Grade 8 English courses. This suggests that knowing how to read and write in a first language predicts success in second language. This is an exciting interdependence finding.

It was disappointing that developmental background variables had extremely low relationships with language and achievement measures. However, it was interesting that a history of schooling for those with no measurable English had some predictive power for high school grades in the examinable subjects. Indeed, this suggests schooling is, after all, important. The DB model was also supported tangentially in that first cultural attitudes toward teaching and learning affected students' and parents' views of the instruction going on in the schools. As Li (2006) observed, parents rejected features of the instructional practices going on in their school and opted for a business model for their children; one in which the students were able to master individual bits of knowledge rather than focus on process.

Students were asked whether they thought knowing how to read in their first languages helped them to learn to read in English. Their answers were mixed and varied, interestingly, in their views of how their first languages contributed to their learning. In many cases first languages were viewed as helpful because students could use their bilingual dictionaries to discover the meanings of unknown English words. Students did suggest that it would be helpful to have someone who could explain vocabulary to them, but not to study in their first language.

COMMON UNDERLYING PROFICIENCY— THE INTERDEPENDENCE HYPOTHESIS

The studies described in this book have resulted in some dramatic long-term evidence to support CUP. Study mortality, although a powerful finding in and of itself, resulted in difficulties in the long-term predictive findings. However, there is interesting and powerful evidence showing that interdependence as a construct does exit. There was a significant relationship between students' first- and second-language compositions (.32, n = 2,778). Some researchers would likely write home to mother about this finding because it is significant. It does show an interdependence effect, but this researcher is somewhat more conservative about being able to explain about 9% of the covariance in the two variables. What is exciting, however, is that L1 composition scores are a better predictor of English and social studies scores than are English composition scores. So, for instance, L1 composition and grades in English 8 showed a correlation of .53 (57), whereas the correlation between English composition and English 8 was .16 (62). This is solid evidence for interdependence. Scores on a math skills test predicted math and science grades better than a math concepts test. L1 compositions scores were better predictors of math and science grades than English composition scores. So, for instance, math skills score predicted grades for Math 8 (.43, n = 194), Math 9 (.42, n = 192), Math 10 (.30, n = 75), and Math 11 (.45, n = 52). The pattern was the same for science courses.

Another effect size of interest is that the math classes had higher enrolments than did the social studies and English classes. This may reflect the interests of the underlying populations in the study. The fascinating interdependence finding is that L1 composition scores predicted math and science grades better than the English composition scores. So, for instance, Math 11 and L1 scores had a correlation of .45 (n = 52), whereas English scores had a correlation of .04 (n = 59), which is essentially zero or no relationship.

However, the most dramatic finding relates to issues not normally associated with interdependence. The results broken down by various linguistic and geolinguistic groups show a consistency of vectors that is intriguing. It suggests there is an educational variable that is strong. Both findings of the analysis of quantitative data and the interview data suggest that instructional strategies are a profoundly significant variable. Indeed, instructional strategies represent a socially situated literacy variable. This variable is extremely powerful. It masks what may be subtle differences in learning due to first-language orthography.

ENGLISH-ONLY VERSUS BILINGUAL INSTRUCTION

Results of the studies presented in this book cannot answer the basic question about which of these approaches best meets the needs of immigrant or native-born ESL students. Students were asked about bilingual classes and argued overwhelmingly that they did not wish to study bilingually, as noted earlier. The interesting finding that supports the notion of the value of learning to read in a first language is that students who arrived with no measurable English skills were more likely to succeed if they had attended school in their home countries. Indeed, the longer they had attended school, the higher their grades in the examinable subjects were. This suggests a transfer of first-language skills to the learning of English, a common underlying proficiency base. Another very strong area of support for common underlying proficiency was that bilingual students, even those who reported they had not studied English before they immigrated, had higher levels of achievement in courses that required CALP than their cohorts who had entered Canada as monolinguals.

The story of Dennis reported in chapter 7 reveals that he was better at reading in Cantonese than he was, by far, in English. The difficulty was that his Cantonese literacy skills were never utilized in his mainstream English-only school. Dennis would have likely benefited from instruction in Cantonese and, perhaps, bilingually. His is an interesting case because it suggests that literacy skills can differ between two languages in a single human being. It may be that he was literate in Cantonese and disabled in English. This is an interesting finding that suggests that reading processes in Chinese may, in fact, differ from those in English.

It was interesting to observe that one of the best predictors of success in high school, particularly in English and social studies, was students' scores on their first-language compositions. It is also interesting that math scores were predictive of students' success in math and science courses. The math test was a basic skills-based test that did not require English skills. Scores on the math tests were also weakly related to grades in English and social studies courses. Students who reported they were bilingual scored higher in their academic classes than those who reported they were monolingual. Personal developmental features such as age they first uttered single words for those with no English skills were a better predictor of secondary school success than they were for those who had some English skills on entering the country.

ENGLISH-ONLY INSTRUCTION

The struggle to learn English and to learn academic content is extremely difficult. Immigrant students deal with the trials and tribulations of growing into adulthood while trying to master a new language, a new culture, a new society, and multiple sets of expectations from their schoolmates, their friends, their teachers, and their parents. Immigrants in this study dealt with acne, angst, and insecurities about whom and what they were. Unlike the people described in the quote from the base of the Statue of Liberty, "the wretched refuse of your teeming shore" and "the homeless," it cannot be said that the immigrants described in this book were either wretched refuse or homeless. Indeed, most were advantaged educationally and/or financially, even many of the refugees. Their lived lives were often, in their views, difficult. Indeed, both their comments and the results of their achievement in the examinable grades in this English-only school system revealed a serious problem that grew worse over the course of secondary school, particularly as they left their ESL umbrella. In general, the English-only instruction caused students great stress and turmoil, and many students disappeared from the examinable courses. More affluent students could afford to employ tutors. However, their scores also decreased after they exited ESL courses.

Examinable Courses: An Elitist View?

The overwhelming majority of human beings in the world succeeds quite well in life without ever having been admitted to or attended a university. A university degree in many respects represents social capital. Education in North America has been viewed by many as a system that has allowed human beings who would not otherwise have access to gain social capital. An amazing number of colleagues of this researcher, including him, are the first members of their families to have attended a university and to have received degrees. Over the last 20 or 30 years, however, the system has seemed to change into one that does not provide students, especially those from diverse cultural and economic backgrounds, with the social capital it did previously. Individuals with a college or university degree do have increased potential to succeed financially. The high school degree has come to be viewed as minimal certification for employment at levels above unskilled labor. Not having a high school diploma or equivalent is a serious shortcoming for individuals in the United States and Canada.

Statistics Canada (1995) reports that students who have not completed high school have a significantly higher level of unemployment than those who have completed their diplomas. Women without high school diplomas have an astounding 70% unemployment rate. Rumberger's (2001) analyses reveal findings that are similar in the United States. He also found that unemployment rates for dropouts were 75% higher than for high school graduates. On the average, students in Australia have a 75% graduation rate (http://www.flinders.edu.au/?news=21), whereas Canada's is about 70% (Statistics Canada, 2004). Dearden, Emmerson, Frayne, and Meghir (2005) report similar completion statistics for students in the United Kingdom. The 2005 National Assessment of Adult Literacy report includes the statement that "Perhaps most sobering was that adult literacy dropped or was flat across every level of education, from people with graduate degrees to those who dropped out of high school." It also reports that those who have higher literacy levels made about $50,000 a year, which is $28,000 more than those who had only minimal literacy skills.

These English-speaking jurisdictions have become increasingly reliant on technology and technical knowledge to compete economically in the world. It is estimated that the loss of potential wages and taxes in the United States alone over the life span of the total number of dropouts in a year, is approximately $260,000,000,000. Haney, Madaus, and Abrams (2003) report that graduation rates in the United States are about 75%. However, they also report on differences related to jurisdictions. They report that "the states with the worst graduation rates in the 2000–2001 academic year were: South Carolina (51%), Florida (52%), Georgia, Mississippi and Tennessee (57%), and New York (58%)."

There is evidence that the dropout rates for immigrant students are even higher than the overall averages reported for these countries (e.g., Rumberger, 1995). As discussed earlier, reported dropout rates for immigrant students in Canada are as high as 73% (Watt & Roessingh, 2001). The disappearance rate in the present study was about 60%. Pirbhai-Illich (2005), convinced that this statistic could not be correct, conducted a careful follow-up study and discovered the percentage of immigrant students who did not complete a high school diploma or equivalent was about 40%. This statistic was computed by following up on those who left school prematurely, but returned or finished a GED in adult school. Even so, this is an extremely high dropout rate. Immigrant students would appear to have less success in receiving the basic certification to allow them to enter the work force at levels higher than as unskilled laborers. The disappearance rate from examinable courses reported in this book supports the conclusion that immigrant students are at risk. Immigrant students and those who are ESL are at risk in the major English-speaking countries. Some groups of immigrant students are more likely to fail and drop out than other students. This is a very troubling finding for all those concerned with school and schooling in the United States, Canada, Australia, New Zealand, and the United Kingdom.

PAIR (2000) revealed that 177 Spanish-speaking students in the entire province of British Columbia graduated from high school and were eligible for admission to university. The sobering finding is that only 14 actually went on to university education. There is a similar pattern for other minority groups. The Ministry of Education (2005) reports that the percentage of minority groups such as the Spanish speakers continues to increase, while the overall population decreases. This suggests that the problems such students face will only increase in the schools and in society.

Conclusion and Some Educational Conundrums

The studies described in this book were not experimental. Variables were not controlled and manipulated. Instead, variables were observed and measured by locally developed assessment measures and a number of standardized reading tests. The standardized tests are not viewed as valid measures by some researchers, but they were viewed as pragmatic alternatives to assessments requiring extended one-on-one testing sessions by school personnel.

Sample sizes were not controlled in any fashion. They differed dramatically from group to group and from year to year as a consequence of funding and staffing. In essence, the dynamic nature of school and schooling is reflected in the results. Indeed, disappearance rate could be considered to be a rather sophisticated measure of effect size, but in a negative way. The bottom line is that the present studies can be criticized in various ways by those who believe that teaching and learning should be subjected to scientific study. The dynamic nature of teaching and learning—some have likened it to chaos—makes scientific study difficult at best, and likely beyond our present-day technical know-how to achieve.

The studies described in this book were designed and thought out. Proposals were written and submitted to funding agencies and financial support was received. There was great enthusiasm for the potential of the long-term predictive portion of the studies, both by school personnel and by the researcher. In many respects, this enthusiasm was naive. The seeming chaos of activities occurring in schools, particularly high schools, masks an underlying entropy that results in the disappearance of students. The observed level of student mobility is astounding. Critics will note that the long-term study has serious subject mortality issues that make it difficult to generate valid and reliable predictive coefficients. And they are correct.

The disappearance rate from the examinable courses, in and of itself, is an extremely powerful finding. The percentage of students who entered the district who were missing at the end of the study is a powerful finding that demonstrates a difficult problem for school personnel. Research suggests it is a problem in Canada, the United States, Australia, the United Kingdom, and New Zealand. So, what's new in the findings reported in this book that will inform policy and research in other school jurisdictions in Canada and in other countries like the United States?

Statistics concerning immigrant students are often reported as though they are a group of human beings who are all the same. The misleading nature of this conclusion was described in considerable detail in this book. The immigrant population who came to Vancouver differs from the population that has entered Toronto, Canada, or Miami, FL, or Los Angeles, CA. An important finding reported here is that significant background differences, such as socioeconomic status, are often communicated by geolinguistic terms. Those individuals identified as Spanish-speaking, Vietnamese-speaking, and Punjabi-speaking, for instance, tended to have a number of other features that were perceived by teachers and the general public to be negative. There was a relationship between those other features and students' success in school. Spanish speakers did less well in school in this study, but not because they were simply Spanish speakers. They did less well because they often had interrupted or no school, had suffered physical and emotional trauma, and came from families of lower socioeconomic status and lowered access to resources. The term *Spanish-speaking* became a signifier filled with negative features associated with a group of students, many of whom shared none of the underlying features. Mandarin speaking, on the other hand (chap. 6), became a signifier for "school success and achievement," even though many Mandarin speakers disappeared from schools and many reported they had extreme difficulties in their studies. Mandarin speakers' grades also decreased after the ESL support structures were gone. The important finding here is that immigrant populations vary dramatically in many ways and great caution should be taken to avoid creating negative images that are signified by words such as "Vietnamese."

In general, findings presented here suggest that English-only instruction at the secondary-school level is not very successful. It is important to acknowledge that the students who tended to succeed came from families that had the financial support to hire tutors who supported their children's learning. The population of immigrants described in these studies had a large majority of students who were Cantonese and Mandarin speakers. A significant number of them are best described as middle-class or higher in terms of socioeconomic status. They also generally shared a cultural view that focused on the importance of school and schooling. Populations in other jurisdictions differ from the population in the present studies. It is vital to consider that a majority of students in the present study were from families best described as financially settled who viewed education as important to their children's potential for success. Results showed that they struggled in this English-only system and that those who did not have such backgrounds were more likely to disappear from the system. English-only instruction worked marginally for those students whose families could pay to support their learning. What about other immigrants who come from families that are not able to support their learning in ways described here?

It is also important to note that the findings of the present studies show that there are some students who are best described as resilient, who manage to learn English and academic content and to graduate and continue on to postsecondary institutions. The research base related to school resilience is an important one that should be read by teachers, school and district administrators, and politicians. A valid criticism of the present study is that the students who were left in the sample at Grade 12 were special, indeed, resilient students who had the resources to struggle and succeed. This should be a very sobering finding for educators and policymakers in other jurisdictions such as the United States whose populations are not comprised of the same high percentage of economically advantaged immigrant students. On the other hand, it would be of great value to look closely at the 14 resilient Spanish-speaking students mentioned earlier to see what made them successful. Such findings might provide educators and policymakers with information that could help them to improve the success rate of such students.

CONUNDRUMS

A number of the findings of the studies presented in this book have raised what can only be called conundrums or dilemmas. The school district was an English-only system in which students were enrolled in academic classes taught in English. They were also enrolled in ESL classes to help them learn the English skills they needed to learn in their academic classes. It was clear that as students left ESL classes their grades decreased. As they lost ESL support, they found it more difficult to learn in their academic classes.

Conundrum 1

Students complained that in an English-only school system they could not find native English speakers with whom they could interact to learn how to communicate in English.

Conundrum 2

The language of the community and of the school was often not English. Students did not hear English in the hallways, in the schoolyard, or in the community. Often the only native English speakers they heard were their teachers. ESL methodology is reportedly based on the notion that the language of the community is the target language. Should ESL methodologies in such communities be reconsidered?

Conundrum 3

Many students and their parents complained that ESL classes were roadblocks to gaining admission to a university, so students got out of such classes as soon as they could. Some referred to ESL classes as a kind of ghetto. After they exited ESL classes their grades went down.

Conundrum 4

Students left ESL support classes after about 3.5 years. On the average they actually seemed to need at least 5 years to be able to contend with the English in their academic classes.

Conundrum 5

Parents were convinced that their children had acquired the skills necessary to contend with their academic studies because they had basic interpersonal communicative skills. They pressured the school to remove their children from ESL classes (sometimes with great anger and determination). Students' grades suffered as a result.

Conundrum 6

Students and teachers concluded that the best way for students to learn to communicate and to learn social conventions was to participate in extracurricular activities. However, students reported that for various cultural and social reasons they could not and did not participate in such activities.

Conundrum 7

Teachers and school administrators were convinced that multicultural education was vitally important for students, both native Canadians and immigrants, to learn about different cultures. A number of attempts were made to include students in such activities. However, typically only Asian girls, it was reported, showed any interest in attending. One event had 95 participants: 94 Asian girls and one Asian boy.

Conundrum 8

Students indicated that they did not want to be enrolled in bilingual education, but that occasional help with vocabulary would be very useful. Teachers generally prohibited the use of any first languages in their classrooms, including bilingual dictionaries.

Conundrum 9

Parents indicated they had moved to Canada so that their children would have better educational opportunities. However, both parents and students, mostly those from more affluent families, rejected the education they were receiving because it did not include hours of homework dedicated to the rote learning of facts (see also Li, 2006).

Conundrum 10

Teachers were generally dedicated to the notion that teaching and learning should be process based and that students should learn to be critical readers and learners, whereas parents and their children believed teaching and learning should be focused on the rote acquisition of facts. Most teachers appeared to have a top-down view of teaching and learning, whereas most parents had a bottom-up view.

Conundrum 11

Students from Hong Kong scored significantly higher on all of the English language and literacy assessments; however, they did not receive better grades in the examinable classes. Mandarin speakers scored higher than Cantonese speakers, and it seems they may have done so because of the scaffolding they received because of their parents' socioeconomic status.

Conundrum 12

It is not clear what happened to the students who disappeared because there is no satisfactory way to track where they are and what they are doing. Even in this age of electronic tracking, students appear to simply disappear.

Conundrum 13

This is, perhaps, the most troubling of the conundrums. Teachers and administrators in the Vancouver school district are caring and thoughtful human beings who are dedicated to providing the best programs for their students. Their ESL programs are designed to support students' learning in many different ways. They are well thought out and research based. The conundrum is that for various reasons beyond the control of teachers, ESL support classes do not result in producing students able to cope with the task of reading and learning in their academic courses because students do not stay in them long enough to develop appropriate levels of CALP. There is little that can be done to change the view of parents and others concerning the value of ESL classes.

These are troubling ironies that must be addressed in some way by teachers and administrators in English-only school systems. They are extremely difficult issues to consider. How is it possible to schedule students from various cultural backgrounds to interact with each other and native speakers, when the mores of their cultures dictate that they not interact with their schoolmates in social situations? How is it possible to make certain that ESL learners have access to English models when the majority of a school is non-English speaking? How is it possible to assure that students receive enough ESL support to allow them to learn in their academic classes when budgets do not support them and there is not enough time before students are forced by age to leave school? How is it possible to get students from different language groups to interact with others? How do educators convince parents that their children are not "disabled" because they are enrolled in ESL support classes?

These are important issues to consider. Immigrant students arrive with complex backgrounds and first-language skills and abilities that they cannot rely on to succeed in their academic classes. The tragedy is that some families have the financial resources to scaffold their students' learning, whereas others do not. Those who do, succeed against great odds. It is unfortunate that schools do not have the resources to support all immigrant students' learning. Those who do not have support disappear from the system altogether. It is a greater tragedy to see that those who fail and disappear are often members of particular groups signified by a linguistic or geolinguistic term.

Bilingual researchers have little to no research that focuses on secondary ESL students. Bilingual education is not feasible for the multiple small linguistic groups in a school population like Vancouver's. It is not possible, for instance, to design and implement a Bengali–English secondary bilingual program for the 42 individuals who speak this language, for a number of reasons: They are not all located in the same school; there are no trained Bengali–English bilingual teachers; and there are no teaching resources available in the school district written in Bengali. This is true for a majority of the language groups represented in the Vancouver school district. It seems like the only feasible alternative is ESL instruction. The task is to make ESL support better than it is.

Secondary schools seem to have lost the ability to provide students the social capital they need to survive in this complex technological society. There are millions of human beings who are successful in society because they were given the social capital they needed to succeed through their studies in public school, even though they were from poor families. It is time to question what has happened to those democratic institutions.

The issues related to English-only versus bilingual instruction are contentious and often discussed in bitter terms. Considerable evidence has been presented in this book to suggest that the English-only environment is a difficult one for immigrant students. Hopefully the results discussed in this book paint a fair picture of the outcomes of English-only programs. Miriam Amada Ferguson, known as Ma Ferguson, and the first woman governor of Texas some 70 years ago, became involved in a debate about which languages should be used in teaching Texas schoolchildren. Her basic argument was, "If English was good enough for Jesus Christ, it's good enough for me" (Cooley, 2001). It seems that English-only instruction may not be good enough in its present form for a large portion of the immigrant population. On the other hand, bilingual education does not appear to be a reasonable alternative for the students in smaller linguistic groups.

As noted on the first page of this book, the Statue of Liberty welcomes immigrants, and Emma Lazarus's poem beckons to the world with the promise of freedom and opportunity. Learning to read and write English alone is not necessarily enough to guarantee that immigrants can participate in society and have equal opportunity or equal access. Researchers must be concerned about social justice, about poverty, about politics, and about social responsibility. The failure to be concerned about and to act on such issues has dire consequences for a rapidly growing segment of our school population: those whose first language is not English.

The riots in France in 2005, described in the first chapter of this book, involved children of immigrants. These children were products of the school system in France where their special needs and abilities were not recognized. They often left school without the preparation they needed to succeed in society. It seems that the school systems in a number of countries are failing to meet the needs of students, especially of immigrants. The fact that failure is marked by geolinguistic and linguistic groups reveals an urgent need for educators to consider the conundrums mentioned earlier. There are no easy answers; however, the consequences of not addressing them have a disastrous potential. We only need to look to France to see the results of not considering such issues.

References

A conversation with Lisa Delpit. (1991). *Language Arts, 68,* 541–547.

Adams, M. J. (1990). *Beginning to read: Thinking and learning about print.* Cambridge, MA: MIT Press.

Adams, M. J., & Collins, A. (1979). A schema-theoretic view of reading. In R. O. Freedle (Ed.), *New directions in discourse processing* (pp. 11–22). Norwood, NJ: Ablex.

Allington, R. (2005). NCLB, reading first, and whither the future? *Reading Today 18,* 23.

American Heritage Dictionaries. (Ed.). (2000). *The American Heritage Dictionary of the English Language* (4th ed.). New York: Houghton Mifflin Company.

Anderson, C. (1964). The psychology of a metaphor. *Journal of Genetic Psychology, 5,* 53–73.

Anderson, J. (1994). Parents' perceptions of emergent literacy. *Reading Psychology, 15*(3), 165–187.

Anderson, J., & Gunderson, L. (1997) Literacy learning from a multicultural perspective. *The Reading Teacher, 50,* 411–412.

Anderson, J., & Gunderson, L. (2001). *You don't read a science book, you study it: An exploration of cultural concepts of reading.* Accessed April 23, 2006, at http://www.readingonline.org/electronic/elec_index.asp?HREF=anderson/index. html

Anderson, J. F., & Powell, R. (1988). Cultural influences on educational processes. In L. A. Samovar & R. E. Porter (Eds.), *Intercultural communication: A reader* (5th ed., pp. 207–214). Belmont, CA: Wadsworth.

Anderson, R. C., Hiebert, E. H., Scott, J. A., & Wilkinson, I. A. G. (1985). *Becoming a nation of readers: The report of the Commission on Reading.* Washington, DC: National Institute of Education, U.S. Department of Education.

Anderson, R. C., & Pearson, P. D. (1984). A schema-theoretic view of basic processes in reading comprehension. In P. D. Pearson, R. Barr, M. L. Kamil, & P. Mosenthall (Eds.), *The handbook of reading research* (pp. 255–292). New York: Longmans.

Anderson, R. C., Reynolds, R. E., Schallert, D. L., & Goetz, E. T. (1977). Frameworks for comprehending discourse. *American Educational Research Journal, 14,* 367–382.

Anderson, R. C., Spiro, R. J., & Anderson, M. C. (1977). *Schemata as scaffolding for the representation of information in connected discourse* (Tech. Rep. No. 24). Urbana: University of Illinois.

Anderson, R. C., Stevens, K. C., Shifrin, Z., & Osborn, J. H. (1978). Instantiation of general terms. *Journal of Reading Behavior, 10*, 149–157.

Andrew, C. M., Lapkin, S., & Swain, M. (1978). *Report on the 1978 evaluation of the Ottawa and Carleton French immersion programs, grades 5–7*. Toronto, CA: Ontario Institute for Studies in Education.

Arlin, P. K. (1978). *Metaphors and thought in children* (Rep. No. 78). Vancouver, Canada: Educational Research Institute of British Columbia.

Aro, M. (2006). Learning to read: The effect of orthography. In R. M. Joshi & P. G. Aaron (Eds.), *Handbook of orthography and literacy* (pp. 531–550). Mahwah, NJ: Lawrence Erlbaum Associates.

Arter, J. L. (1976). *The effects of metaphor on reading comprehension*. Unpublished doctoral dissertation, University of Illinois, Urbana.

Ashton-Warner, S. (1963). *Teacher*. New York: Bantam Books.

Ashworth, M. N. (1991). Foreword, viewpoint 2. In L. Gunderson (Ed.), *ESL literacy instruction: A guidebook to theory and practice* (p. x). Englewood Cliffs, NJ: Prentice Hall Regents.

Ashworth, N. M., Cummins, J., & Handscomb, G. (1989). *The report of the external review team on the Vancouver school board's ESL programmes*. Vancouver: Vancouver School Board.

Asimov, N. (1997, January). California schools rate D-minus in report: Exhaustive study blames Prop 13 for the damage. *The San Francisco Chronicle*, p. A2.

Au, K. H. (1993). *Literacy instruction in multicultural settings*. Forth Worth, TX: Harcourt Brace Jovanovich.

Auerbach, E. R. (1993). Reexamining English only in the ESL classroom. *TESOL Quarterly, 27*, 9–29.

Baker, K. A., & deKanter, A. A. (1981). *Effectiveness of bilingual education: A review of the literature*. Washington, DC: Office of Planning and Budget, U.S. Department of Education.

Baldwin, R. S., Luce, T. S., & Readence, J. S. (1982). The impact of subschemata on metaphorical processing. *Reading Research Quarterly, 17*, 528–543.

Banks, J. A. (1991) *Teaching strategies for ethnic studies* (4th ed.). Needham Heights, MA: Allyn and Bacon.

Barik, H. C., & Swain, M. (1975). Three-year evaluation of a large scale early grade French immersion program: The Ottawa study. *Language Learning, 25*, 1–30.

Barnlund, D. C. (1987). Verbal self-disclosure: Topics, targets, depth. In L. F. Luce & E. C. Smith (Eds.), *Toward internationalism: Readings in cross-cultural communication* (2nd ed., pp. 147–165). Rowley, MA: Newbury House.

Bartlett, F. C. (1932). *Remembering*. Cambridge: Cambridge University Press.

Bates, E. (1976). *Language and context: The acquisition of pragmatics*. New York: Academic Press.

Bates, E., Benigni, L., Bretherton, I., Camaioni, L., & Volterra, V. (1977). From gesture to the first word: On cognitive and social prerequisites. In L. Rosenblum (Ed.), *Conversation, interaction, and the development of language* (pp. 247–307). New York: John Wiley & Sons.

Becker, C. B. (1988). Reasons for the lack of argumentation and debate in the Far East. In L. A. Samovar & R. E. Porter (Eds.), *Intercultural communication: A reader* (5th ed., pp. 243–252). Belmont, CA: Wadsworth.

Bell, J. S. (1995). The relationship between L1 and L2 literacy: Some complicating factors. *TESOL Quarterly, 29*, 687–704.

Bendor-Samuel, J. (1996). African languages. In P. T. Daniels & W. Bright (Eds.), *The world's writing systems* (pp. 689–691). New York: Oxford University Press.

Berlin, B., & Kay, P. (1969). *Basic color terms: Their universality and evolution.* Berkeley: University of California Press.

Bernhardt, E. B. (1991). *Reading development in a second language.* Norwood, NJ: Ablex.

Bernhardt E. B. (2000). Second-language reading as a case study of reading in the 20th century. In M. L. Kamil, P. B. Mosenthal, P. D. Pearson, & R. Barr (Eds.), *Handbook of reading research* (3rd ed., pp. 791–811). Mahwah, NJ: Lawrence Erlbaum Associates.

Bernhardt, E. B., & Kamil, M. (1995). Interpreting relationships between L1 and L2 reading: Consolidating the linguistic threshold and the linguistic interdependence hypotheses. *Applied Linguistics, 16*, 15–34.

Betts, E. A. (1946) *Foundations of reading instruction with emphasis on differentiated guidance.* New York: American Books Company.

Billow, R. M. (1975). A cognitive developmental study of metaphor comprehension. *Developmental Psychology, 11*, 415–423.

Boyarin, D. (1993). Placing reading: Ancient Israel and medieval Europe. In J. Boyarin (Ed.) *The ethnography of reading* (pp. 10–37). Berkeley: University of California Press.

Bradley, L., & Bryant, P. E. (1985). *Rhyme and reason in reading and spelling.* Ann Arbor: University of Michigan Press.

Brewer, W. (1976). Is reading a letter-by-letter process? A discussion of Gough's paper. In H. Singer & R. B. Ruddell (Eds.), *Theoretical models and processes of reading* (3rd ed., pp. 722–750). Newark, DE: International Reading Association.

Brinton, D. M., Snow, M. A., & Wesche, M. B. (2003). *Content-based second language instruction.* Ann Arbor: University of Michigan Press.

Brown, R. (1973). *A first language: The early stages.* London: George Allen & Unwin.

Brown, I. S., & Felton, R. H. (1990). Effects of instruction on beginning reading skills in children at risk for reading disability. *Reading and Writing: An Interdisciplinary Journal, 2*, 223–241.

Cambourne, B. (1988). *The whole story: Natural learning and the acquisition of literacy in the classroom.* Auckland, NZ: Scholastic. (Sydney: PETA.)

Cambourne, B., & Turbill, J. B. (1988). *From guinea pigs to coresearchers.* Brisbane: Pre-Conference Institute, World Reading Conference.

Cambourne, B., & Turbill, J. B. (1989). *Whole language all day, every day.* New Orleans: Pre-Conference Institute, International Reading Association Annual Conference.

Cambourne, B., & Turbill, J. (1990). Assessment in whole-language classrooms: Theory into practice. *Elementary School Journal 90*, 337–349.

Canale, M. (1983). From communicative competence to communicative language pedagogy. In J. C. Richards & R. W. Schmidt (Eds.), *Language and communication* (pp. 2–27). London: Longman.

Canale, M., & Swain, M. (1980). Theoretical bases of communicative approaches to second language teaching and testing. *Applied Linguistics, 1*, 1–47.

Carrell, P. L. (1981). Culture-specific schemata in L2 comprehension. In R. Orem & J. Haskell (Eds.), *Selected papers from the ninth Illinois TESOL/BE annual convention, The first Midwest TESOL conference* (pp. 123–132). Chicago: TESOL/BE.

Carrell, P. L. (1983). Some issues in studying the role of schemata, or background knowledge, in second language comprehension. *Reading in a Foreign Language, 1*, 81–92.

Carrell, P. L. (1984). Schema theory and ESL reading: Classroom implications and applications. *Modern Language Journal, 68*, 332–343.

Carrell, P. L. (1987a). Content and formal schemata in ESL reading. *TESOL Quarterly, 21*, 461–481.

Carrell, P. L. (1987b). Introduction. In J. Devine, P. L. Carrell, & D. E. Eskey (Eds.), *Research in reading in English as a second language* (pp. 1–7). Washington, DC: TESOL.

Carrell, P. L. (1988a). Interactive text processing: Implications for ESL/second language reading classrooms. In P. L. Carrell & D. Eskey (Eds.), *Interactive approaches to second language reading* (pp. 239–259). New York: Cambridge University Press.

Carrell, P. L. (1988b). Some causes of text-boundedness and schema-interference in ESL reading. In P. L. Carrell, J. Devine, & D. Eskey (Eds.), *Interactive approaches to second language reading* (pp. 101–113). New York: Cambridge University Press.

Carrell, P. L., Devine, J., & Eskey, D. (Eds.). (1988). *Interactive approaches to second language reading*. New York: Cambridge University Press.

Carrell, P. L., & Eisterhold, J. (1983). Schema theory and ESL reading pedagogy. *TESOL Quarterly, 17*, 553–573.

Carrigan, T. (1986, December). *Reading achievement of grade one students involved in language experience programs vs. basal programs*. Paper presented at the National Reading Conference, Austin, TX.

Carrigan, T. (1994). *An ESL report: Richmond school district*. Richmond, British Columbia: Richmond School Board.

Carrigan, T. (2000). *ESL students*. Richmond, British Columbia: Richmond School District.

Cazabon, M. T., Nicoladis, E., & Lambert, W. E. (1998). *Becoming bilingual in the Amigo two-way immersion program*. Santa Cruz: University of California at Santa Cruz. Available at http://repositories.cdlib.org/crede/rsrchrpts/rr03

Chall, J. S. (1958). *Readability: An appraisal of research and application*. Athens: Bureau of Education Research, Ohio University.

Chen, H. S., & Graves, M. (1995). Effects of previewing and providing background knowledge. *TESOL Quarterly, 29*, 663–682.

Cho, K., & Krashen, S. D. (1994). Acquisition of vocabulary for the Sweet Valley Kids series: Adult ESL acquisition. *Journal of reading, 37*, 662–667.

Clark, H. H., & Clark, E. V. (1977). *Psychology and language: An introduction to psycholinguistics*. New York: Harcourt, Brace, Jovanovich.

Clarke, D. (1997). *A study of ESL support and immigrants' success in secondary school*. Unpublished MA thesis, University of British Columbia, Vancouver.

Clarke, M. (1979). Reading in Spanish and English: Evidence from adult ESL learners. *Language Learning. 29*, 121–150.

Clarke, M., & Silberstein, S. (1977). Toward a realization of psycholinguistic principles for the ESL reading class. *Language Learning, 27*, 135–154.

Clay, M. (1979). *Reading: The patterning of complex behavior* (2nd ed.). Portsmouth, NH: Heinemann.

Clay, M. (1985). *The early detection of reading difficulties* (3rd ed.). Portsmouth, NH: Heinemann.

Clay, M. (1991). *Becoming literate: The construction of inner control*. Portsmouth, NH: Heinemann.

Coady, J. (1979). A psycholinguistic model of the ESL reader. In R. Mackay, B. Barkman, & R. R. Jordan (Eds.), *Reading in a second language* (pp. 5–12). Rowley, MA: Newbury House.

Collier, V. P. (1987). Age and rate of acquisition of second language for academic purposes. *TESOL Quarterly, 21*, 617–641.

Collier, V. P. (1994, March). *Sociocultural processes in academic, cognitive, and language development*. Plenary Address, TESOL International, Baltimore, MD.

Connor, U. M. (1981). The application of reading miscue analysis to diagnosis of English-as-a-second-language learners' reading skills. In C. Twyford, W. Diehl, & K. Feathers (Eds.), *Reading English as a second language: Moving from theory* (pp. 47–55). Bloomington: Indiana University School of Education.

Cooley, J. A. (2001). Are the Clintons channeling Ma and Pa Ferguson? *The Houston Review*. Accessed December 12, 2005, at http://www.houstonreview.com/articles/ClintonsFerguson.html

Crago, M. B. (1992). Communicative interaction and second language acquisition: An Inuit example. *TESOL Quarterly, 26*, 487–505.

Crawford, J. (1989). *Bilingual education: History, politics, theory, and practice*. Trenton, NJ: Crane.

Crawford, J. (1997). *Best evidence: Research foundation of the Bilingual Education Act*. National Clearing House for Bilingual Education. Accessed April 23, 2006, at http://www.ncbe.gwu.edu/ncbepubs/reports/bestevidence/index. htm

Crawford, J. (1999, May). *Life in a politicized climate: What role of educational researchers?* Paper presented at the Linguistic Minority Conference on the Schooling of English Language Learners in the Post 227 Era. Sacramento, CA. Paper available at http://ourworld.compuserve.com/homepages/JWCRAWFORD/LMRI.htm

Cummins, J. (1978). The cognitive development of children in immersion programs. *The Canadian Modern Language Review, 34*, 855–883.

Cummins, J. (1979). Cognitive/academic language proficiency, linguistic interdependence, the optimum age question and some other matters. *Working Papers on Bilingualism, 19*, 197–205.

Cummins, J. (1980). The entry and exit fallacy in bilingual education. *NABE Journal, 4*, 25–59.

Cummins, J. (1981a). Age on arrival and immigrant second language learning in Canada: A reassessment. *Applied Linguistics, 2*, 132–149.

Cummins, J. (1981b). The role of primary language development in promoting educational success for language minority students. In *Schooling and language minority students* (pp. 3–49). Los Angeles: California State University.

Cummins, J. (1982). Tests, achievement and bilingual students. *FOCUS, 9*. Washington, DC: National Clearing House for Bilingual Education.

Cummins, J. (1983a). *Heritage language education: A literature review*. Toronto, Ontario: Ministry of Education.

Cummins, J. (1983b). Language proficiency and academic achievement. In J. W. Oller, Jr. (Ed.), *Issues in language testing research* (pp. 108–129). Rowley, MA: Newbury House.

Cummins, J. (1984). *Bilingualism and special education: Issues in assessment and pedagogy*. Clevedon, England: Multicultural Matters.

Cummins, J. (1991). Empowering minority students: A framework for intervention. In M. Minami & B. P. Kennedy (Eds.), *Language issues in literacy and bilingual/multicultural education* (pp. 372–390). Cambridge, MA: Harvard Educational Review, Reprint Series No. 22. (Original work published 1985)

Cummins, J. (1998). *Beyond adversarial discourse: Searching for common ground in the education of bilingual students*. Presentation to the California State Board of Education. Accessed January 8, 2004, at http://ourworld.compuserve.com/homepages/JWCRAWFORD/cummins.htm

Cummins, J. (2000). *Language, power and pedagogy*. Toronto: Multilingual Matters Limited.

Cummins, J., & Swain, M. (1983). Analysis-by-rhetoric: Reading the text or the reader's own projections? A reply to Edelsky et al. *Applied Linguistics, 4*, 23–41.

Cummins, J., & Swain, M. (1986). Linguistic interdependence: A central principle of bilingual education. In *Bilingualism in education* (pp. 80–95). New York: Longman.

Cunningham, A. E. (1990). Explicit versus implicit instruction in phonemic awareness. *Journal of Experimental Child Psychology, 50*, 429–444.

Cunningham, J. E. (1976). Metaphor and reading comprehension. *Journal of Reading Behavior, 8*, 363–368.

Daniels, P. T., & Bright, W. (Eds.). (1996). *The world's writing systems*. New York: Oxford University Press.

Dank, M., & McEachern, W. (1979). A psycholinguistic description comparing the native language oral reading behavior of French immersion students with traditional English language students. *Canadian Modern Language Review, 35*, 336–371.

Dearden, L., Emmerson, C., Frayne, C., & Meghir, J. (2005). *Education subsidies and school drop-out rates*. London: Institute for Fiscal Studies.

DeFrancis, J. (1989). *Visible speech: The diverse oneness of writing systems*. Honolulu, HI: University of Hawaii Press.

Delpit, L. D. (1988). The silenced dialogue: Power and pedagogy in educating other people's children. *Harvard Educational Review 58, 3*, 280–298.

Dinh-Hoa, N. (1996). Vietnamese. In P. T. Daniels & W. Bright (Eds.), *The world's writing systems* (pp. 691–695). New York: Oxford University Press.

Diringer, D. (1968). *The alphabet* (Vols. 1 & 2). New York: Funk & Wagnalls.

Duff, P. A., & Uchida, Y. (1997). The negotiation of teachers' sociocultural identities and practices in postsecondary EFL classes. *TESOL Quarterly, 31,* 451–486.

Durkin, D. (1978–1979). What classroom observations reveal about reading comprehension instruction. *Reading Research Quarterly 14,* 481–533.

Dyson, A. H. (1981). Oral language: The rooting system for learning to write. *Language Arts, 58,* 776–84.

Early, M. (1989). A snapshot of ESL students' integration patterns. *TESL Canada Journal, 7,* 52–60.

Early, M. (1990). Enabling first- and second-language learners in the classroom. *Language Arts, 67,* 565–575.

Early, M., & Gunderson, L. (1993). Linking home, school, and community language learning. *TESL Canada Journal, 11,* 99–111.

Eddy, C. (1994). *A report on the screening and assignment of students at the Oakridge reception and orientation centre.* Vancouver: Vancouver School Board.

Eddy, C. (1995). *Statistics from the Oakridge Orientation and Reception Centre.* Vancouver: Vancouver School Board.

Eddy, C. (2005). *Statistics from the Vancouver placement and reception centre.* Vancouver: Vancouver School Board.

Edelsky, C. (1990a). Whose agenda is this anyway? A response to McKenna, Robinson, and Miller. *Educational Researcher, 19,* 7–11.

Edelsky, C. (1990b). *With literacy and justice for all: Rethinking the social in language and education.* London: Falmer Press.

Elley, W. (1991). Acquiring literacy in a second language; The effect of book-based programs. *Language Learning, 41,* 375–411.

Elley, W. B. (1992). *How in the world do students read?* Grindeldruck, Germany: International Association for the Evaluation of Educational Achievement.

Elley, W., & Mangubhai, F. (1983). The impact of reading on second language learning. *Reading Research Quarterly, 19,* 53–67.

Ellis, R. (1994). *The study of second language acquisition.* Oxford: Oxford University Press.

Eskey, D. (1973). A model program for teaching advanced reading to students of English as a foreign language. *Language Learning, 23,* 169–184.

Eskey, D., & Grabe, W. (1988). Interactive models for second language reading: Perspectives on instruction. In P. L. Carrell, J. Devine, & D. Eskey (Eds.), *Interactive approaches to second language reading* (pp. 223–238). New York: Cambridge University Press.

Evans, M. A., & Carr, T. H. (1985). Cognitive abilities, conditions of learning, and the early development of reading skill. *Reading Research Quarterly, 20,* 327–350.

Fabian, J. (1993). Keep listening: Ethnography and reading. In J. Boyarin (Ed.), *The ethnography of reading* (pp. 80–97). Berkeley: University of California Press.

Favreau, M., Komodo, M. K., & Segalowitz, N. (1980). Second language reading: Implications of the word superiority effect in skilled bilinguals. *Canadian Journal of Psychology, 34,* 370–380.

Favreau, M., & Segalowitz, N. (1983). Second language reading in fluent bilinguals. *Applied Psycholinguistics, 3,* 329–341.

Ferreiro, E. (1986). The interplay between information and assimilation in beginning literacy. In W. H. Teale & E. Sulzby (Eds.), *Emergent literacy: Writing and reading* (pp. 15–49). Norwood, NJ: Ablex.

Field, M. L., & Aebersold, J. A. (1990). Cultural attitudes toward reading: Implications for teachers of ESL/bilingual readers. *Journal of Reading, 33*, 406–410.

Floyd, P., & Carrell, P. L. (1987). Effects on ESL reading of teaching cultural content schemata. *Language Learning, 37*, 89–108.

Fraser Institute. (2000). *Report card on secondary schools, 2000.* Accessed April 23, 2006, at http://www.fraserinstitute.ca/publications/studies/education/report_card/2000/bc/tables/vancouver.html

Freeman, Y. S., & Freeman, D. E. (1992). *Whole language for second language learners.* Portsmouth, NH: Heinemann.

Frost, R., & Bentin, S. (1992). Reading consonants and guessing vowels: Visual word recognition in Hebrew orthography. In R. Frost & L. Katz (Eds.), *Orthography, phonology, morphology, and meaning* (pp. 27–44). Amsterdam: Elsevier.

Fry, E. (1968). *Graph for estimating readability—Extended.* New Brunswick, NJ: Rutgers University Reading Center.

Gaffield-Vile, N. (1996). Content-based second language instruction at the tertiary level. *ELT Journal 50*, 108–114.

Gambrell, T. J., & McFeteridge, P. A. (1981). Children, similes, metaphors and reading go together. *Reading-Canada-Lecture, 1*, 9–35.

Gamez, G. I. (1979). Reading in a second language: 'Native language approach' vs 'direct method'. *The Reading Teacher, 32*, 665–670.

Gardner, H. (1974). Metaphors and modalities: How children project polar adjectives onto diverse domains. *Child Development, 45*, 84–91.

Gardner, H., Kircher, M., Winner, E., & Perkins, D. (1974). Children's metaphoric productions and preferences. *Journal of Child Language, 2*, 125–141.

Gatbonton, E. C., & Tucker (1971). Cultural orientation and the study of foreign literature. *TESOL Quarterly, 5*, 137–143.

Gecker, J. (2005, November 8). France to order curfews as riots spread. *The Vancouver Sun*, p. A12.

Genisio, M. (1996, Spring). An assembly bill mandating phonics: The implications are many. *WSRA Journal*, pp. 50–53.

Gersten, R., Woodward, J., & Schneider, S. (1992). Bilingual immersion: A longitudinal evaluation of the El Paso program. *READ*, ERIC Document Reproductions, pp. 1–42.

Geva, E. (1995). Orthographic and cognitive processing in learning to read. In I. Taylor & D. R. Olson (Eds.), *Scripts and literacy* (pp. 277–291). Dordrecht: Kluwer Academic.

Gibson, E. J., Osser, H., Schiff, W., & Smith, J. (1963). An analysis of critical features of letters tested by a confusion matrix. In *Final report on a basic research program on reading.* Final report, Project #639, Ithica, New York: Cornell University.

Goodman, K. S. (1967). Reading: A psycholinguistic guessing game. *Journal of the Reading Specialist, 6*, 126–135.

Goodman, K. (1976). Reading: A psycholinguistic guessing game. In H. Singer & R. Ruddell (Eds.), *Theoretical models and processes of reading* (2nd ed., pp. 497–508). Newark, DE: International Reading Association.

Goodman, K. S. (1981). Letters to the editor. *Reading Research Quarterly, 16,* 477–478.

Goodman, K. S. (1985). Unity in all reading. In H. Singer & R. B. Ruddell (Eds.), *Theoretical models and processes of reading* (3rd ed., pp. 813–840). Newark, DE: International Reading Association.

Goodman, K. S., & Gollasch, F. V. (1980). Word omissions: Deliberate and non-deliberate. *Reading Research Quarterly, 16,* 6–31.

Goodman, K. S., & Goodman, Y. (1978). *Reading of American children whose language is a stable rural dialect of English or other than English* (ED 173 754). Washington, DC: ERIC Document Reproduction Service.

Goodman, Y. M. (1989). Roots of the whole language movement. *Elementary School Journal, 90*(2), 113–127.

Gough, P. (1976). One second of reading. In H. Singer and R. B. Ruddell (Eds.), *Theoretical models and processes of reading* (3rd ed., pp. 722–750). Newark, DE: International Reading Association. (Original work published 1972)

Grabe, W. (1988). Reassessing the term interactive. In P. L. Carrell, J. Devine, & D. Eskey (Eds.), *Interactive approaches to second language reading* (pp. 56–72). New York: Cambridge University Press.

Grabe, W. (1991). Current developments in second language reading research. *TESOL Quarterly, 26,* 375–406.

Gradman, H. L., & Hanania, E. (1991). Language learning background factors and ESL proficiency. *Modern Language Journal, 75,* 39–51.

Gray, W. S., & Leary, B. E. (1935). *What makes a book readable?* Chicago: University of Chicago Press.

Greene, J. P. (1998). *A meta-analysis of the effectiveness of bilingual education.* Austin, TX: University of Texas. http://ourworld.compuserve.com/homepages/jwcrawford/greene.htm

Grindstaff, F. L., & Muller, A. L. (1975). The national assessment of literature: Two reviews. *Research in the Teaching of English, 9,* 80–106.

Gunderson, L. (1979). *A study of Burmese phonemes.* Berkley, CA: University of California Berkley Phonological Archives.

Gunderson, L. (1981). *A developmental study of the role of letter features in word recognition.* Unpublished doctoral dissertation, University of California, Berkeley.

Gunderson, L. (1983). ESL students: Don't throw them to the sharks. *Highway One, 6,* 34–44.

Gunderson, L. (1985a). A survey of ESL reading instruction in British Columbia. *Canadian Modern Language Review, 42,* 44–55.

Gunderson, L. (1985b). L2 reading instruction in ESL and mainstream classrooms. In J. Niles & R. Lalik (Eds.), *Issues in literacy: A research perspective* (pp. 65–69). Rochester, NY: National Reading Conference.

Gunderson, L. (1985c). Basal reading instruction and ESL students. *Reading Horizons, 25,* 162–168.

Gunderson, L. (1986). ESL students and content reading. *TESL Canada Journal, 4,* 49–53.

Gunderson, L. (1989). *A whole language primer.* Richmond Hills, Ontario: Scholastic Canada.

Gunderson, L. (1991a). *ESL literacy instruction: A guidebook to theory and practice.* Englewood Cliffs, NJ: Prentice Hall Regents.

Gunderson, L. (1991b). *A theoretical model of the differential effects of cognitive demand and context embeddedness on second language reading.* Paper presented at the Regional English Language Centre Conference, Singapore.

Gunderson, L. (1994). English as a second language instruction. In A. Purvis (Ed.), *The encyclopedia of English studies and language arts (pp. 437–439).* New York: Longmans.

Gunderson, L. (1995) *Monday morning guide to comprehension.* Markham, Ontario: Pippin.

Gunderson, L. (1997). Whole-language approaches to reading and writing. In S. Stahl & D. Hayes (Eds.), *Instructional models in reading* (pp. 221–247). Englewood Cliffs, NJ: Lawrence Erlbaum Associates.

Gunderson, L. (1996). *An ESL research report.* Richmond, BC: Richmond School District.

Gunderson, L. (2000). Voices of the teenage diasporas. *Journal of Adolescent and Adult Literacy, 43,* 692–706.

Gunderson, L. (2001). Different cultural views of whole language. In S. Boran & B. Comber (Eds.), *Critiquing whole language and classroom inquiry* (pp. 242–271). Urbana, IL: National Council of Teachers of English.

Gunderson, L. (2003). Whole language and inquiry:The issue of voice from a multicultural perspective. In S. Boran & B. Comber (Eds.), *Critiquing whole language and classroom inquiry* (pp. 242–271). Urbana, IL: Whole Language Umbrella and the National Council of Teachers of English.

Gunderson, L. (2004). The Language, Literacy, Achievement, and Social Consequences of English-Only programs for Immigrant Students. In J. Hoffman & D. Schallert (Eds.), *The NRC Yearbook* (pp. 1–27). Milwaukee, WI: National Reading Conference.

Gunderson, L., & Anderson, J. (2003). Multicultural views of literacy learning and teaching. In A. I. Willis, G. E. Garcia, R. Barrera & Harris, V. J. (Eds.), *Multicultural issue in literacy research and practice* (pp. 123–144). Mahwah, NJ: Lawrence Erlbaum Associates.

Gunderson, L., & Carrigan, T. (1993). *An analysis of the English achievement of ESL students: A three year study.* Paper presented at the National Reading Conference, Charleston, NC.

Gunderson, L., & Clarke, D. K. (1998). An exploration of the relationship between ESL students' backgrounds and their English and academic achievement. In T. Shanahan & F. V. Rodrigues-Brown (Eds.), *National reading conference yearbook* (pp. 264–273). Chicago: National Reading Conference.

Gunderson, L., Slade, K., & Rosenke, D. (1988). A study of the cloze response of L1 and L2 students in response to literal and idiomatic passages. *TESL Canada Journal, 5,* 49–56.

Gunderson, L., & Shapiro, J. (1987). Some findings on whole language instruction. *Reading-Canada-Lecture, 5,* 22–26.

Gunderson, L., & Shapiro, J. (1988). Whole language instruction: Writing in 1st grade. *The Reading Teacher, 41,* 430–437.

Gunderson, L., & Siegel, L. (2001). The evils of the use of IQ tests to define learning disabilities in first- and second-language learners. *The Reading Teacher, 55,* 48–55.

Gunnison, R. B. (1996, December). State rejects 2 texts, citing phonics law. *San Francisco Chronicle*, p. A1.

Guttierrez, A. L. (1975). Bilingual education: Reading through two languages. In D. E. Critchlow (Ed.), *Reading and the Spanish speaking child* (pp. 2–6). Laredo: Texas State Council of the International Reading Association.

Haddad, F. (1981). First language illiteracy—second language reading: A case study. In S. Hudelson (Ed.), *Learning to read in different languages* (pp. 32–44). Washington, DC: Center for Applied Linguistics.

Hafiz, F. M., & Tudor, I. (1989). Extensive reading and the development of language skills. *English Language Teaching Journal, 43*, 4–13.

Hakuta, K. (1986). *Mirror of language: The debate on bilingualism*. New York: Basic Books.

Hakuta, K., Butler, Y. G., & Witt, D. (2000). *How long does it take English learners to attain proficiency?* Santa Barbara: University of California Linguistic Minority Research Institute.

Haney, W., Madaus, G., & Abrams, L. (2003). *Where have all the students gone?* Accessed April 23, 2006, at http://www. bc.edu/research/nbetpp/statements/nbr3_press.pdf

Harley, B., Cummins, J., Swain, M., & Allen, P. (1990). The nature of language proficiency. In B. Harley, P. Allen, J. Cummins & M. Swain (Eds.), *The development of second language proficiency* (pp. 7–25). Cambridge: Cambridge University Press.

Harris, D. P., & Palmer, L. (1986). *CELT examiner's instructions and technical manual*. New York: McGraw-Hill.

Harste, J. C. (1993). Curriculum for the millennium: Putting an edge on learning through inquiry. *Australian Journal of Language and Literacy 16*, 6–22.

Harste, J. C., & Burke, C. L. (1977). A new hypothesis for reading research: Both teaching and learning of reading are theoretically based. In P. D. Pearson (Ed.), *Twenty-sixth yearbook of the national reading conference* (pp. 32–40). Clemson, SC: National Reading Conference.

Hatcher, P., Hulme, C., & Ellis, A. W. (1994). Ameliorating early reading failure by integrating the teaching of reading and phonological skills: The phonological linkage hypothesis. *Child Development, 65*, 41–57.

Hayashi, C. (1994). A study of politeness features in Japanese exchange students' English and Japanese. An unpublished Master of Arts thesis, Department of Language and Literacy Education, University of British Columbia, Vancouver, Canada.

Haynes, M., & Carr, T. H. (1990). Writing system background and second language reading: A component skills analysis of English reading by native-speaker-readers of Chinese. In T. H. Carr & B. A. Levy (Eds.), *Reading and its development: Component skills approaches* (pp. 375–398). New York: Academic Press.

Heald-Taylor, G. (1986). *Whole language strategies for ESL students*. Toronto: OISE Press.

Heald-Taylor, G. (1989). *The administrator's guide to whole language*. Katonah, NY: Richard C. Owen.

Heath, S. B. (1983). *Ways with words: Language life and work in communities and classrooms*. Cambridge: Cambridge University Press.

Heine, B., & Nurse, D. (Eds.). (2000). *African languages: An introduction*. Cambridge: Cambridge University Press.

Helmer, S., & Eddy, C. (1996). *Look at me when I talk to you: ESL learners in non-ESL classrooms.* Toronto, ON: Pippin.

Herman, K. (1959). *Reading disability: A medical study of word blindness and related handicaps.* Springfield, IL: Charles C. Thomas Company.

Hillerich, R. L. (1970). ERMAS: A beginning reading project for Mexican American children. *National Elementary Principal, 1,* 80–84.

Hipple, M. L. (1985). Journal writing in kindergarten. *Language Arts, 62,* 255–261.

Ho, C. S., & Bryant, P. (1997). Learning to read Chinese beyond the logographic phase. *Reading Research Quarterly, 32,* 276–289.

Holdaway, D. (1979). *The foundations of literacy.* Sydney, Australia: Ashton Scholastic.

Honey, P. J. (1987). Vietnamese speakers. In M. Swan & B. Smith (Eds.), *Learner English: A teacher's guide to interference and other problems* (pp. 238–251). Cambridge: Cambirdge University Press.

Hornberger, N. (1989). Continua of biliteracy. *Review of Educational Research, 59,* 271–296.

Howard, E. R., & Sugarman, J. (2001). *Two-way immersion programs in the U.S.* Washington, DC: Center for Applied Linguistics,

Howe, N. (1993). The cultural construction of reading in Anglo-Saxon England. In J. Boyarin (Ed.), *The ethnography of reading* (pp. 58–79). Berkeley: University of California Press.

Hudelson, S. (1984). Kan yu ret and rayt en ingles: Children become literate in English as a second language. *TESOL Quarterly, 18,* 221–238.

Hudson, T. (1982). The effects of induced schemata on the 'short circuit' in L2 reading: Non-decoding factors in L2 reading performance. *Language Learning, 32,* 1–31.

Hudson-Ross, S., & Dong, Y. R. (1990). Literacy learning as a reflection of language and culture: Chinese elementary school education. *The Reading Teacher, 44,* 110–123.

Huey, E. B. (1968). *The psychology and pedagogy of reading.* Cambridge, MA: MIT Press. (Original work published 1908)

Hung, D. L., & Tzeng, O. J. L. (1981). Orthographic variations and visual information processing. *Psychological Bulletin, 90,* 377–414.

IDEA. (1997). *The individuals with disabilities education act amendments of 1997.* Accessed April 23, 2006, at http://www.ed.gov/offices/OSERS/Policy/IDEA/index.html

Irujo, S. (1986). Don't put your leg in your mouth: Transfer in the acquisition of idioms in a second language. *TESOL Quarterly, 20,* 287–304.

Iverson, S., & Tunmer, W. E. (1993). Phonological processing skills and the reading recovery program. *Journal of Educational Psychology, 85,* 112–126.

Jamieson, J., & Lazaruk, S. (2001, August 15). A fortune in his future. *Vancouver Sun,* p. A6.

Malgrady, R. G., & Johnson, M. G. (1980). Towards a perceptual theory of metaphor. In R. P. Honeck & R. R. Hoffman (Eds.), *Cognition and figurative language* (pp. 239–258). Hillsdale, NJ: Lawrence Erlbaum Associates.

Johnson, P. (1981). Effects on reading comprehension of language complexity and cultural background background of a text. *TESOL Quarterly, 15,* 503–516.

Johnson, P. (1982). Effects on reading comprehension of building background. *TESOL Quarterly, 16,* 503–516.

Johnston, P. H. (1992). *Constructive evaluation of literate activity.* White Plains, NY: Longman.

Jordans, P. (1979). Rules, grammatical intuitions and strategies in foreign language learning. *Interlanguage Studies Bulletin, 2,* 58–146.

Joshi, R. M., & Aaron, P. G. (Eds.). (2006). *Handbook of orthography and literacy.* Mahwah, NJ: Lawrence Erlbaum Associates.

Juel, C. (1988). Learning to read and write: A longitudinal study of fifty-four children from first through fourth grade. *Journal of Educational Psychology. 80,* 437–47.

Juel, C. (1994). *Learning to read and write in one elementary school.* New York: Springer-Verlag.

Katz, L., & Frost, R. (1992). The reading process is different for different orthographies. In R. Frost & L. Katz (Eds.), *Orthography, phonology, morphology, and meaning* (pp. 67–84). Amsterdam: Elsevier.

Kaufman, M. (1968.). Will instruction in reading Spanish affect reading ability in English? *Journal of Reading, 11,* 521–527.

Keaton, J. (2005, November 8). Anger simmers among youth in Paris projects. *The Vancouver Sun,* p. A 12.

Kellerman, E. (1977). Towards a characterization of the strategy of transfer in second language learning. *Interlanguage Studies Bulletin, 2,* 5–77.

Kintsch, W. (1974.) *The representation of meaning in memory.* Hillsdale, NJ: Lawrence Erlbaum Associates.

Klare, G. (1963). *The measurement of readability.* Ames: Iowa State University Press.

Koda, K. (1995). Cognitive consequences of L1 and L2 orthographies. In I. Taylor & D. R. Olson (Eds.), *Scripts and literacy* (pp. 310–324). Dordrecht: Kluwer Academic.

Kolers, P. A. (1972). Experiments in reading. *Scientific American, 227,* 84–91.

Korkeamäki, R., & Dreher, M. J. (1993). Finland, phonics and whole language: Beginning reading in a regular letter-sound correspondence language. *Language Arts, 70,* 475–482.

Krashen, S. D. (1982). Accounting for child–adult differences in second language rate and attainment. In S. D. Krashen, R. C. Scarcella & M. A. Long (Eds.), *Child–adult differences in second language acquisition* (pp. 202–226). Rowley, MA: Newbury House.

Krashen, S. D. (1993). *The power of reading.* Englewood, CO: Libraries Unlimited.

Krashen, S. D., Long, M. A., & Scarcella, R. C. (1979). Age, rate, and eventual attainment in second language acquisition. *TESOL Quarterly, 13,* 573–582.

Krashen, S. (1999). *Why Malherbe (1946) is NOT evidence against bilingual education.* Accessed July 24, 2005 at http://ourworld.compuserve. com/homepages/JWCRAWFORD/Krashen4. htm

Krashen, S. D., Scarcella, R. C., & Long, M. A. (Eds.). (1982). *Child–adult differences in second language acquisition.* Rowley, MA: Newbury House.

Kroeber, A., & Kluckhohn, C. (1954). *Culture: A critical review of concepts and definitions.* New York: Random House.

LaBerge, D., & Samuels, S. J. (1974). Toward a theory of automatic information processing in reading. *Cognitive Psychology, 6,* 293–323.

Lara, J. (1994). Demographic overview: Changes in student enrollment in American schools. In K. Sprangenberg-Urbschat & R. Pritchard (Eds.), *Kids come in all languages: Reading instruction for ESL students* (pp. 9–21). Newark, DE: International Reading Association.

Larsen-Freeman, D. 1986. *Techniques and principles in language teaching.* Oxford: Oxford University Press.

Larson, D. N., & Smalley, W. A. (1972). *Becoming bilingual: A guide to language learning.* Pasadena, CA: William Carey Library.

Lau vs. Nichols. (1974). 414 U.S. 563.

Leu, D. (1981). Questions from a metatheoretical perspective: The interdependence of solutions to issues involved in the development of reading comprehension models. In M. Kamil (Ed.), *Directions in reading: Research and instruction* (pp. 96–107). Washington, DC: National Reading Conference.

Leu, D. J. (1982). Oral reading error analysis: A criticial review of research and application. *Reading Research Quarterly. 17,* 420–437.

Levin, H., & Kaplan, E. L. (1970). *Basic studies in reading.* New York: Basic Books.

Lewis, G. L. (1965). *Bilingualism—Some aspects of its history. Report on an international seminar on bilingualism in education.* London: Her Majesty's Stationery.

Leyba, C. F. (1978). *Longitudinal study: Title VII bilingual programs.* Los Angeles: Santa Fe Public Schools, National Dissemination and Assessment Center.

Li, G. (2006). *Culturally contested pedagogy: Battles of literacy and schooling between mainstream teachers and Asian immigrant parents.* Albany, NY: State University of New York Press.

Lie, A. (1991). Effects of a training program for stimulating skills in word analysis in first-grade children. *Reading Research Quarterly, 26,* 234–250.

Lono, L. P. (1987.) Cultural aspects in the development of reading comprehension skills. In C. Cargill (Ed.), *A TESOL professional anthology* (pp. 79–92). Lincolnwood, IL: National Textbook Company.

Lucas, G., & Asimov, N. (1995, October). Sacramento: Governor signs bills on basic spelling, math. *The San Francisco Chronicle,* p. A17.

Lucas, T., & Katz, A. (1994) Reframing the debate: The roles of native languages in English-only programs for language minority students. *TESOL Quarterly, 28,* 537–561.

Mabry, M. (1995). Review of the Wide Range Achievement test 3. In J. C. Conoley & J. C. Impara (Eds.), *The twelfth mental measurements yearbook* (pp. 1108–1110). Lincoln: Buros Institute of Mental Measurements, University of Nebraska-Lincoln.

Mackay, R., & Mountford, A. (1979). Reading for information. In R. Mackay, B. Barkman, & R. R. Jordan (Eds.), *Reading in a second language* (pp. 106–141). Rowley, MA: Newbury House.

Mackey, W. F. (1972). *Bilingual education in a binational school.* Rowley, MA: Newbury House.

Maley, A. (1985). On chalk and cheese, babies and bathwater and squared circles: Can traditional and communicative approaches be reconciled? In P. Larson, E. L. Judd, & D. S. Messerschmitt (Eds.), *On TESOL'84* (pp. 159–170). Washington, DC: TESOL.

Maley, A. (1987). XANADU—A miracle of rare device: The teaching of English in China. In J. M. Valdes (Ed.), *Culture bound: Bridging the culture gap in language teaching* (pp. 102–111). Cambridge: Cambridge University Press.

Marchbanks, G., & Levin, H. (1965). Cues by which children recognize words. *Journal of Educational Psychology. 56*, 57–61.

Matalene, C. (1985). Contrastive rhetoric: An American writing teacher in China. *College English, 47*, 789–808.

Mathews, M. M. (1966). *Teaching to read: Historically considered.* Chicago: University of Chicago Press.

Matsumura, S. (2001). Modeling the relationships among interlanguage pragmatic development, L2 proficiency, and exposure to L2. *Applied Linguistics, 24*, 465–491.

McCallum, R. D., Whitlow, R. F., & Moore, S. (1991, December). *Standardized tests as measures of achievement in whole language programs: A question of validity.* Paper presented at the National Reading Conference, Palm Springs, CA.

McKenna, M. C., Robinson, R. D., & Miller, J. W. (1993). Whole language and research: The case for caution. In D. Leu & C. K. Kinzer (Eds.), *Examining central issues in literacy research, theory, and practice* (pp. 141–152). Chicago: National Reading Conference.

McLeod, J., & McLeod, R. (1990). *NewGAP.* Novato, CA: Academic Therapy Publications.

McLeod, J., & McLeod, R. (1977). *GAP.* Sydney, Australia: Heinemann.

Mes-Prat, M., & Edwards, H. P. (1981). Elementary French immersion children's use of orthographic structure for reading. *Canadian Modern Language Review, 37*, 682–693.

Miller, R. (1990). *What are schools for: Holistic education in American culture.* Brandon, VT: Holistic Education Press.

Minister of Industry, Science and Technology. (1992). *Statistics Canada: Knowledge of languages. The Nation, 91 Census.* Ottawa: Statistics Canada. Catalogue 93–318.

Ministry of Education (2005). *Students whose primary language spoken at home in not English, 1995/96–2004/05 (public and independent).* Victoria, Canada: British Columbia Ministry of Education Information Department.

Minsky, M. (1975). A framework for for representing knowledge. In P. H. Winston (Ed.), *The psychology of computer vision* (pp. 211–277). New York: McGraw Hill.

Modiano, N. (1968). National or mother tongue language in beginning reading? *Research in the Teaching of English, 2*, 32–43.

Mohan, B. (1986). *Knowledge and content.* New York: Allyn and Bacon.

Moll, L. (1992). Bilingual classroom studies and community analysis: Some recent trends. *Educational Researcher, 21*, 20–24.

Moore, S. (1998). Bilingual betrayal. *National Review.* Accessed April 23, 2006, at http://www.onenation.org/1098/101298a.html

Morris, D. (1981). Concept of word: A developmental phenomenon in the beginning reading and writing process. *Language Arts, 58*, 659–668.

Murdock, G. P. (1945). The common denominator of cultures. In R. Linton (Ed.), *The science of man in the world crisis* (pp. 123–142). New York: Columbia University Press.

Natalicio, D. S.(1979). Reading and the bilingual child. In L. B. Resnick & P. A. Weaver (Eds.), *Theory and practice of early reading* (Vol. 3, pp. 186–200). Hillsdale, NJ: Lawrence Erlbaum Associates.

National Center for Education Statistics. (2004). *Language minorities and their educational and labor market indicators—Recent trends.* U.S. Department of Education, Institute of Education Sciences, number 2004–2009.

National Joint Committee on Learning Disabilities. (2000, January). *Learning disabilities: Issues on definition.* http://www.ldonline.org/njcld/defn_91.html

National Literacy Panel. (2003). Accessed December 12, 2005 at http://www.cal.org/natl-lit-panel/index.html

Neisser, U. (1967). *Cognitive psychology.* New York: Appleton-Century-Crofts.

Nelson, G. L. (1987). Culture's role in reading comprehension: A schema theoretical approach. *Journal of Reading, 30,* 424–429.

Nicholson, T. (1991). Do children read words better in context or in lists? A classic study revisited. *Journal of Educational Psychology, 83,* 444–450.

Noakes, S. (1993). Gracious words: Luke's Jesus and the reading of sacred poetry at the beginning of the Christian era. In J. Boyarin (Ed.), *The ethnography of reading* (pp. 38–57). Berkeley: University of California Press.

Norton-Peirce, B (1997). Language, identity, and the ownership of English. *TESOL Quarterly, 31,* 409–429.

Norton, B. (2000). *Identity and language learning: Gender, ethnicity and educational change.* Essex, England: Longman.

Ohala, J. (1978, September). *Lecture in phonology.* Berkeley: University of California.

Olofsson, A. (1993). The relevance of phonological awareness in learning to read: Scandinavian longitudinal and quasi-experimental studies. In R. M. Joshi & C. K. Leong (Eds.), *Reading disabilities: Diagnosis and component processes* (pp. 185–198). Dordrecht, The Netherlands: Kluwer Academic.

Olson, D. (1986). Learning to mean what you say: Toward a psychology of literacy. In S. de Castell, A. Luke, & K. Egan (Eds.), *Literacy, society and schooling: A reader* (pp. 145–158). Cambridge: Cambridge University Press.

Olson, D. (1989). Literate thought. In C. K. Leong & B. S. Randhawa (Eds.), *Understanding literacy and cognition: Theory, research, and application* (pp. 3–15). New York: Plenum Press.

Olson, D. (1992). When a learner attempts to become literate in a second language, what is he or she attempting? The forum. *TESL Canada Journal, 20,* 18–22.

Ortony, A. (1975). Why metaphors are necessary and not just nice. *Educational Theory, 25,* 45–53.

Ortony, A. (1993). The role of similarity in similes and metaphors. In A. Ortony (Ed.) *Metaphor and thought* (pp. 342–356). Cambridge: Cambridge University Press.

Ortony, A., Reynolds, R. E., & Arter. J. L. (1978). Metaphor: Theoretical and empirical research. *Psychological Bulletin, 85,* 919–943.

Ortony, A., Schallert, D. L., Reynolds, R. E., & Antos. S. J. (1978). Interpreting metaphors and idioms: Some effects of context on comprehension. *Journal of Verbal Learning and Verbal Behavior, 17,* 465–477.

Oster, J. (1989). Seeing with different eyes: Another view of literature in the ESL class. *TESOL Quarterly, 23,* 85–103.

Osterloh, K. (1987). Intercultural differences and communicative approaches to foreign-language teaching in the Third World. In J. M. Valdes (Ed.), *Culture bound:*

Bridging the culture gap in language teaching (pp. 77–84). Cambridge: Cambridge University Press.

Ovando, C. J. (2003). Bilingual education in the United States: Historical development and current issues. *Bilingual Research Journal, 27*, 1–24.

Planning and Institutional Research. (2002). *Transitions for 1999/00 graduates from BC secondary schools to BC universities in fall* 2000. Accessed April 23, 2006, at http://www.pair.ubc.ca

Palmer, B. M., Gambrell, L. B., & Almasi, J. F. (1991, December). *Whole language research: A methodological analysis.* Paper presented at the National Reading Conference, Palm Springs, CA.

Paradis, M., Hagiwara, H., & Hildebrandt, N. (1985). *Neurolinguistic aspects of the Japanese writing system.* New York: Academic Press.

Parker, O. D., and Educational Services Staff of AFME. (1986). Cultural clues to the Middle Eastern student. In J. M. Valdes (Ed.), *Culture bound: Bridging the culture gap in language teaching* (pp. 94–101). Cambridge: Cambridge University Press.

Parry, K. (1996). Culture, literacy, and L2 reading. *TESOL Quarterly, 30*, 665–692.

Pearson, P. D., Raphael, T. E., TePaske, N., & Hyser, C. (1979). *The function of metaphor in children's recall of expository passages* (Tech. Rep. No. 131). Urbana, IL: Center for the Study of Reading.

Perreman, R. (1992). Lecture, ecritures, orthographes. In P. Lecocq (Ed.), *La lecture: Processus, apprentissage, troubles* (pp. 55–77). Lille, France: Presses Universitaires de Lille.

Petrie, H. G. (1979). Metaphor and learning. In A. Ortony (Ed.), *Metaphor and thought* (pp. 438–461). Cambridge: Cambridge University Press.

Pflaum, S., Walberg, H. J., Karegianes, M., & Rasher, S. (1980). Reading instruction: A quantitative analysis. *Educational Researcher, 9*,12–18.

Pichert, J. A., & Anderson, R. C. (1977). Taking different perspectives on a story. *Journal of Educational Psychology, 69*, 309–315.

Piper, T. (2001). *And then there were two: Children and second language learning.* Markham, ON: Pippin.

Pirbhai-Illich, F. (2005). *The educational pathways and outcomes of ethnic and linguistic minority students.* Unpublished doctoral dissertation, University of British Columbia, Vancouver.

Pittman, R. S., & Grimes, J. E. (Eds.). (2000). *Ethnologue: Languages of the world. SIL International* (14th ed). http://www.sil.org/ethnologue/countries/Viet.html#MOO

Pollio, M., & Pollio, H. (1974). The development of figurative language in school children. *Journal of Psycholinguistic Research, 3*, 185–201.

Poole, D. (1992). Language socialization in the second language classroom. *Language Learning, 42*, 593–616.

Popkewitz, T. S. (1984). *Paradigm and ideology in educational research: The social functions of the intellectual.* New York: Falmer Press.

Prah, K. K. (Ed.). (1998). *Between distinction and extinction: The harmonisation and standardization of African Languages.* Johannesburg: Witwaterstrand University Press.

Radwanski, G. (1987). *Ontario study of the relevance of education, and the issue of dropouts.* Toronto: Ontario Ministry of Education.

Ramirez, J. D. (1992). Executive summary. *Bilingual Research Journal, 16*, 1–62.

Ramirez, J. D., Yuen, S. D., & Ramey, D. R. (1991). *Executive summary of final report: Longitudinal study of structured English immersion strategy early-exit and late-exit transitional bilingual education program for language minority students*. San Mateo, CA: Aguirre International.

Read, C. (1971). Preschool children's knowledge of English phonology. *Harvard Educational Review. 41*, 1–14.

Regier, T., Kay, P., & Cook, R. S. (in press). *Universal foci and varying boundaries in linguistic color categories*. Accessed April 23, 2006 at http://www.icsi.berkeley.edu/~kay/cogsci05.pdf

Rego, L. (1991). The role of early linguistic awareness in children's reading and writing. *Dissertation Abstracts International, 53*, 1391A. (University Microfilms No. BRD-96830)

Reynolds, R. E., & Schwartz, R. M. (1979, April). *The relation of metaphoric processing to the comprehension and memory of prose*. Paper presented at the American Educational Research Association Conference, San Francisco. Xerox copy.

Richard-Amato, P. A. (1988). *Making it happen: Interaction in the second language classroom: From theory to practice*. New York: Longman.

Rigg, P. (1986). Reading in ESL: Learning from kids. In P. Rigg & S. Enright (Eds.), *Children and ESL: Integrating perspectives* (pp. 55–92). Washington, DC: TESOL.

Rigg, P. (1991). Whole language in TESOL. *TESOL Quarterly, 25*, 521–542.

Rigg, P. (1977). The miscue-ESL project. In H. Brown, C. Yorio, & R. Crymes (Eds.), *On TESOL '77: Teaching and learning English as a second language: Trends in research and practice* (pp. 106–118). Washington, DC: TESOL.

Rivera, C. (Ed.). (1984). *Language proficiency and academic achievement*. Clevedon, England: Multilingual Matters.

Robson, B. (1981). *Alternatives in ESL and literacy: Ban vinai. Asia Foundation Final Report*. Arlington, VA: Center for Applied Linguistics.

Roessingh, H., & Field, D. (2000). Time, timing, timetabling: Critical elements of successful graduation of high school ESL learners. *TESL Canada Journal, 18*, 17–31.

Rosch, E. (1977). Human categorization. In N. Warren (Ed.), *Studies in cross-cultural psychology* (pp. 1–72). London: Academic Press.

Rosen, C. L. (1970). *Assessment and relative effects of reading programs for Mexican Americans: A position paper* (ED061 000). Arlington, VA: ERIC Document Reproduction Services.

Rosowsky, A. (2001). Decoding as a cultural practice and its effects on the reading process of bilingual pupils. *Language and Education, 15*, 56–70.

Rossell, C. H. (1998) *Mystery on the bilingual express: A critique of the Thomas and Collier study*. Accessed December 8, 2005, at http://www.ceousa.org/READ/collier.html

Rossell, C., & Baker, K. (1996). The educational effectiveness of bilingual education. *Research in the Teaching of English, 30*, 7–74.

Rossier, P., & Holm, W. (1980). *The rock point experience: A longitudinal study of a Navajo school*. Washington, DC: Center for Applied Linguistics.

Royer, J. M., & Carlo, M. S. (1991). Transfer of comprehension skills from native to second language. *Journal of Reading, 34*, 450–455.

Rumberger, R. W. (1995). Dropping out of middle school: A multilevel analysis of students and schools. *American Educational Research Journal, 32*, 583–625.

Rumelhart, D. E. (1977). Toward an interactive model of reading. In S. Dornic (Ed.), *Attention and performance VI* (pp. 573–603). Hillsdale, NJ: Lawrence Erlbaum Associates.

Rumelhart, D. E. (1985). Toward an interactive model of reading. In H. Singer & R. B. Ruddell (Eds.), *Theoretical models and processes of reading* (3rd ed., pp. 722–750). Newark, DE: International Reading Association.

Rystrom, R. (1969). Evaluating letter discrimination problems in the primary grades. *Journal of Reading Behavior, 1*, 38–48.

Sacks, O. (1990). *Seeing voices*. New York: HarperCollins.

Samad, A. A. (2002). *Brief review of Somali caste systems: Statement to the committee on the eliminations of racial discrimination.* Accessed April 23, 2006, at http://www.idsn.org/pdf/Africa/somalia.pdf

Saville-Troike, M. (1984). What really matters in second language learning for academic achievement? *TESOL Quarterly, 17*, 199–219.

Scarcella, R. C. (1990). *Teaching language minority students in the multicultural classroom.* Englewood Cliffs, NJ: Prentice Hall.

Scarf, B., Zamansky, H. S., & Brightbill, R. F. (1966). Word recognition with meaning. *Perception and Psychophysics, 1*, 110–112.

Schank, R. C., & Abelson, R. P. (1977). *Scripts, plans, goals, and understanding.* Hillsdale, NJ: Lawrence Erlbaum Associates.

Schecter, S. R., & Bayley, R. (1997). Language socialization practices and cultural identity: Case studies of Mexican-descent families in California and Texas. *TESOL Quarterly, 31*, 513–541.

Schieffelin, B. B. (1982). Talking like birds: Sound play in cultural perspective. In J. Loy (Ed.), *The paradoxes of play* (pp. 177–184). West Point, NY: Leisure Press.

Schieffelin, B. B., & Ochs, E. (Eds.). (1986a). *Language socialization across cultures.* New York: Cambridge University Press.

Schieffelin, B. B., & Ochs, E. (1986b). Language socialization. *Annual Review of Anthropology, 15*, 163–191.

Schiller, E. (1996). Khmer writing. In P. T. Daniels & W. Bright (Eds.), *The world's writing systems* (pp. 467–473). New York: Oxford University Press.

Schumann, J. (1978a). The acculturation model for second-language acquisition. In R. C. Gingras (Ed.), *Second language acquisition and foreign language teaching* (pp. 27–50). Washington, DC: Center for Applied Linguistics.

Schumann, J. (1978b). Psychological factors in second language acquisition. In J. Richards (Ed.), *Understanding second and foreign language learning: Issues and approaches* (pp. 163–178). Rowley MA: Newbury.

Schumann, J. (1986). Research on the acculturalization model for second language acquisition. *Journal of Multilingual and Multicultural Development, 7*, 379–392.

Scribner, S., & Cole, M. (1981). *The psychology of literacy.* Cambridge, MA: Harvard University Press.

Séror, J., Chen, L., & Gunderson, L. (2005). Multiple perspectives on educationally resilient immigrant students. *TESL Canada Journal, 22*, 55–74.

Shannon, P. (1989). *Broken promises.* Cambridge, MA: Bergin and Garvey.

Shapiro, J. (1994). Research perspectives on whole language. In V. Froese (Ed.), *Whole language: Practice and theory* (pp. 433–470). Scarborough, ON: Allyn & Bacon Canada.

Shapiro, J., & Gunderson, L. (1988). A comparison of vocabulary generated by grade 1 students in whole language classrooms and basal reader vocabulary. *Reading Research and Instruction, 27*, 40–46.

Sherman, L. A. (1893). *The literary sentence-length in English prose and the decrease of prediction. Analysis of literature.* Boston: Ginn and Company.

Silva, T. (1993). Toward an understanding of the distinct nature of L1 writing: The ESL research and its implications. *TESOL Quarterly, 24*, 657–677.

Slavin, R. E., & Cheung, A. (2005). A synthesis of research on language of reading instruction for English language learners. *Review of Educational Research 75*, 247–284.

Smith, F. (1973). *Psycholinguistics and reading.* New York: Holt, Rinehart and Winston.

Smith, F. (1979). *Reading without nonsense.* New York: Teachers College Press.

Smith, F. (1982). *Understanding reading* (3rd ed.). New York: Holt, Rinehart and Winston.

Smith, N. B. (1928). Matching ability as a factor in first grade reading. *Journal of Educational Psychology, 19*, 560.

Sperling, G. (1960). The information available in brief visual presentations. *Psychological Monographs, 74*, 11, 19–38.

Sperling, G. (1963). A model for some kinds of visual memory tasks. *Human Factors, 5*, 19–31.

Spiro, R. J., & Myers, A. (1984). Individual differences and underlying cognitive processes. In P. D. Pearson (Ed.), *Handbook of reading research* (Vol. 1, pp. 471–501). New York: Longman.

Staff Writer. (2005). U.S. department of education declines to publish report on literacy education of bilingual children. *Reading Today, 23*, 1.

Stahl, S. A., & Miller, P. D. (1989). Whole language and language experiences approaches for beginning reading: Quantitative synthesis. *Review of Educational Research, 16*, 32–71.

Stanovich, K. E. (1981). Toward an interactive-compensatory model of individual differences in the development of reading fluency. *Reading Research Quarterly, 16*, 32–71.

Stanovich, K., & West, R. F. (1979). The effect of orthographic structure on the word search performance of good and poor readers. *Journal of Experimental Child Psychology, 28*, 258–267.

Statistics Canada. (2001). *Neighborhood income and demographics.* Accessed April 23, 2006, at http://www.satcan.ca/english/IPS/Data/13C0015.htm

Steffenhagen, J. (2001, September 1) Dropout rates in Canadian schools shocking. *The Vancouver Sun*, p. A1.

Steffensen, M. S., Joag-dev, L., & Anderson, R. C. (1979). A cross-cultural perspective on reading comprehension. *Reading Research Quarterly, 15*(1), 10–29.

Sulzby, E. (1986). Writing and reading: Signs of oral and written organization in the young child. In W. H. Teale & E. Sulzby (Eds.), *Emergent literacy: Writing and reading* (pp. 50–89). Norwood, NJ: Ablex.

Super, S. (1969). Spatial perception of language symbols and a description of a test designed to assess this function. *Journal of Optomological Science, Archives of the American Academy of Optomology, 46,* 426–433.

Swain, M. (1981). Bilingual education for majority and minority language children. *Studia Linguistica, 15,* 15–31.

Swain, M. (1996). Integrating language and content in immersion classrooms: Research perspectives. *Canadian Modern Language Review, 52,* 529–548.

Swain, M., & Lapkin, S. (1982). *Evaluating bilingual education: A Canadian case study.* Clevedon, England: Multicultural Matters.

Swiniarski, L. B. (1992). Voices from down under: Impressions of New Zealand's schooling. *Childhood Education, 68,* 225–228.

Tabachnick, B. G., & Fidell, L. S. (1996). *Using multivariate statistics* (3rd ed.). New York: Harper Collins College Publishers.

Taglieber, L., Johnson, P., & Yarbrough. B. (1988). Effects of prereading activities on EFL reading comprehension. *TESOL Quarterly, 22,* 455–472.

Tanner, A. (2001, August 13). Cuts hurt immigrants. *The Vancouver Sun,* p. A7.

The Education Forum (2003). High school drop-outs—What do they cost us? *The Newsletter of the Education Forum.* Accessed December 7, 2005, at www.educationforum.org.nz

Thomas, W. P., & Collier, V. (1997). *School effectiveness for language minority students.* National Clearinghouse for Bilingual Education. Accessed April 23, 2006, at http://www.ncbe.gwu.edu/ncbepubs/resource/effectiveness

Thomas, W. P., & Collier, V. P. (2002). *A national study of school effectiveness for language minority students' long-term academic achievement.* Santa Cruz, CA: Center for Research on Education, Diversity, & Excellence.

Thompson, G. B. (1981). Commentary: Toward a theoretical account of individual differences in the acquisition of reading skills. *Reading Research Quarterly, 14(4),* 596–599.

Thonis, E. W. (1970). *Teaching reading to non-English speakers.* New York: Collier Macmillan International.

Toppo, G. (2005). *Is bilingual education report being downplayed?* Accessed December 14, 2005, at http://www.nabe.org/press/Clips/clip091605b.htm

Tucker, G. R., Lambert, W. E., & d'Anglejan, A. (1973) Cognitive and attitudinal consequences of bilingual schooling: The St. Lambert project through grade five. *Journal of Educational Psychology, 65,* 141–149.

Tunmer, W. E., & Nesdale, A. R. (1985). Phonemic segmentation skill and beginning reading. *Journal of Educational Psychology, 77,* 417–427.

Turvey, M. T., Feldman, L. B., & Lukatela, G. (1984). The Serbo-Croatian orthography constrains the reader to a phonologically analytic strategy. In L. Henderson (Ed.), *Orthographies and reading* (pp. 81–89). London: Lawrence Erlbaum Associates.

Tzeng, O. J. L., & Wang, W. S. Y. (1983). The first two r's: The way different languages reduce speech to script affects how visual information is processed in the brain. *American Scientist. 71,* 238–243.

U.S. Office of Education. (1977). Definition and criteria for defining students as learning disabled. *Federal Register, 42(50),* 65083.

Valdes, J. M. (Ed.). (1987). *Culture bound: Bridging the culture gap in language teaching.* Cambridge: Cambridge University Press.

Valdes, J. M. (1986). Cultural differences and similarities. In J. M. Valdes (Ed.), *Culture bound: Bridging the cultural gap in language teaching* (pp. 49–51). New York: Cambridge University Press.

Verhoeven, L. T. (1990). Acquisition of reading in a second language. *Reading Research Quarterly, 25,* 90–114.

Vontress, C. E. (1976). Counseling the racial and ethnic minorities. In G. S. Belkin (Ed.), *Counseling: Directions in theory and practice* (pp. 277–290). Belmont, CA: Wadsworth.

Walters, K., & Gunderson, L. (1985). Using oral reading activities with ESL students in L1 to improve English achievement. *The Reading Teacher, 39,* 118–122.

Watt, D., & Roessingh, H. (2001). The dynamics of ESL drop-outs: Plus ça change... *The Canadian Modern Language Journal, 58,* 203–222.

Watt, D., & Roessingh, H. (2000). *ESL students at higher risk of school dropout.* University of Calgary. http://www.ucalgary.ca/unicomm/NewsReleases/esldrop.htm

Widdowson, H. G. (1978). *Teaching language as communication.* London: Oxford University Press.

Wilkinson, G. S. (1993). *Wide range achievement test 3.* Wilmington, DE: Jastak Associates/Wide Range.

Willett, J. (1995). Becoming first graders in an L2: An ethnographic study of language socialization. *TESOL Quarterly, 29,* 473–504.

Williams, J. P., Blumberg, E. L., & Williams, D. V. (1970). Cues used in visual word recognition. *Journal of Educational Psychology. 61,* 310–315.

Willig, A. (1985). A meta-analysis of selected studies on the effectiveness of bilingual education. *Review of Educational Research, 55,* 269–317.

Winkeljohann, R. J. (1979). *The effects of the extent to which metaphors appear in prose on the reading comprehension of selected fifth and eighth grade elementary school students.* Unpublished doctoral dissertation. University of Illinois, Urbana.

Winner, E., Engel, M., & Gardner, H. (1980). Misunderstanding metaphor: What's the problem? *Journal of Experimental Child Psychology, 30,* 22–32.

Winner, E., Rosentiel, A. K., & Gardner, H. (1976). The development of metaphoric understanding. *Developmental psychology, 14,* 433–442.

Winsor, P., & Pearson, P. D. (1992). *Children at risk: Their phonemic awareness development in holistic instruction* (Tech. Rep. No. 143). Urbana, IL: Center for the Study of Reading.

Wong-Fillmore, L. (1983). The language learner as an individual. In *On TESOL '82: Pacific perspectives on language learning and teaching* (pp. 157–171). Washington, DC: TESOL International.

Woodcock, R. W. (1973). *Woodcock reading mastery tests.* Circle Pines, MN: American Guidance Service.

Woodward, K. (Ed.). (1997). *Concepts of identity and difference.* London: Sage.

Wright, E. N., & Ramsey, C. (1970). *Students of non-Canadian origin: Age on arrival, academic achievement and ability* (Research Rep. No. 88). Toronto: Toronto School Board.

Yau, M. (1995). *Refugee students in Toronto schools: An exploratory study.* Toronto: Toronto Board of Education. Microfiche.

YEAR 2000. (1988). *The British Columbia primary program.* Victoria, Canada: The Queens Printers.

Yoes, D., Jr. (1967). Reading programs for Mexican-American children of Texas. *The reading teacher. 20,* 313–18, 323.

Yopp, H. K. (1992). Developing phonemic awareness in young children. *Reading Teacher, 45,* 696–703.

Young, R., & Lee, S. (1985). EFL curriculum innovation and teachers' attitudes. In P. Larson, E. L. Judd., & D. S. Messerschmitt (Eds.), *On TESOL'84.* (pp. 183–194). Washington, DC: TESOL.

Zehr, M. A. (2001). California's English fluency rate helps fuel debate. *Education Week, 21,* 23.

Zehr, M. A. (2003). Reports spotlight Latino dropout rates, college attendance. *Education Week, 22,* 12.

Zumbo, B. D., Sireci, S. G., & Hambleton, R. K. (2003, April). *Re-visiting exploratory methods for construct comparability: Is there something to be gained from the ways of old?* Presented at the meeting of the National Council on Measurement in Education (NCME), Chicago.

Author Index

A

Aaron, P. G., 50
Abelson, R. P., 28
Abrams, L., 264
Adams, M. J., 24, 27, 33
Aebersold, J. A., 12
Allen, P., 43
Allington, R., 243
Almassi, J., 32
Anderson, C., 39
Anderson, J., 11, 30, 31, 48, 54, 55, 186, 210, 254
Anderson, J. F., 12
Anderson, M., 24
Anderson, R. C., 24, 28, 39, 47
Andrew, C. M., 14
Antos, S., 40
Arlin, P. K., 40
Aro, M., 132
Arter, J. L., 40
Ashton-Warner, S., 31
Ashworth, M. N., 63, 159
Asimov, N., 7, 13, 14, 34
Au, K. H., 29, 37
Auerbach, E. R., 14

B

Baker, K., 16, 17
Baker, K. A., 37
Baldwin, R. S., 40
Banks, J. A., 11
Barik, H. C., 14
Barnlund, D. C., 12

Bartlett, F. C., 27
Bates, E., 105
Bayley, R., 51
Becker, C. B., 12
Bell, J. S., 44
Bendor-Samuel, J., 135
Benigni, L., 105
Bentin, S., 36
Berlin, B., 252
Bernhardt, E., 21, 24, 25, 44, 46, 48, 49, 50, 51, 59, 61, 126, 131, 148, 149, 152, 159, 259
Betts, E. A., 25
Billow, R. M., 40
Blumberg, E. L., 27
Boyarin, D., 20
Bradley, L., 59
Bretherton, I., 105
Brewer, W., 23
Bright, W., 134
Brightbill, R. F., 22, 23
Brinton, D. M., 60
Brown I. S., 59
Brown, R., 173
Bryant, P. E., 36, 59, 110
Burke, C. L., 29
Butler, Y. G., 37

C

Camaioni, L., 105
Cambourne, B., 31
Canale, M., 43
Carlo, M. S., 44

297

Subject Index